CLIMB TO CONQUER

THE UNTOLD STORY OF WORLD WAR II'S 10TH MOUNTAIN DIVISION SKI TROOPS

PETER SHELTON

SCRIBNER

NEW YORK LONDON TORONTO SYDNEY SINGAPORE

D1005272

I

SCRIBNER
1230 Avenue of the Americas
New York, NY 10020

SCRIBNER   and design are trademarks of Macmillan Library Reference USA, Inc.,
used under license by Simon & Schuster, the publisher of this work.

For information about special discounts for bulk purchases,
please contact Simon & Schuster Special Sales:
1-800-456-6798 or business@simonandschuster.com

Unless otherwise noted, all photos are courtesy of
the Denver Public Library—10th Mountain Division Collection.

Designed by Colin Joh
Text set in Janson

Manufactured in the United States of America

1   2   3   4   5   6   7   8   9   10

Library of Congress Cataloging-in-Publication Data
Shelton, Peter.
Climb to conquer : the untold story of WWII's Tenth Mountain Division
ski troops / Peter Shelton.
p.   cm.
Includes bibliographical references and index.
1. United States. Army. Mountain Division, 10th—History.   2. United States. Army—Ski
troops.   3. World War, 1939–1945—Regimental histories—United States.
4.World War, 1939–1945—Campaigns—Italy.   I. Title.
D769.310th .S48 2003
940.54'1273—dc22
2003061619

ISBN 978-1-4516-5510-0

To Ellen, Cloe, and Cecily.
And to my father who, like the men of
the 10th Mountain Division, modestly downplays
his contributions in World War II.

CONTENTS

We conquer men and mountains.
—Motto of the 87th Regiment, 10th Mountain Division

Higher.
—Motto of the 86th Regiment, 10th Mountain Division

Always Forward.
—Motto of the 85th Regiment, 10th Mountain Division

CLIMB
TO
CONQUER

Prologue

John Jennings, a twenty-one-year-old infantryman with the 87th Regiment of the 10th Mountain Division, steadied his ski and slipped one leather boot between the toe irons. In the darkness, he felt for the cable loop and positioned it around his heel. Then he snapped the forward throw closed—a familiar, comforting sound—locking his boot to the ski. Kneeling, he repeated the process with the other boot and binding. It was January 1945. Snow coated the cobblestone streets of Vidiciatico, a medieval farming village in Italy's Northern Apennine Mountains. A few miles to the north, the German army had dug in for the winter along a series of high ridges, forming a defensive shield that U.S. Army mapmakers dubbed the Winter Line.

The hills here reminded Jennings of the hills around Hanover, New Hampshire, where he had completed three semesters at Dartmouth College before reporting to the Army in February 1943. Monte Belvedere, the mountain directly in front of Vidiciatico, sloped up gradually to a long, whaleback ridge at 3,800 feet. Sharp ravines etched the mountain face in a few places, but most of the ground was cultivated in a patchwork of tilted fields and hedgerows, woods and orchards nearly to the top. Now, of course, the fields lay dormant under a thin, midwinter snowpack. Lit by a partial moon, individual crystals sparkled between the shadows. It was the kind of night that Jennings would have considered beautiful back home in Massachusetts. It *was* beautiful, in spite of the deadly game he was playing.

Jennings's ten-man patrol would have to maneuver, at least part of the night, in the open, and so they wore their camouflage "whites," knee-length poplin anoraks, over their olive-drab uniforms. Their skis were painted white too, as were the bamboo shafts of their ski poles and the camo-white pack covers. A lot of their gear, though, developed specifically for the 10th Mountain Division during its training in Colorado, had not made the crossing to Italy. Or if it had, not much of it had been delivered to the front lines. The soldiers missed their lug-soled mountain boots and their custom mountain rucksacks. They didn't have their white pants or their white canvas gaiters to keep snow out of their boots. Their high-peaked, four-man mountain tents were nowhere to be seen, and instead of cozy, double-down sleeping bags the soldiers huddled under thin army blankets. Fortunately, most of them were billeted indoors, out of sight of German observation, in nearby barns and farmhouses. The supply sergeant who had brought the skis and anoraks up from Florence couldn't find any climbing wax, so Jennings and the patrol had "borrowed" candles from Italian families and rubbed candle wax onto their ski bases instead. At midnight, they slipped out of Vidiciatico toward Belvedere. It felt good, Jennings thought to himself, to have the boards on his feet again.

At Dartmouth he'd been a four-event man—jumping, cross-country, downhill, and slalom. But his first choice following Pearl Harbor had not been the Army's newly formed ski troops. He had wanted to join the Navy. His mother's family came from the Vermont side of Lake Champlain, near where the Battle of Plattsburgh was fought during the War of 1812. Relatives told stories about the British invaders sailing down the lake from Canada raiding farms along the way only to be defeated in the decisive naval battle off Plattsburgh. The smaller American fleet won with stunning certainty, thus preventing the invasion of New York via the Hudson River valley. Sailing held the real romance for Jennings. But the Navy wouldn't take him because he wore glasses. As his second choice, he volunteered for the 10th Mountain Division. "At least," his father reasoned, wrongly, as it happened, "you won't be sent overseas."

The patrol skied in silence, single-file through moonlit stands of leafless oak and chestnut trees. Warm days and freezing nights had left an icy crust on the snow surface. It supported the skiers' weight most of the time. Now and then, the crust collapsed, and their skis broke through, knee-deep, into the sugary hollow below. Without skis, it would not have been possible to go even a hundred yards; a man on foot would simply flounder. Jennings labored under the extra weight of a Browning Automatic Rifle, a heavy though effective relic of World War I. Its firepower lay somewhere between that of a machine gun, which would have been too cumbersome for one man to ski with, and the standard-issue M-1 rifle. It took a twenty-round clip and could fire singly or in automatic bursts. Still, the BAR weighed twenty pounds, more than double the heft of the M-1, and Jennings also lugged twenty pounds of .30-caliber ammunition on his belt.

Because of the weight, Jennings broke through more often than the riflemen did. It took more energy to free his ski tips and climb back to the surface, but he was a strong kid and a good skier. He'd grown early, to six feet and 175 pounds while still in high school at Cushing Academy. His 1939 football team went undefeated and untied as New England prep school champs, and as a member of Cushing's traveling ski team, he had competed on the boards for years. At Camp Hale, Jennings's skills had led him into the elite Mountain Training Group, or MTG, with the men who designed and taught the courses in skiing and mountaineering, the ones who led the training missions onto the rocks and snow. Jennings thought back now to those halcyon days in Colorado. The war hadn't seemed quite real then, and it still didn't—not at the deepest gut level. The 10th had been on the line only a few days. Except for the patrols, there hadn't been much to do but stay hidden and keep warm. Jennings had not squeezed off even one shot with the BAR.

For three hours the squad zigzagged uphill toward its objective on Belvedere's west flank. The goal was an abandoned farm near the ridgeline. Were there Germans there? If so, how many? Did it look as if they'd occupied the place for a while? Were they dug in to defend or just passing through? The goal was not to fight any German soldiers they might find there, or win territory. Neither side was attempting, at this point in the winter, to gain ground. The cold and snow, the inability to move vehicles and artillery, had locked both sides into an uneasy stalemate. Still, both sides sent patrols across the line nearly every night, to probe, to learn what they could, and if they happened to get lucky, to bring back a prisoner for interrogation.

Most patrols never fired a shot. Medic Bud Lovett joined a predawn ski patrol west of Belvedere outside the town of Bagni di Lucca. The squad skied quietly uphill until sometime after sunrise, when they spotted a lone German in camouflage whites standing on a connecting ridge. The patrol's orders included bringing back prisoners if possible, so the squad leader called out for the trooper to halt, put his hands on his head, and "come in." A beat elapsed. Then another. Then the German jumped his skis 90 degrees into the fall line and schussed straight down the steep slope in front of him—

"like going down Tuckerman's," Lovett thought. "He was some skier." So impressed were the Americans that no one even thought to take a shot at him as he fled.

When Jennings's squad found the farmhouse, the officer in charge spread the men out in the field below it. Jennings was to set up his BAR on a haystack and provide cover while two scouts moved forward toward the buildings. Jennings wondered why. From where he crouched, he could hear Germans talking and digging in the rocky ground, digging a machine-gun placement perhaps. The Americans should get out now, before it got too light. They were right under the enemy's nose, and in full daylight they would surely be spotted.

The eastern sky brightened. Shadows sharpened as the snow took on a dawn glow. Seconds felt like minutes. And minutes stretched too far in both directions, into memory and fear. "Why is it taking so long?" Jennings thought. "We're not going to be able to take a prisoner in broad daylight. We're way out in the open here. No trees for hundreds of feet below the meadow. No cover. If the enemy has even one machine gun . . . Why don't they hurry up?" Jennings, a private first class, was not in charge. All he could do was shift his feet—skis attached—to a slightly more comfortable position under him, and wait. He hadn't exactly volunteered for these patrols. The S2 (intelligence officer) for the 2nd Battalion had spotted him in Vidiciatico, knew him to be a Dartmouth skier and MTG guy, and "volunteered" him for these night patrols. He hadn't minded the duty until now. The skiing with heavy packs, that was okay—they'd trained for that—but this agonizing waiting . . .

When the scouts finally scrambled back, the sun was nearly up. Jennings flung the BAR on his back and pushed off down the hill, skating and poling as fast as he could. All ten squad members raced through the growing light for the trees at the base of the meadow, certain that the enemy at their backs had spotted them. Jennings fought for balance on the collapsing crust. Climbing slowly uphill through tricky snow was one thing; this high-speed flight was quite another. The weight of the BAR threatened constantly to pitch him on his face. Now they were in the first small trees, just sticks really, dodging left and right around them. "This has got to be the hardest slalom I've ever raced," Jennings thought. And then he saw the machine-gun fire kicking up puffs of snow on either side of him. They had been discovered.

The bullets swept the snow in a predictable geometry a few feet behind the fleeing Americans. If any one of the patrol were to fall, he would surely be raked where he lay. Out of the corners of his eyes, Jennings checked the others flying as he was over the snow, all still upright, skiing for their lives.

Legs pumping, skis singing with the speed, Jennings and his BAR dodged the last scrub oak into the clear, out of sight from above. They'd made it. They were free now to coast back down their ascent track, almost as if they were out for a casual ski tour in the Berkshires, say, or the Adirondacks, back to the safety of the line—and what awaited them next.

CHAPTER 1:

Minnie's Ski Troops

The idea for America's first and only Army mountain division grew out of a conversation before the fire at Johnny Seesaw's, a one-time roadhouse turned ski lodge near Manchester, Vermont.

February 1940 was a bitter month in the Green Mountains. Storms swirled down from the Arctic whipping snow into drifts six feet high. Travel was dicey on slick roads, and the cold tested even hardy New Englanders. Still, skiers up from the cities, from Boston and New York and points south, soldiered up and down the trails at nearby Bromley Mountain. There was but one lift then, a rope tow with a turn in the middle that threw many an unwary rider. Gloved hands strained to grip the heavy rope. Snow from the swirling sky, and from the occasional fall, plastered wool jackets and blowsy gabardine pants, penetrated inside goggles and knit caps. After three or four runs, it was generally time to head for shelter.

Following one particularly bracing session on the hill, four ski friends gathered in Johnny Seesaw's common room to warm their outsides before the fire and their insides with a hot rum or two. Looking back, each member of the quartet could legitimately be called a founding father of the new sport of skiing in America, though they probably wouldn't have described themselves that way; downhill skiing was simply too new, and their passions had yet to gain the perspective of history. First among equals was Roger Langley of Boston, president of the National Ski Association. The NSA organized and sanctioned amateur ski competitions going back to the late 1800s—first jumping, when that was the only form of competitive skiing, and then, beginning in 1933, alpine (or downhill) competitions as well. The NSA staged the national championships and selected U.S. Olympic team members. As president, Langley influenced everything from competition rules to the public face of American ski racing.

Second before the fire, Harvard University grad Robert Livermore had raced for the United States at the first Winter Olympics to include alpine skiing, at Garmisch-Partenkirchen, Germany, in 1936. Next to him sat Alex Bright, the leader of an influential Boston ski club and, at forty-something, considered the dean of American downhillers. And finally, there was Charles Minot "Minnie" Dole, a Connecticut insurance executive and enthusiastic amateur skier who had just organized the country's first volunteer ski patrols, known collectively as the National Ski Patrol System.

Talk turned, as it did in countless living rooms that winter, to the Russo-Finnish war. Pearl Harbor was still almost two years away. Isolationist America was not at war and not at all sure that it would be drawn again, so soon after "the war to end all wars," into conflict in Europe. But the topic pressed inevitably into conversation, fueled by radio and newspaper accounts, and by the movie newsreels. Beginning in October, the newsreels had given graphic immediacy to Hitler's blitzkrieg through the Polish army and the shocking partition of Poland by the Nazis and the Soviets. Soon the Russians had also occupied Estonia, Latvia, and Lithuania, and were pressuring the Finns for access to ice-free ports on the Gulf of Finland.

The Finns said no. On November 29, 1939, with no formal declaration of war, a massive Soviet force of seventy divisions and over a thousand tanks invaded from the south and east. But instead of the expected walkover, the Soviets met determined and surprisingly successful resistance from the tiny Finnish defense force. At the time of the invasion, the Finnish army consisted of perhaps thirty thousand men, the equivalent of three small divisions, with a few antique tanks and aircraft. By the time the so-called Winter War ended, Finnish troop numbers had jumped to two hundred thousand, but the Soviets deployed nearly a million men and vastly outgunned their northern neighbors. And still the Finns managed to stymie the lumbering Russian columns.

They did this with stealth raids on skis. They used the climate and the terrain to their advantage, as do guerilla fighters everywhere. In a landscape dominated by countless snow-covered lakes, thick woods, and very few roads, the heavily mechanized Soviets were forced to advance in long, vulnerable lines over the established roadways. Rather than sit back in defensive positions, the Finns went on the offensive. Well camouflaged in head-to-toe white uniforms, they streamed out of the woods on skis, cut the Soviet columns from the sides, as if snipping a ribbon, and then, with cold and hunger weakening the invaders, proceeded over days to destroy the isolated pockets one by one. The Russians, in ill-conceived khaki and mostly without skis, were powerless to outmaneuver their assailants. The few Russians who were equipped with skis didn't know how to use them. Finnish troops found how-to skiing manuals on many a body sprawled in the bloodstained snow.

In the early weeks of the war, Finnish victories all out of proportion to their numbers netted more captured materiel than the country's small industrial base could possibly have manufactured. Again and again, the Finns appeared from out of the forest, wreaked havoc on the enemy's flanks, and melted back into the trees, hauling their wounded on ski sleds. Light artillery was likewise moved around by horse-drawn sleigh. Victories at Suomussalmi and Tolvajärvi in December destroyed most of two Soviet divisions and forced the once-haughty Russians to rethink the whole affair. The Finns knew how to live in the snow, how to conceal sparks from their stoves and how to stay warm in tents and snow caves through nights that reached 60 degrees below zero. The Russians, by contrast, slept in freezing metal sheds and huddled around bonfires in the open air, which made them easy targets for Finnish snipers. Soviet commanders asked for and did finally receive a brigade of ski troopers from Siberia, but these men were accustomed to fighting out in the open. The entire brigade skied out onto a frozen lake and was gunned down by unseen riflemen in the trees.

The Finns held out for three months, but in the end, the huge Soviet advantage in artillery and air power—and the coming of the spring thaw—finally bludgeoned the Finns into acceding. On March 13, the Russians got the territory they wanted on the Karelian Isthmus and a leased naval base at the mouth of the Baltic Sea. But the adventure had cost the Russians dearly: fifty thousand dead and three times that many wounded. And the damage to Soviet military prestige was even more devastating. The mighty Red Army had been embarrassed by the scrappy, resourceful Finns, and this fact would contribute to Hitler's decision in 1941 to take on what he perceived to be a weak Soviet military. Western news organizations loved the Winter War: It was a classic underdog tale, the heroes vastly outnumbered but fighting with guile and success far greater than anyone could have expected—a kind of updated, snowy version of the Battle of Bunker Hill. What's more, the fighting was photogenic. Camera crews sent back dramatic footage of the white-coated good guys and the swift grace of their running on skis.

Dole and company not only admired what the Finns were doing in February 1940, they also wondered aloud if there might not be an important lesson there. The Finnish resistance was "a perfect example," Minnie wrote later in *Birth Pains of the 10th Mountain Division*, "of men fighting in an environment with which they were entirely at home and for which they were trained." What if Germany decided to invade North America? Would we be able to defend our northern border? In winter? In a winter like the one raging outside that very night?

There had been no firm indication that Hitler's territorial ambitions extended across the Atlantic. But American paranoia, following two decades of isolationism, ran wild, and not without justification. German U-boats were sinking merchant ships bound for England. There were documented cases of Nazi-inspired sabotage and propaganda here at home. The publication in 1939 of *Nazi Spies in America*, by FBI agent Leon Turrou, caused a near panic, especially in New York. Turrou claimed that evidence gained through the use of a lie detector, a new technology (not yet discredited), proved the German-American Volksbund, a cultural organization based in New York, was actually a front for a Nazi spy ring. In a January 1939 article for the *Charlotte News*, the writer W. J. Cash enumerated what most Americans believed to be true, that "the Nazis do have an extended chain of spies scattered throughout this country, in shipyards, in ammunition plants, in key industrial spots, in air bases, in the army and navy—all busily engaged in stealing and smuggling out information designed to give the high command in Berlin a complete picture of our readiness for war and our points best open to attack."

Would Germany attack? Hitler's dream of Lebensraum, of "living space" for a pure Aryan race beyond the borders of the Fatherland, had always pointed east to the fertile plains of the Ukraine. And he seemed to be moving in that direction with the Anschluss, the forced merger with Austria in 1938, and then the annexation of Czechoslovakia and the rout of Poland a year later. But what if Hitler's armies were simply unstoppable and his appetite grew for dominion beyond Europe?

Minnie Dole and friends certainly wouldn't have been alone if they had engaged in a bit of speculation, a round of fireside "what-if?" What if England and her still-vast empire were forced somehow to surrender to the Nazis? In 1940 the British navy still ruled the waves, but her army and air forces, purposely small and reeling from the horrors of 1914–18, were not up to challenging a continental German war machine that had been modernizing for half a decade. What if England were to fall and, along with her, our massive neighbor to the north?

If Hitler could use Canada as a staging area, surely the United States would face a daunting threat. Minnie Dole knew his history and his geography. All four New Englanders at Johnny Seesaw's that night knew that an invasion route from Montreal south held real strategic promise. It had happened before. British and French troops fought up and down the Champlain Valley during the French and Indian War, some of the time on snowshoes. The British had raided down the broad valley separating Vermont and New York as far south as Fort Ticonderoga during the American War of Independence. And then barely thirty years later, they tried it again before they were stopped at the Battle of Plattsburgh. Had the redcoats not been defeated there, they would have had a straight shot at Albany and the Hudson River. A quick thrust down the Hudson would have brought them to New York City, effectively severing the Northeast from the rest of the nation. "What chance would we have today of defending against such an attack," the skiers wondered aloud, "especially in winter in mountainous New England?"

Not much, they concluded. Particularly against Germany's Jaegers, Hitler's mountain troops. The Reich counted three specially trained mountain divisions at the beginning of the war and would add as many as eleven more as fighting spread into Scandinavia, the Balkans, and the Carpathians. All three original mountain divisions had contributed to the "lightning war" in Poland the previous autumn. The United States had no troops trained and equipped for either vertical landscapes or cold weather. Our most recent conflicts abroad had been in Cuba and the Philippines, and almost all of our training facilities were in the Deep South, Hawaii, and Panama. The U.S. Army, small and underequipped as it was, was a tropical army. The most recent military study to be found on equipment for winter warfare had come out of Alaska and was dated 1914. It included advice on the proper use of the polar bear harpoon.

Dole and Langley decided that evening at Johnny Seesaw's to write the War Department and offer the services of their respective organizations in the nation's defense. The premise was rather vague, but Dole in particular had something valuable to offer. The National Ski Patrol System had in slightly more than a year become a grassroots network of some three thousand members—all hearty outdoorsmen and women—spread across the nation's northern tier. Ski patrollers might help map the northern frontier or train Army draftees in skiing technique. Or the patrol itself might be organized into volunteer units that could later be incorporated into the Army. The National Ski Association, for its part, might serve as a clearinghouse for mountaineering information. Actually, neither Dole nor Langley knew exactly how they might be of use. The point was to make the case for winter-ready troops. And in Dole's case, that plea would soon become an obsession.

The reply to Dole and Langley's first letter, which arrived later that spring signed by an underling, was in Dole's words little more than "polite derision"—"The Secretary of War has instructed me to thank you . . ." and so on. The officer wrote that his department fielded every sort of wacky if well-intentioned offer, including one from a man who claimed he had invented bullets that shot around corners.

Minnie Dole refused to be discouraged. Born in 1900, he had grown into a soft-faced man with a high forehead and studious wire rims who was partial to silk ascots and a walnut burl pipe. But regardless of his gentle exterior, Dole could be imperious; he was a patrician by birth and temperament, a man used to getting his way. The only other circumstances in his life that had similarly thwarted his will had also had to do with war. At seventeen, when the United States entered World War I, he tried to enlist in the ambulance corps, but his father had refused to give his permission. Minnie was "sick with frustration" when he heard the battle stories of former classmates fighting in France. As soon as he turned eighteen, he applied to Officer Training School but arrived at Fort Lee, Virginia, to the wailing of sirens and the cheering of cadets who had just heard news of the Armistice.

The National Ski Patrol was born out of Minnie's personal response to two skiing accidents. The first occurred on New Year's Day 1937, in Stowe, Vermont, when Dole fell awkwardly in tricky wet snow and heard bones in his ankle snap. There were no trained ski patrolmen on the mountain in those days, no rescue sleds. It was hours before his friends were able to haul him, shivering and near shock, down the hill on a scrap of roofing tin. Two months later, Minnie was hobbling around on crutches when he learned that the same friend who'd helped him down the hill in Stowe was now dead, having flown into the trees while downhill racing on the

Ghost Trail near Pittsfield, Massachusetts. Devastated, Minnie turned his grief to work and, not much more than a year later, in March 1938, with encouragement from Roger Langley and help from the American Red Cross, announced the birth of the National Ski Patrol System. He organized courses, designed certification exams, standardized practices on the hill—including the placement of rescue toboggans—and wrote the first Red Cross *Winter First Aid Manual*. By 1939, the NSPS had thousands of members in ninety-three chapters, at least one chapter in every state where snow regularly blanketed the hills.

Now, after watching the Finns fight on skis, Minnie Dole was convinced the United States needed specialized cold-weather and mountain troops. The Germans had their Jaegers, the French their Chasseurs Alpins, the Italians their Alpini. The United States should be similarly prepared—either for defense or to fight on foreign mountains—and Minnie, with his organizational skills and grassroots connection to American skiers, could help. Over the next twenty months, he rained letters on official Washington, two thousand of them by some estimates, pecked out on his Royal typewriter in the small home office that doubled as National Ski Patrol headquarters.

Dole followed every lead with the tenacity of a crusader. When one avenue appeared to close him off, he tried another, or he went over the top. He wrote directly to President Franklin Delano Roosevelt and to Army Chief of Staff Gen. George C. Marshall and to Secretary of War Henry Stimson. The Army, in turn, resisted at first the very idea of specialized troops. This wasn't the Army way, and considering the limited money and time, there were more pressing matters, namely the need to build regular infantry divisions from scratch. Dole persisted. In one letter, he wrote, "If the Army will not entertain [the idea of mountain troops], I am seriously thinking of organizing a Voluntary Group myself and putting such Corps through a month's training next winter, with the aid of foreign teachers who are familiar with maneuvers as carried on in their own countries."

By "foreign teachers," Dole meant the many ski instructors who had emigrated to the States from Central Europe during the 1930s. Some had fought in the mountains in World War I, and others had served in mountain divisions after the war. Now they were the vanguard of American skiing. As the first U.S. ski schools were being organized, these Austrians and Germans and Swiss became the first professional instructors—at Peckett's-on-Sugar-Hill in New Hampshire, at Stowe, and at Sun Valley, Idaho, which opened in 1936 with the world's first chairlift, an engineering marvel based on overhead-cable systems for loading banana boats. The United States had produced a handful of fine, homegrown skiers in the early years of the sport, but the imported Europeans were the shining stars of the sudden 1930s skiing boom.

One might have expected skiing to decline during the Depression years, but in fact, the numbers grew dramatically. In 1936 *Time* magazine referred to alpine skiing as "a nationwide mania" and opined that "winter sports in the U.S. have ceased to be a patrician fad and have become instead a national pastime." Between the late 1920s and the late 1930s, the number of American recreational skiers ballooned from around twenty thousand to at least two hundred thousand.

Time may have overstated skiing's egalitarian appeal. Most of the best skiers still came from well-to-do families who had traveled in Europe and could afford to send their sons and daughters to college, where the most serious competition (and coaching) was to be found. But the explosive growth did cross class lines. The biggest reason was the invention of the continuous-loop rope tow. Before, everyone had had to make the sweaty, if soulful, uphill hike on skis for the much briefer pleasure of sliding back down. Cross-country and downhill skiing were essentially one and the same; it was the arrival of lift-served skiing that ultimately separated the two endeavors. A ride to the top, even if it did cost a dollar a day, made all the difference. The first U.S. rope went up at Woodstock, Vermont, in 1934, and within three years there were hundreds of tows coast-to-coast. They were cheap and relatively easy to install; many were powered by Model T Fords, which could come down off their blocks in summer and be driven away.

Suddenly, farmers in hill country with fields and orchards that held good snow had a way to make a little extra money in the winter months. Farm wives with an extra bedroom or two hung SKIERS WELCOME signs in the window. Roosevelt's New Deal work crews, the Civilian Conservation Corps, cut ski trails on virgin state lands. Snow trains brought skiers from the cities out into the country for a day or a weekend, and then hauled them back, partying all the way, on Sunday night.

Skiing's glamour trickled down to a growing middle class that tapped into its fashion and lingo and songs. No other winter sport threw off such sparks; it was exhilarating, healthy exercise in an era with no superhighways leading to warmer climes, no television, no Internet. Plus, it was a great way to meet the opposite sex, even before the invention of stretch pants in the 1950s.

The final piece in skiing's amazing growth spurt was Minnie Dole's "foreign teachers." Americans needed instruction in "controlled skiing," and the resorts, particularly the more exclusive ones like Peckett's and Stowe, were willing to import the best. The acknowledged masters came from the Arlberg School, in Austria, where Hannes Schneider had perfected a teaching progression based on the snowplow, the stem turn, and the stem christiania—terms that soon worked their way into the American skiing lexicon.

These men brought their alpine charm, along with the first instruction books and films, to an enthusiastic reception in the States even as talk of war darkened the mountains at home.

By mid-year 1940, with progress slow at the War Department, Minnie took it upon himself to compile a skiing manual that might aid in training a future ski army. He used parts of existing texts by Otto Lang, an Austrian protégé of the great Schneider; by Benno Rybizka, another Arlberg instructor; and by the Swiss Walter Prager, who coached the Dartmouth College ski team. Minnie also began collecting information on ski mountaineering and equipment with the help of the California mountaineer Bestor Robinson.

Meanwhile, in April, Germany invaded Norway, occupying all of her major port cities. A relatively small force of German Jaegers held its ground for more than a month against heavily reinforced British counterattacks in the fjords at Narvik, proving again the value of trained mountain troops. In May, Hitler launched his western offensive, rolling quickly through Belgium and Holland and into northern France. And in June, when France capitulated, Nazi armies marched east into Romania to secure that country's oil resources. In the Far East, the Japanese conquest extended beyond Manchuria into the rest of China, and Japanese war planners openly coveted the raw materials, including oil, in the Dutch East Indies (now Indonesia), in French Indochina, and in British-held Malaya. By September, the Japanese would formally join the Axis powers, Germany and Italy, forming the Tripartite Pact. In less than a year, the war had widened into what John Jay, 10th Mountain Division public relations man, would later call "total war." Most of the planet would be drawn in, and battles would be fought in every kind of weather and terrain. Mountains, which had in past wars served as barriers to be avoided or bypassed, would surely see fighting in this total war. Minnie Dole was certain of it.

The barrage of letter writing intensified and finally paid dividends during the stifling late summer of 1940, when Dole and NSPS treasurer John E. P. Morgan traveled to Washington to see the Army's top man, Chief of Staff Gen. George C. Marshall himself. Marshall met them in his summer dress uniform and mirror-polished black cavalry boots. The irony of the scene could not have been lost on any of them, sweating in the September heat and talking about ice and snow.

Marshall listened more than he spoke, and at the end he told his visitors that a decision had been made to keep some existing U.S. Army units in the snowbelt through the coming winter to experiment with training and equipment for cold-weather fighting. Clipped and formal, he said he appreciated Dole's interest and very likely would call upon the NSA and the NSPS for advice on gear and ski-teaching technique.

Marshall never told Dole what had changed the Army's thinking, whether Dole's letters had finally been persuasive or whether the lessons of Finland and Narvik had tipped the scales, or a combination of the two. For whatever reasons, Marshall had apparently become a convert. In a formal letter of November 9, 1940, he charged:

> the National Ski Patrol, acting as a volunteer civilian agency, to become fully familiar with local terrain; to locate existing shelter and to experiment with means of shelter, such as light tents, which may be found suitable for the sustained field operations of military ski patrol units; to perfect an organization prepared to furnish guides to the Army in event of training or of actual operations in the local areas; and to cooperate with and extend into inaccessible areas the antiaircraft and antiparachute warning services.

*　　*　　*

Despite the military's distaste for working with civilian organizations, Marshall had let Dole and the National Ski Patrol into the mix. There had been no promise of a mountain division, and indeed it would be another year before the commitment was made to create one, but, in Minnie's phrase, "the pot was bubbling." The reality was, Army higher-ups knew nothing about mountains and skiing. They needed help, and they knew it—and they would get it that first winter from enlisted men and civilians who'd grown up in the snow.

Marshall's order created six Army "ski patrols" (not to be confused with the NSPS patrollers who volunteered at ski areas around the country). These were small, detached units patched together from the skiers and woodsmen already in established infantry divisions. Each patrol was given $1,200 to purchase ski equipment locally, not nearly enough to equip each man but enough, it was thought, to train groups of men in turn.

The 1st Division patrol operated out of Plattsburgh Barracks in upstate New York. They skied strictly cross-country on the rolling trails built for the 1932 Olympics at Lake Placid. Their instructor was three-time captain of the U.S. Olympic jumping team, Rolf Monsen. The men liked the training, understandably; it was what they had done for fun as kids. Their commanding officer, Col. John Muir, liked it too. "I believe that ski training is an asset," he wrote in a subsequent report. "Like the Texan's six-shooter, you may not need it, but if you ever do, you will need it in a hurry, awful bad."

Men from the 44th Division trained at Old Forge, New York, under newly inducted Pvt. Harald Sorenson, an Olympic skier from Norway. These soldiers were challenged to races by local snowshoers—some of the best in the Adirondacks—who considered their mode of locomotion more versatile than skis. The snowshoers set the courses, which included lots of uphill and tight trees, but the skiers won every time, proving that skis, as ungainly as they might seem, were faster for general snow travel.

In Washington state, a patrol of twenty-five men from the 41st Division spent the winter at a Civilian Conservation Corps camp outside Rainier National Park under the guidance of Sgt. Karl Hindeman, a ski instructor from Montana.

Another northwestern outfit from the 3rd Division trained under former University of Oregon ski coach Paul Lafferty. Eighteen officers and men bunked together in a converted garage at Longmire, a National Park Service camp on the south slope of Mount Rainier. At the end of their winter's training, Lafferty led the men on a two-week circumnavigation of Rainier's massive, dormant cone, crossing along the way many of the twenty-six glaciers that creep down its flanks. As they went, they tested a hodgepodge of civilian ski and winter camping gear—there being no standard military issue at the time—and what passed then for lightweight camping food: dehydrated cereals, dried potatoes, chipped beef, powdered eggs, spaghetti.

The 41st Division ski patrol undertook a graduation exercise of sorts too, skiing across Washington's Olympic Mountains in four days, west to east, under the leadership of Lt. John Woodward, a former University of Washington ski team captain. "I didn't have the rank," says Woodward sheepishly now, "but there was so little mountaineering experience, they said, 'John, you're in charge.'"

Woodward's trek across the Olympics confirmed what top skiers at the time already knew, that skis with metal edges far outperformed edgeless models. Soldiers on the edgeless skis reported great frustration as rounded wooden edges slipped out from beneath them on slopes of wind-hardened or icy snow.

These first limited cadres did learn to ski. And they reported their findings regarding improvised training methods and equipment, but the Army clearly had a long way to go toward understanding the needs of a mountain division.

Indeed, the military still wasn't convinced it wanted a mountain division. Winter over, the Army deemed the ski patrol experiments a success and disbanded them in the spring of 1941. Minnie Dole despaired. The patrols had not led to a permanent force as he had hoped; specialized units remained in disfavor within the Army hierarchy. Why not, some in the War Department argued, just move flatland units up to the mountains for short periods of training? Or adapt existing infantry divisions to operations in different kinds of terrain? Minnie believed that neither of these options would be adequate for defending Alaska, say, or for fighting in the Appalachian Mountains for that matter, when the real cold and snow set in. He got back on his typewriter and agitated for the creation, at the very least, of a small permanent test force that could be the nucleus of some future division. But the matter languished in Washington for the better part of the summer.

Meanwhile, Minnie and his team continued working outside the official purview of the War Department. They formed the Volunteer Winter Defense Committee of the National Ski Association and set to work answering the reams of questions posed by the ski patrol "experiments." Their equipment committee was chaired by Bestor Robinson, the California mountaineer, and included Monsen from Lake Placid, Dole, Langley, Alfred Lindley, who had climbed Mount McKinley on skis, Douglas Burkett of the Appalachian Mountain Club, and a well-known Alaskan explorer from the American Geophysical Society named Walter Wood.

They faced a huge job. Most of the gear available in 1941 was suited to the burgeoning mass of "practice-slope skiers" in America, few of whom ventured off-trail. Mountaineering and snow-camping gear, what little there was, came primarily from Europe.

The only lightweight camp stoves, for instance, which were essential for melting snow for drinking and cooking, had to be imported from Sweden.

The committee's first step was to round up all of the foreign manuals on winter warfare that members could find, translate them, and learn what they could. What they discovered was that not much applied to the American landscape. (They were still thinking in terms of defending against invasion.) European and Scandinavian mountain troops could often count on existing alpine huts, farms, and villages for shelter. And the Swiss were practiced at hollowing out caves in their glaciers to house and protect large numbers of soldiers. But America's high country was largely uninhabited wilderness. And there were no glaciers in New England or indeed along most of the northern frontier. Americans would have to develop their own portable mountain tents.

The committee learned that the Finns transported heavy equipment, including artillery, by horse-drawn sleigh along their frozen roadways. But Finland is mostly flat, and this technique wasn't likely to work in the powdery snow and roadless expanses of North America. They read reports on Arctic and Antarctic expeditions, but these were dependent on dog teams and motor tractors for transport. The committee figured there weren't enough sled dogs on the planet to support an army division, and they knew that no over-snow vehicle then in existence could get up steep pitches or through deep, soft snow.

The one manual that did provide real guidance was the Sierra Club's *Manual of Ski Mountaineering*, edited by David Brower, a twenty-nine-year-old Berkeley, California native. Written as a series of articles by club members, it offered sound advice on everything from avalanche awareness to putting together a lightweight kit of backcountry essentials. In the equipment chapter, Bestor Robinson, a club member, a lawyer, and a stickler for detail, even suggested drilling holes in your toothbrush to save an ounce or two. Climbers are notorious gear freaks, and Robinson, a pioneer of vertical climbing in Yosemite Valley in the 1930s, knew better than most the value of worrying his gear to perfection.

In April 1941, Robinson and Paul Lafferty (of the 3rd Division ski patrol) and about twenty other experienced skiers, including David Brower, set off into the still-snowy backcountry of the eastern Sierra Nevadas. They camped in Little Lakes Valley at 10,000 feet elevation, just beneath the jagged granite crest of the range. They carried with them every piece of mountain gear they believed might work for the Army, all of it from civilian suppliers: skis from Northland and Anderson & Thompson, boots by the Bass Company and L.L. Bean, sleeping bags and tents from Abercrombie & Fitch, winter clothing from Montgomery Ward and Marshall Field. They tested gasoline stoves and different ski waxes. Snowshoes, repair kits, rucksacks, pack boards, pitons, snap rings, climbing ropes, knit caps, knives, sun screens, mess kits, mittens, goggles, gaiters, wool pants, poplin pants, poplin parkas, and caribou-hide parkas.

Robinson, who had joined the staff of the Quartermaster General, took the results to Washington, where specifications for GI gear began to take shape. But the Army still didn't seem any closer, despite the testing and Minnie Dole's furious letter writing, to creating a real mountain force.

Then in August, proponents of a mountain division got a boost from the U.S. military attaché to Italy. The war had expanded into southern and eastern Europe. While Hitler's Panzers drove into the Soviet Union, Italian dictator Benito Mussolini decided, as part of his "parallel war" strategy, to invade Italy's ancient enemy, Greece, through the mountains of Albania. The attaché's report described an Italian army ill-equipped for cold. When the Greeks counterattacked and the Italians were forced to retreat back into the mountains, an estimated ten thousand of them froze to death. Twenty-five thousand were killed in mountain fighting, and many thousands more were taken prisoner. The blow to Italian morale and prestige turned out to be irreparable.

In a memorandum on the Italian fiasco, Lt. Col. L. S. Gerow of the General Staff Corps wrote: "Important lesson learned: an army which may have to fight anywhere in the world must have . . . units especially organized, trained, and equipped for fighting in the mountains and in winter . . . such units cannot be improvised hurriedly from line divisions. They require long periods of hardening and experience, for which there is no substitute for time."

Minnie Dole couldn't have asked for a better testimonial, and on October 22, 1941, he received letters from Secretary of War Stimson and General Marshall stating that on November 15, 1941, the 1st Battalion (Reinforced) 87th Mountain Infantry Regiment would be activated at Fort Lewis, Washington. The first element of what would become the 10th Mountain Division was officially launched. Whether it had come about because of Minnie's tireless advocacy or because of the experiences of allies and enemies in winter settings was not ultimately important. On December 8, 1941, the day after the Japanese attack on Pearl Harbor, the first recruit arrived in Washington. His was a profile that would come to characterize, fairly or unfairly, the "elite" nature of the new division. He was Charles McLane of Manchester, New Hampshire, a Dartmouth racer from a well-known skiing family. He carried his own rucksack and his own skis, and he stood in the Puget Sound drizzle in his green Dartmouth sweater with the white *D* on it. He told the duty officer that he was there to report for the ski troops. To which the officer replied: "Corporal, as far as I can figure out, you *are* the ski troops."

The mountain troops truly had arrived when the February 21, 1942, issue of *The New Yorker* magazine ran a "Notes and Comment" piece entitled "Minnie's Ski Troops." The story summarized Dole's twenty-month effort to establish a cold-weather, high-altitude division and ended with this: "Minnie is gratified with results, but he thinks this winter's Russian campaign would have sold the idea anyhow."

Once again, the newsreels showed a mighty army stopped in its tracks by snow and cold. This time it was the German army on the eastern front, caught short of Moscow and freezing to death by the thousands in summer boots and light jackets.

CHAPTER 2:

Paradise

A s the first would-be ski troops arrived at Fort Lewis early in the winter of 1941–42, there was more to feel gloomy about than the coastal Washington weather. The war in Europe and the Far East, with few exceptions, was going the Axis way. For a full year, from June 1940 to June 1941, Great Britain battled Germany alone. Had it not been for the miraculous evacuation at Dunkirk, where 198,000 British and 140,000 French and Belgian soldiers escaped in a motley seven-hundred-ship armada across the English Channel, there might not have been any Allied powers for the United States to join. But after Dunkirk, Hitler's planned invasion of the British Isles, code-named "Operation Sea Lion," had to be postponed until the Luftwaffe, the German air force, gained control of the skies over the Channel.

The Royal Air Force, in what came to be known as the Battle of

Britain, made sure that never happened. Throughout the summer of 1940, wave after wave of German bombers and their fighter escorts were intercepted by RAF Spitfires and Hurricanes. The British fighters turned out to be more maneuverable and their pilots more focused than the tactically disorganized Germans. By mid-September the RAF knew it could shoot down Luftwaffe bombers faster than German industry could produce new ones. In frustration, Hitler ordered the night-bombing of major English cities. But "the Blitz" only served to steel English resolve, and by late winter 1941, the bombing campaign had withered. Hitler put off Sea Lion indefinitely and turned his attention to Lebensraum and the Soviet heartland.

Meanwhile, Italy had joined with Germany and had declared war on both France and Britain (but not until it was clear France had fallen before the German blitzkrieg). Though Mussolini had once thought of the younger Adolf Hitler as his protégé, Hitler had nothing but disdain for Il Duce and his undisciplined military. Back in March 1940, Hitler had told Mussolini that Germany didn't need Italy's help to win the war, but that Italy would be allowed to participate and thus escape second-rate status in the Mediterranean. On returning to Rome, Mussolini decided that Italy would fight its own "parallel war" to forge "a new Roman Empire." Soon thereafter came the disastrous defeat at the hands of the Greeks in the mountains of Albania and ill-conceived adventures in Abyssinia (now Ethiopia), Kenya, and Sudan.

On the eastern front, Hitler reneged on his nonaggression pact with Stalin and invaded the Soviet Union in June 1941. As they had in the west, his Panzer divisions streaked across the Russian steppes, outflanking and surrounding whole Soviet armies with lightning pincer movements. But October and November brought early and bitter cold snaps, and winter snows immobilized the underdressed Germans within sight of Moscow.

In the Pacific, Japan's expansion would soon reach its zenith with the fall of Hong Kong, French Indochina (Vietnam), Malaya, Sumatra, Burma, Borneo, Java, Wake, and Guam. On January 9, 1942, U.S. troops on the Bataan peninsula surrendered, effectively turning the Philippines over to the Japanese as well. Japanese strategists had taken full advantage of Britain's desperate home defense and of the inability of the United States to fight back following the surprise attack on Pearl Harbor. But that event, far from demoralizing the Americans, as Admiral Isoroku Yamamoto, commander in chief of the Japanese fleet, had hoped, served to galvanize the United States for war. Already committed to being "the arsenal of democracy," in FDR's phrase, the United States was now on track to fight and win wherever necessary. The creation of the 87th Mountain Regiment was one small piece in the jigsaw puzzle of a massive war effort.

The Army could hardly have picked a better location for the fledgling mountain regiment. The soldiers felt no affection for Fort (Meriwether) Lewis itself, just outside Tacoma, but the presence nearby of Mount Rainier made up in spades for Lewis's coastal fog and mud.

On clear days, Rainier's volcanic dome towers over the lowlands of Puget Sound—an American Fuji with a perpetual, ice-cream cone summit. At 14,410 feet it is the highest peak in the Cascade Range and fifth highest in the Lower 48 (after California's Mount Whitney and three summits in Colorado). Its twenty-six glaciers pour down all sides of the mountain into dense stands of conifer, summer meadows full of wildflowers, waterfalls, and trout streams. The entire massif was set aside as a national park in 1899. And since 1870, when the mountain was first climbed, Rainier has been the signature challenge for northwestern mountaineers. It is so big, and so close to the ocean, that it makes its own weather; snowstorms wrap the summit any month of the year. Climbers die every year attempting the summit. They freeze to death in sudden squalls or fall into hidden crevasses. The mountaineers in the 87th knew this was a serious peak and eagerly claimed Rainier as home.

Beginning in the mid 1930s, there was organized skiing on Rainier too, on its lower slopes, where seasonal snow depths of twenty feet were common. Once the road was plowed following a storm, weekenders from Seattle and Tacoma flocked to the rope tows at two National Park Service lodges at Longmire and Paradise. A smooth-skiing émigré from Salzburg named Otto Lang had started the first official Arlberg ski school in the western United States at Paradise in 1936. The slopes were good enough to host the 1935 National Championships. Minnie Dole's friends, Robert Livermore, Jr., and Alex Bright, earned their spots on the 1936 Olympic team in those races on the "Silver Skis" course.

When the snow began to fly that first winter of 1941–42, the 87th's commanding officer, Col. Onslow S. Rolfe, negotiated a deal with the National Park Service to lease Paradise Lodge through May. These were luxury digs by Army standards and a big-mountain fantasy for those recruits who had been skiers at home in the East and Midwest. A twenty-eight-year-old enlisted man from Wisconsin named Charles Bradley described it thus in his book *Aleutian Echoes*: "The 87th was rolled up and transported by bus to Paradise . . . where the well-plowed roads lay in snow canyons deeper than the buses and where my quarters on the first floor of the lodge required me to climb to the third floor to step out of doors. Paradise? Right on! A place to study war? Too weird to think about."

Colonel Rolfe knew about war, but he admittedly didn't know much about skiing or surviving in the mountains. He was a West Point graduate and had been a decorated cavalryman in World War I, but the only reason he could figure he'd been assigned the job at

Rainier was that he was a native of New Hampshire and someone back at the War Department must have assumed that meant he was a skier.

He wasn't a skier, but he learned fast. Pinkie, as he was known to the men, took instruction from some of the best in world, because, as the companies of the first battalion filled up—A Company, then B Company, and so on—the roster at Paradise became a kind of who's who of American skiing.

Some joined the Army specifically to be a part of the 87th; others, already in the service, transferred to the ski troops from their old outfits. Robert Livermore, Jr., signed up, as did a young racing sensation out of the University of New Hampshire named Steve Knowlton. Lt. John Jay, namesake and direct descendant of the first chief justice of the Supreme Court, transferred in from the Army Signal Corps. He was a budding ski filmmaker. Dev Jennings was a Utah mountain climber and ski racer. And Nelson Bennett and Tap Tapley left skiing jobs at the resort in Sun Valley to join the troops at Paradise. More than a few veterans of the Army "ski patrols" met them there, including Capt. Paul Lafferty and Lt. John Woodward.

A significant number of the men who signed up were not Americans but the great European skiers who had left the old country to seek their fortunes on this side of the pond. The most famous name of all was that of Torger Tokle, a ski jumper from Norway who had been in the United States only since 1939. At this time, downhill racing was too new to have much of a following, but ski jumping was enormously popular, one of the biggest spectator sports of the day. And Tokle had no equal on the barnstorming professional tour. Thousands came out to watch the jumpers at each stop, from Madison Square Garden to the Los Angeles Coliseum, where tons of crushed ice had to be hauled in to coat the in-run and landing zone. A newspaper photo of a jump constructed at the Los Angeles County Fair in the 1930s shows a tremendous, curving scaffold with a thin ribbon of ice down its middle while palm trees wave in a cloudless Southern California sky. The jumping tour had its roots in winter and mountains and genuine competition, but it also had its circus side and competed with horse racing and baseball for the biggest crowds on some weekends.

The jumpers were called "birdmen." And they did fly: crouching at sixty miles an hour on the in-run, skis clattering in the icy grooves, then bursting off the lip, legs together, body leaning out into the wind, chin nearly reaching the ski tips, arms pinwheeling for balance until, at the last second, the legs split into a telemark landing and a final skid to a stop. It all seemed too incredible, each succeeding jumper outdoing the last, riding the air on their "Norwegian snowshoes."

During the winter of 1942, on one of the big outdoor hills at Iron Springs, Michigan, Tokle set a world distance record of 289 feet. He didn't look much like an athlete. He was only five feet seven inches and 160 pounds. But he had tremendous spring in his legs and an ability to hang in the air until the last possible moment before touching down. Humble and cheerful, he had worked as a carpenter before joining the Army, sending money home to family in Nazi-occupied Norway. Now he loved to amaze his fellow enlisted men with standing leaps onto flatbed trucks or over the supply room counter. Later, when the 10th was sent overseas, he would be the only ski trooper mentioned by name in newspaper stories from the front.

One of the first draftees to arrive on Rainier was Sgt. Walter Prager, a Swiss world champion who had most recently coached the Dartmouth College racing team. Dartmouth in the 1930s was the New York Yankees of collegiate skiing, and Prager was a legend on both sides of the Atlantic. He'd won the most important Alps ski race, the Arlberg-Kandahar, in St. Anton, Austria—twice—first in 1930 and again in 1933. At Dartmouth, he ran the most venerable, most successful program in the United States, attracting the best young skiers and dominating competition year after year. Four of the eight men on the 1936 Olympic team were Prager's boys. His commanding officer at Fort Lewis, Lt. John Woodward, said, "With ten or fifteen of the world's top skiers in the battalion, Walter Prager might have been the only man with the ability to keep all of the greats in line."

Among the other greats there at Paradise were Austrians Friedl Pfeifer, who had emigrated before the Anschluss, and Toni Matt, who had managed to leave in 1939 after Germany's political union with Austria. Matt was a brash young racer, a cherubic and barrel-chested junior champion at home who immediately seized a place in American skiing history by straight-lining the Inferno, an infamous annual dash down 4,200 vertical feet from the summit of New Hampshire's wind-whipped Mount Washington. All the other skiers in the race, including defending champion (and Dartmouth hero) Dick Durrance, made turns on the super-steep Headwall to keep their speed in check. But Matt schussed it, knocked six minutes off the old record time, and, at age nineteen, created an instant legend.

Friedl Pfeifer was also a downhill champion, a world champion in fact, somewhat older than Matt and already established as one of the top instructors at Sun Valley. From its opening, Sun Valley epitomized skiing's high end, its glittering romance. The resort's founder, Averell Harriman, meant it to be that way. Diplomat, railroad magnate, future governor of New York, and avid skier, Harriman set out to recreate in the Idaho wilderness the grand resorts he'd skied in the Alps. As part of the plan, he invited most of Hollywood to the opening party, and he imported the best Austrian skiers to teach in his ski school. Friedl was one of the most celebrated, and with his dark hair slicked back and silk ascot peeking out of perfectly pressed white shirts, he fit right into the scene. Framed pho-

tographs in the hallways of the Sun Valley Lodge show Friedl leading the way for the likes of Gary Cooper and Clark Gable,
Claudette Colbert, Errol Flynn, and Norma Shearer. It didn't hurt
that Friedl swooped across the snow low and fast in the Arlberg
style, effortlessly, like a hawk.

But Pfeifer's transition to the ski army was anything but smooth.
On the day Pearl Harbor was bombed, FBI agents, who suspected
some Sun Valley instructors of Nazi leanings, quickly arrested
Friedl and a handful of other German-speakers, including the
school's director, Hans Hauser. Pfeifer felt he had been unjustly
detained, but he did understand the panicked mindset that gripped
his adopted nation. He told an interviewer in the film *The Sun Valley Skiers*, "Some rumor was that I was up on Galena Pass. I had a
hidden radio station to, to communicate with the Nazis, well with
Hitler. I was terribly shocked when they put some handcuffs on me
at two o'clock in the morning and wouldn't even let me go back to
say goodbye to my wife and my little baby that was a year old."

Jailed in Salt Lake City, the Austrians were given a choice:
deportation home, where service with Axis armies was a near certainty; join the U.S. military and perhaps fight against friends and
countrymen; or spend the rest of the war in jail. Hauser, who didn't
disguise his sympathy for Hitler, chose jail. Pfeifer, whose strong
anti-Nazi feelings soon came out, joined the 87th Mountain
Infantry Regiment as one of its top instructors.

Learning to ski the military way involved a change of approach
for everyone, famous or not. Out went the fancy jump turns and fast
christies, and in came a far less glamorous slogging, the practical
moving of men and equipment across the snow for the purpose of
doing battle. Day trips from Paradise Lodge grew longer and
longer with gradually heavier loads. Muscles grew sinewy and hard.
Faces bronzed in the high sun. Bradley recalled in *Aleutian Echoes*:

As time went on the loads increased to include overnight and cooking equipment, in addition to extra clothing, sleeping bags, matches, food, etc. Our backs and shoulders were toughening up, and we were learning some of the difficulties arising from barreling downhill with a heavy load riding on our backs that has its own inertia, power, and direction. When we were finally carrying rifles, a common misjudgment of speed and control could end in the load lifting the skier off the snow, rolling him forward in the air, and driving him head first in the snow. The rifle, lagging slightly, would catch up and deliver the coup de grace by whacking the skier on the head.

Pinkie Rolfe took his licks along with everyone else, in what would become a hallmark of the 10th Mountain Division—the submission of senior officers to instruction from experts of lower rank. It would be one of many anomalies peculiar to the mountain troops and a big part of the outfit's egalitarian nature. Colonel Rolfe got a small measure of revenge, though. The 87th Regiment at Fort Lewis kept a large stable of mules and horses. As a light division, designed to operate in largely roadless terrain, the Army planned for the 10th to haul its artillery and other supplies with the sturdy, long-eared Missouri mules. A sign overarching the camp gate said it all: THROUGH THESE PORTALS PASS THE MOST BEAUTIFUL MULES IN THE WORLD.

As an old cavalryman, Rolfe insisted that his officers spend at least some time riding. After a particularly galling experience that ended with the rider on the ground and the horse standing calmly over him, Lt. John Jay explained in skiers' terms to the snickering faces above him, "I must have caught an edge."

The soldiers' packs grew still heavier until, fully loaded for multiple nights out in the snow, they weighed ninety pounds—one hundred, if you counted the rifle strapped to the side. When they fell, smaller skiers couldn't get up off the snow without first wriggling out of their shoulder straps. And then there was the problem of hoisting the bursting rucksack back up. The men learned to pull each other up off the ground or to offer to hold the pack while a comrade maneuvered beneath it on his long, slippery feet. Friedl Pfeifer said in the film *Fire on the Mountain*, "We had a philosophy to helping each other. That's the main thing in the mountains."

Commanders realized eventually that this sort of backbreaking load would not do in combat; the troopers would have no energy left for fighting. But the ninety-pound pack bonded soldiers who suffered through the training and were stronger for it. A group of 87th men even wrote a song about it. The self-styled 87th Mountain Infantry Glee Club was made up mostly of eastern college men with a history of irreverent, satirical singing. John Jay, of Williams College, was one, as was Dartmouth's Charles McLane. The best lyricist in the bunch turned out to be Ralph Bromaghin, a Sun Valley ski instructor. He came up with the words to "Ninety Pounds of Rucksack," which was sung to the Navy tune "Bell Bottom Trousers."

> *I was a barmaid in a mountain inn.*
> *There I learned the wages, the miseries of sin.*
> *Along came a skier fresh from the slopes.*
> *He's the one that ruined me and shattered all my hopes.*
>
> *Singing ninety pounds of rucksack, a pound of grub or two.*
> *He'll schuss the mountains like his daddy used to do.*
>
> *He asked me for a candle to light his way to bed.*
> *He asked me for a kerchief to cover up his head.*

I like a foolish maid and thinking it no harm
Jumped into the skier's bed to keep the skier warm.

Singing ninety pounds of rucksack, a pound of grub or two.
He'll schuss the mountains like his daddy used to do.

Early in the morning before the break of day
He handed me a five note and with it he did say:
Take this my darling for the damage I have done.
You may have a daughter, you may have a son.
Now, if you have a daughter, bounce her on your knee.
But if you have a son, send the bastard out to ski.

Singing ninety pounds of rucksack, a pound of grub or two.
He'll schuss the mountains like his daddy used to do.

The moral of this story, as you can plainly see
Is never trust a skier an inch above your knee.
For I trusted one, and now look at me—
I've got a bastard in the Mountain Infantry.

Singing ninety pounds of rucksack, a pound of grub or two.
He'll schuss the mountains like his daddy used to do.

This would become the 87th's, and later the division's, trademark drinking, marching, all-around good-time song. The men regularly belted out at least a dozen others. Some were send-ups of popular tunes, and many more were inspired by the singing and yodeling traditions of the Europeans.

The Gemütlichkeit—the camaraderie—flowed, but inevitably, Paradise had to end. The lodge wasn't big enough to accommodate even one battalion (about a thousand men), let alone a full regiment (three battalions) or the three regiments it would take to fill out a division. And the lease with the National Park Service was up. The Army knew from the start that it would have to find a permanent home for the 10th somewhere else. Preferably one that was outside the confines of a national park. Paradise had been perfect for skiing but was not ideal for a skiing army. The Park Service had grudgingly allowed the men of the 87th to carry rifles, for example, but they couldn't fire them, not even blanks. Too disruptive to wildlife.

The Army needed a place big enough for division-sized maneuvers, a place it could fire live ammunition, a place far enough from the public eye to screen the young division's missteps. And there would be plenty of those. No one involved had done this before—build a mountain division from scratch. Not even Minnie Dole knew what it should look like, how it should be equipped and organized. Paradise was a start, a good start, but just one in what would become a long line of experiments. The men who got to know Paradise weren't told at the time, but by the spring of 1942, well before the snow had melted, a new, permanent home for the mountain infantry was under construction in Colorado.

Meanwhile, in May, a cadre of some of the 87th's most experienced skiers finished the season on Rainier with a bravura ski ascent to the summit. The idea of, or justification for, the climb was to test equipment and rations under conditions more extreme than those at the lodge's five-thousand-foot elevation—as if any of the skiers needed justification to climb the peak that had hovered all winter, in Charles Bradley's words, "almost straight overhead, a detached mass of ice, rock and swirling snow, floating in the sky, inaccessible, threatening, beckoning." The Quartermaster General's office had been working tirelessly to come up with equipment that would meet the imagined needs of a winter fighting force. The trouble was, there were no specifications (no one knew, for example, how much loft was needed in a down sleeping bag to keep a body warm at a given air temperature) and little in the way of test results.

The troops at Paradise had experimented all winter with a variety of civilian-made boots and rucksacks, sleeping bags and mountain tents, socks and sweaters, and so on. They'd tested, briefly, a diet of pure Indian pemmican: dried meat, fat, and berries pressed into near-indigestible loaves. They'd tried different kinds of snowshoes and skis and tinkered with a motorized sled that looked like a giant shoehorn with a lawnmower engine on the back. This precursor to the snowmobile was as difficult to control as a bumper car and a good deal more dangerous. Minnie Dole himself test-drove the thing on one of his visits to Rainier. "Pinkie Rolfe did his best to kill me off," he wrote later, "by sending me off on a test motorized toboggan to climb a 75-degree grade on which the toboggan turned over backwards. Somehow I survived."

The Rainier climbers meant to put this gear (minus the toboggan) to the test at altitude, on the glaciers, in wind and cold and avalanche conditions. Should the 10th be called on to fight in the Alps—the Austrian Jaegers and Italian Alpini had battled to a bloody draw on the peaks of the Sud Tyrol in World War I—then this knowledge could prove invaluable.

Ten men started out on May 8 under the command of Capt. Albert Jackman. John Jay kept the weather records and brought along his movie camera. A well-known Swiss mountaineer, Peter Gabriel, was in charge of technical climbing. And Charles Bradley went along as "co-ordinator of 87th menus."

At two intermediate camps along the route, they spent time acclimating and trying to figure out the new, waterproof, zip-together tents. But mostly, in brilliant, sunny weather, it seems they practiced cooking and eating and making pretty tracks in the wide-open snowfields. Or so it appears in the rough footage John Jay shot. There's a lot of melting of snow for hot chocolate, scenes of dehydrated flakes (of what, it is not clear) being added to cans of boiling water. At Camp 2, the last stop before the summit, the camera lingers on a grinning soldier, his one-burner stove sputtering away in a nicely carved snow kitchen, frying bacon.

In Jay's unofficial report after the fact, he mentions three "findings." First, that the stoves "produced deadly gas when used inside the tents." Mystified at first by their wooziness, Jackman radioed down to a doctor at the base who "cleared the matter up." They were lucky somebody hadn't died from carbon monoxide fumes, and thereafter they either cooked outside on the snow or made sure to have proper ventilation inside the tent.

Second, the pyramid tents themselves were a disaster. Made of coated, waterproof nylon, the walls were impervious, in either direction. Condensed breath from the four men inside froze on the ceiling and showered "snowstorms" on anyone who bumped the material even slightly. Zippers froze and broke. The whole setup was heavy and recalcitrant. Nevertheless, the Army ordered forty thousand of them.

The third finding was that the food was generally excellent, especially the cocoa, the powdered bouillon, and the canned meat, which became the basic ingredients in the much-maligned but effective and universal "U.S. Army Field Ration K," or K ration. Jay did recommend more sugar in the diet for high altitude and cautioned that "cooking times need to be doubled and tripled thanks to [the low boiling temperature of water at] elevation and the need to melt snow."

In all, the Rainier ski expedition tested the following (listed in the Army's particular style, nouns first):

Bags, sleeping
Tents, ski, sectional & Modified Mead (by Abercrombie,
    NY $68.00)

Boots, universal, felt, mukluks
Goggles
Rucksacks
Packframes
Poles, ski
Radiophones
Stoves
Kettles
Sweaters
Toque
Snowshovel, Bernina [type]
Trousers, ski, wool; and trousers, mountain, windproof
Gaiters
Crampons (copied from a pair of imported Eckensteins)
Rope, climbing, manila
Mitt, ski, outer
Mittens, wool
Gloves, wool
Climbers, ski, mohair
Headband
Mattress, rubber, pneumatic, double cell & single cell
Mattress, tampico fibre
Parka, ski
Axes, ice

On May 16, 1942, the party left Camp 2 at 12,300 feet, without their skis, for the push to the summit. Corporal Peter Gabriel had decided that they would be safer on foot as they crossed the crevasses. What's more, he correctly assumed that most of the soft snow had been blown from the summit dome, exposing an icy surface too dangerous to attempt on skis. Gabriel probably hadn't read the account of the first (and only previous) ski ascent of Mount

Rainier on July 2, 1939, but it would only have confirmed his decision. Sigurd Hall, one of the summiteers three years before, told a Seattle newspaper that his party had to crampon down to 12,000 feet before getting back on skis: "We couldn't ski down [from the summit]. It was wash-boardy and hard as a stone. Even metal edges wouldn't hold. I'm glad I made it, but I never want to try it again." The men of the 87th would have liked to be the first to complete a ski ascent and descent of Rainier, but they recognized that conditions didn't warrant the risk, and besides, they had a 7,000-foot ski descent still to look forward to, from Camp 2 back down to Paradise.

The day proved to be a fine one, nearly windless and domed with blue. Slowly, surely, they advanced, kicking steps in the snow. The fangs of their crampons bit into the ice, and their axes, like sharp walking sticks, provided a third point of balance. At last they were on top. Midwesterner Bradley was moved to rapture:

> Finally at the summit, elevation 14,000+ feet and way above the cloud deck, we stood on the crown of the king. From there we could see the rest of the army of volcanic cones, strung out far to the south [Mounts Adams, St. Helens, Hood, et al], visible almost across the face of Oregon. Their white summits were well above the crest of the Cascade Range . . . a mountain range on top of a mountain range. We were looking at a small sector of the Ring of Fire, a belt of volcanoes that encircles the Pacific Ocean.

It was perhaps inevitable, from this vantage, for the soldiers to wonder which direction they'd ultimately be heading. The Alps? Norway? Many had thought that an Allied invasion of Europe would begin in Norway. This had been Churchill's initial plan, and it made sense to the troopers on Rainier learning to live in the snow. Not that they ever were told where they might be deployed.

Burma? The Balkans? In the Army, rumor took the place of hard information. Norway seemed as logical as any place else.

But Norway would be scrapped in favor of a planned landing in Normandy—where there were no mountains and no need of mountain troops. Perhaps, then, the 10th would be called to make its way north and west from Rainier, out the Aleutian chain, across the Pacific and down the Kurils, along the volcanic necklace that led, one freezing, windswept, mountainous island at a time, to the Japanese homeland.

CHAPTER 3:

"I Love a Soldier"

The first elements of the 87th Regiment arrived at Camp Hale just as the snow began to fly in late 1942. They came by train from Colorado Springs, up over the Continental Divide at Tennessee Pass and down three miles to an alpine meadow at 9,250 feet. Thick swaths of spruce and fir covered the slopes on all sides of the little valley to about 11,000 feet and then gave way to bare, broad-shouldered ridges 13,000 feet high. The train pulled in to a Denver & Rio Grande siding at the foot of the meadow, where a sign by the tracks identified the place as Pando, Colorado.

Camp Hale filled the valley—an instant city, built over one short summer at a cost of $30 million, specifically for the ski troops. (It was named for Brig. Gen. Irving Hale, a Colorado hero of the Spanish-American War.) White-painted barracks marched in precise rows beside the headwaters of the Eagle River, dredged ruler straight by the Army Corps of Engineers. Hale had bunks for fifteen thousand soldiers. The current 87th Regiment filled only about one-fifth of them. It was clear the outfit needed bodies.

From the beginning the War Department had taken the extraordinary step of authorizing the National Ski Patrol System to recruit skiers for the new division, believing, as Bestor Robinson had written in the Sierra Club *Manual of Ski Mountaineering*, that it "is easier to train a skier to be a soldier than to train a soldier to be a skier." This was the first time a civilian organization had been given such a charge, and early on, it worked well enough. Minnie Dole contacted each of the ninety-three NSPS chapters asking them to spread the word to local patrols, schools, clubs, race teams, search-and-rescue teams, first-aiders, and so on. He felt he had to be selective, given the special nature of the force (and his own particular nature), so he required each applicant to submit three letters of recommendation, attesting to skiing and/or outdoor experience and character, before he would recommend a young man to the 87th. An eighteen-year-old intent on joining any other Army unit had merely to pass a physical and pick up his orders.

Most of the letters came from ski coaches or teachers or family members. All revealed something about the times. Many were funny or touching, and even heartbreaking.

Private Elmer Johnson of Houston submitted a letter from his brother:

Pvt. Elmer Wallace Johnson was raised on a farm far from modern conveniences. He has been taught to live from the many things Nature put on this Earth. He can find food and shelter when the snows have fallen and everything is frozen over. He can tell the direction he is going when there is no sun or moon to go by. He knows how to catch and kill small game without the use of a gun, and to sleep warm without blankets or cover of any kind. All these things he can do, I taught him myself.

His Brother, Floyd G. Johnson.

A letter in support of Stanley Pingree of Portsmouth, New Hampshire, read:

He is an excellent skier and has the stamina to be one. He has always been a natural athlete and has never had to strive to be good at any sport. He just plain IS. I am not trying to get rid of my husband, but I do feel that my temporary loss will be your great gain.

[signed] Elinor Manscom Pingree.

Harold Loudon sent this letter.

My Dear Son:
You ask for a recommend. I think you are fit for the mountain troops. You always were a good boy and a hard worker. And I also think you are a brave boy and willing to do the work that is set before you.

Your Mother.

From Horace Stafford, who was in basic training in California:

Last year I decided to join the ski troops and you sent me a blank to fill out. Boy, I was really rarin' to go—but! A certain lil' gal I knew in college winked her eye and wriggled a little and before I knew it I was standing at the altar and saying, "I do." When I thought I had better send my application in, the little woman said, (quote) You are *not* going to join the ski troops and get your neck busted! (unquote) Furthermore, she tore the application up and gave me definite orders to have the generals put me in the air corps when I got drafted, so here I am in the infantry. . . . Seriously, I am very happily married and I love my wife very much, but she doesn't seem to understand how I feel about skiing. Shoot the application out here and if I get in the mountains I'll think of some way of telling my wife.

Volunteers trickled in that first winter, but the National Ski Patrol's limited net could be thrown only so far. And the war effort, ironically, made it harder to get the word out. Following the Japanese attack on Pearl Harbor, the West Coast became a war zone. Japanese Americans were rounded up and sent to detention camps inland. Defense industries and installations from California to Washington were camouflaged in order to fool potential spy planes; the roof of Boeing's aircraft plant outside Seattle was painted to look like a city street. Fear of a second attack led to the mobilization of coastal observers and blackouts and to tight censorship of military movements and training exercises. This meant that no public word, via print or other media, on the doings of the Army's nascent mountain division was allowed. Outside of the Seattle-Tacoma area, not many Americans knew about the ski troops on Mount Rainier. This made Minnie Dole's recruiting job that much harder.

Help came from, of all places, Hollywood. In the spring of 1942, Darryl Zanuck, head of Twentieth Century Fox Studios, had just finished shooting *Sun Valley Serenade*, a light musical comedy starring Sonja Henie, the Olympic gold medalist in figure skating, as a war refugee traveling with Glen Miller and His Orchestra. On location in Idaho, Zanuck had hired the multi-talented Otto Lang, Sun Valley's new ski school director, post Hans Hauser, to shoot the ski action for *Serenade*. (One of the first St. Anton instructors to emigrate to the States—and founder of the ski school on Mount Rainier—Lang had already made one ski movie, *Ski Flight*, which premiered in 1937 at Radio City Music Hall with *Snow White and the Seven Dwarfs*.) Zanuck, a passionate recreational skier himself, decided to make a film on the latest ski instruction theory and practice, so that the future ski troops would have a paradigm to follow. He asked Lang to direct the instructional film.

They began without help or permission from the Signal Corps, the outfit responsible for Army training films. But the Army did authorize a five-man detachment of its own best skiers to appear in the movie, including Lt. John Woodward and the unchallenged "best skier in the world," Walter Prager. John Jay, former ski-film lecturer, was brought in to assist. Lang wanted exactly ten skiers in his action sequences, so he put white anoraks and caps on some of his top ski instructors: Johnny Litchfield, who would succeed Lang as director at Sun Valley; Sigi Engl, who would succeed Litchfield; Fred Iselin, a future director of ski schools in Aspen; and Peppi Teichner, who would go on to found three Midwestern ski schools.

Zanuck made sure that the production quality far exceeded any previous military training film and maybe any ski movie that had come before. Most ski movies were shot in 16-mm. Lang had teams of men and toboggans to haul his 35-mm cameras to the summits. He shot in slow motion and from astonishing angles above and below the skiers. He insisted on shooting every scene in trackless snow. Jay recalled, "We had powder snow, and Otto got so excited at its pictorial possibilities that he practically laid down martial law over the entire area. No one was to move from a designated spot without his written permission, lest the virgin slope be violated by a lusty track or two."

Lang called his film simply *The Basic Principles of Skiing*. The opening sequence shows a fictional recruit, played by the young unknown Alan Ladd, receiving his equipment in a "cabin" erected on a Hollywood sound stage. (Ladd confided to John Woodward that this role was a relief after his last one, an Army cautionary tale shot in a VD ward.) All of the ski action takes place outside on perfect Idaho spring snow. The film is a primer on the Arlberg technique, the one Lang had mastered in St. Anton at the knee of its inventor, Hannes Schneider. From the humble snowplow to sweeping, high-speed christies, Lang and his synchronous skiers made every movement look beautiful. Ten elegant skiers in white uniforms, swooping in line through perfect snow under a sky so clear it looked black on film. Lang may have made it look a little too beautiful. *The Basic Principles of Skiing* was not, strictly speaking, a recruiting film, but it did get around. And more than a few recruits arrived at Fort Lewis or later at Camp Hale grousing that this man's army didn't look anything like the one they'd seen in the movie.

Hollywood fell in love with the 10th. Once Camp Hale was established, film crews descended on Colorado to take advantage of the stark beauty and the charisma of soldiers on skis. *I Love a Soldier*, starring Paulette Goddard and Sonny Tufts (released in 1944), examined the problems in a wartime marriage. Paramount "borrowed" companies of 10th men to show close-order marching drills with skis on shoulders (something that was rarely seen day-to-day at Hale), and had members of the elite Mountain Training Group perform in full whites for the ski action scenes.

During the winter of 1943 Warner Brothers shot a home-front propaganda movie at Hale called *Mountain Fighters*. It mixed patriotic fervor ("And here they come," the narrator's voice fairly sang, "shooting down the long slope like a string of comets! What a vital role they will play in the destruction of the Axis!") with a simple action plot. The hero is a trooper named Sven Torger—an obvious play on Torger Tokle. The real Torger Tokle never commented on *Mountain Fighters*, but the release of the film, in May 1943, produced a major upsurge in volunteers.

Generating volunteers became Lt. John Jay's full-time job. With the move to Colorado and the lifting of media censorship on the mountain troops, Jay was handed the job of public relations officer. He took up the task with missionary zeal. John Jay came from a long line of New York aristocracy, the great-great-great-grandson of the Supreme Court justice. He had been expected to carry on the family traditions of statesmanship and finance (his father served on the boards of the Globe and Rutgers Fire Insurance Company and the Pierce Arrow Motor Company), but he fell in love with skiing and cameras instead. At Williams College, young Jay spliced together footage from various family ski trips and called the film *Ski the Americas, North and South*. Jay often filmed on the move, holding his 16-mm camera at waist level while skiing along beside his. subjects. Audiences loved the sense of flying, the spray of snow virtually in their faces. They also enjoyed Jay's dry Yankee wit. There was no sound track to the film; each showing was narrated in person by the filmmaker. There had been a smattering of amateur ski-film lecturers before; Jay perfected the form, which was later successfully imitated by Warren Miller, Dick Barrymore, and others.

After graduating in 1938, Jay turned down a Rhodes Scholarship and instead took a job managing the Chilean national ski team. He used that job in his second film, *Ski Here, Señor*. But by then, the war was on, Jay was a private in the Signal Corps—in their training-film unit—and he couldn't take his movie on the road. He did convince his new bosses to send someone out in his place, however, in the person of the "comely" ski school director from Oak Hill at Hanover, New Hampshire. "I figured Debbie Bankart ought to be exempt from the draft, at least," Jay wrote later, tongue firmly in cheek. The military paid for Bankart, a pretty brunette, to crisscross the country with *Ski Here, Señor* as a recruiting tool.

Robert Woody was sixteen, too young to enlist, when he saw *Ski Here, Señor* at a theater in his hometown of Springfield, Massachusetts. "When the first snow of the season arrived in New England," Woody remembers, "and the John Jay film came to town, it really got your juices flowing." As a boy, Woody had devoured the writings of Edward Whymper, including *Scrambles amongst the Alps: 1860–69*. In it, Whymper describes the first successful climb of the Matterhorn, after many attempts, and the tragic descent during which four of the seven summiteers fell to their deaths. This was the so-called golden age of alpinism, and Woody inhaled the literature: "the romance, the imagery of climbing and skiing became part of my mindset," he remembers. Woody also remembers Debbie Bankart as "a very witty girl." "Cute, too. She heard a yawn in one of the audiences and said, very quick-witted, 'Need a pillow?'" Later, when he was old enough to join, Woody remembers, "The romance is what got me into it. Not noble thoughts about saving the world for democracy. We got the idea that [in the 10th] you skied a lot, and you got to go to Mount Rainier."

Woody joined up too late for Rainier; that chapter in the legend of the 10th was already history. A seductive chapter it was, though, and John Jay took full advantage of the mystique that grew up around Paradise. As public relations officer, he flooded newspapers and magazines with releases about the mountain troops, often with pictures he'd taken on Rainier's slopes. He arranged press tours to and radio broadcasts from Camp Hale. He convinced Lowell Thomas, the voice of NBC radio news and a well-known skier, to promote the ski troops on his evening broadcasts. *Life* magazine ran a November 1942 cover story, "The Mountain Infantry." A *Saturday Evening Post* cover illustration of a ski trooper dressed head-to-toe in camouflage-white became a widely distributed recruiting poster and an enduring 10th icon. Minnie Dole bought a thousand copies of the magazine with his own money.

The mountain troops were now competing for recruits with the sexy Army Air Corps and Navy recruitment campaigns. Jay dug deep for ideas. He and Minnie Dole arranged for National Ski Patrol men to receive extra gasoline rations on the theory that each one was an Army recruiter. One NSPS patroller drove a white-clad dummy around a Chicago Fourth of July parade that drew 150,000 spectators. Jay sent full sets of the distinctive white uniforms to department stores around the country whose window dressers used them in patriotic displays. He and Dole went to the American Alpine Club for potential volunteers and asked the U.S. Forest Service and the National Park Service to distribute applications to their rangers.

Probably Jay's single most effective PR coup was his third film, *Ski Patrol*. This one he cobbled together from film shot during the 87th's winter on Mount Rainier plus early footage from Camp Hale. There are scenes from the dramatic summit climb and clips of soldiers marching and practicing strict-protocol military skiing. But what must really have grabbed the young men watching it were the crystal blue-and-white days, icicles flashing in the sunlight, and very good skiers, off-duty (without packs or rifles), streaming down the big, treeless shapes above Paradise, their powder wakes like crystalline smoke hanging in the air behind them.

Jay was already a consummate pro. He made sure to weave in snippets of ski humor, which would become a staple of later films. On weekends, the public was welcome to ski Paradise, and Jay's camera caught all of the standard bits of slapstick: the poor kid trying to walk uphill on his impossibly slippery boards; the inevitable disaster when first-timers try to grab the moving rope tow; the flailing and the look of astonishment on a beginner's face when he realizes he will not keep his balance on this run down; the smiles under funny hats; the pretty girls and their GI escorts.

Debbie Bankart took *Ski Patrol* on the road too, to even bigger houses than had seen *Ski Here, Señor*—an estimated seventy-five thousand viewers all told at outdoor clubs and community centers across the country. At every stop she handed out applications for the ski troops.

Taken together, it was an extraordinary marketing effort in an era before the country was knit together by television—an effort that burned an image (whether it was strictly accurate or not) of an army mountain division into the public mind. But it wasn't enough. Over the winter, the 86th and 85th Regiments had been activated to join the 87th and together constitute a division, but by the spring of 1943, the two newer regiments were still undermanned. Minnie Dole realized that there probably were not enough skiers of the right age and inclination to fill the entire division. So, he rewrote the application in a concerted drive to land men with broader expertise: "mountaineers, loggers, timber cruisers, prospectors, cowboys and rugged outdoor men." Thus was born the oft-used description of the 10th's makeup—"from college boys to cowboys." The Army approved of the expanded list, there being some in the War Department who still openly decried Minnie's "ski club."

In the end, although numbers are not precise, of the fourteen thousand soldiers who constituted the 10th Mountain Division at full strength, about half were volunteers who came through the National Ski Patrol System. The remainder were supplied by the Army through transfers from flatland divisions, primarily the 30th, 31st, and 33rd Divisions from Louisiana and Tennessee. Most of the NSPS volunteers, whether they were skiers or not, came in with at least some outdoor experience. They'd supplied the three letters of recommendation. They were keen and physically fit, and they had an affinity for the mountains, or thought they might. And they generally took to the mountaineering ethos created by the 87th, with its singing and camaraderie and willingness—joy even—for strenuous work in the high country. These men adored Camp Hale and took to the training with gusto.

Many of the transfers had a much harder time of it in Colorado, which for them became Camp Hell. They hadn't asked to be there, and they hated every part of it. They hated the snow, the skiing, the cold. The air at 9,200 feet didn't supply nearly enough oxygen for men used to the altitude in Memphis. And to make matters worse, the air in the valley floor was frequently polluted with smoke from the camp's five hundred coal stoves and the Denver & Rio Grande locomotives chugging over the Divide three times a day. In fact, the air was so bad during high-pressure inversions, it sickened scores of men, and not just the Southerners. Many a committed mountaineer also developed what was called the "Pando hack."

Unlike other camps, Hale was largely cut off from the rest of the world. Even if you could wrangle a pass, Denver was a nine-hour train ride away. By car the trip took half that, but almost no one had a car. The nearest town was Leadville, a once grand silver camp fallen on hard times. But Leadville was off-limits to the troops, because, in this busted, Depression-era mine town, one ancient profession continued to flourish. Nowhere to go; nothing to do. USO troupes feared the altitude and shunned the place, and the service clubs offered nothing stronger than 3.2 beer.

Worst of all for the flatlanders was the prospect of strapping long, recalcitrant, slippery wooden boards to their feet. Skiing was a mystery designed to humiliate and embarrass. Warm-country soldiers took to calling their skis torture boards—"toe-chah boahds." One sergeant became so enraged after a day of floundering in deep snow, he chopped his skis into tiny pieces and fed them into a fire. When Robert Woody arrived at Camp Hale, a ski trooper at last in April 1944, the first man he ran into at his barracks was an unhappy noncom with a distinctive drawl. "Where are the skis?" Woody asked with innocent enthusiasm. "So, ye want to ski?" his bunkmate asked, spitting tobacco. "Well, I hope ye bust your ass."

Many of these men asked for and received transfers out of the 10th. But there was a common wisecrack among those who stayed and learned to survive the mountains. They said: "Anyone who transfers to combat from the mountain troops is yellow!"

In truth, transferring out might very well land you in a unit bound soon for combat. The United States and its ninety combat divisions had begun to play a major role in pushing back Axis advances in the Pacific and North Africa. In early November 1942, the first U.S. troops in the European theater had landed on the Moroccan coast near Casablanca as part of Operation Torch. Together with coordinated British landings behind German lines in Libya, Torch spelled the beginning of the end for Hitler's forces in the desert. By January 1943, U.S. planes were flying alongside the British Royal Air Force on bombing missions over Germany. By February, after nearly six months of fighting, Allied forces recaptured Guadalcanal in the Solomon Islands from the Japanese. And, most portentously for the men of the 10th Mountain Division, in May 1943, U.S. and Canadian infantry stormed the snowy Aleutian island of Attu, held for nearly a year by dug-in Japanese.

CHAPTER 4:

The Homestake Fiasco

O n June 7, 1942, a small Japanese naval force steamed into
the northern Pacific and placed approximately eighty-five
hundred soldiers on the barren and undefended islands of
Attu and Kiska, at the western end of the Aleutians, the chain of
islands lying southwest of Alaska. The idea was to create a diversion
for the much more strategically important attack on Midway
Island, midway between Tokyo and Honolulu. Japanese war planners had no intention of hopscotching the Aleutians fifteen hundred miles to Alaska, but the incursion had a chilling effect on the
American public. U.S. territory had been invaded and occupied,
and the islands did look on a map like stepping-stones to the North
American mainland.

Meanwhile, the bulk of the Japanese fleet was on its way to Midway with plans to knock out what remained (after Pearl Harbor) of

the U.S. North Pacific Fleet. The Japanese brought a tremendous numerical advantage: 4 heavy and 3 light aircraft carriers, 11 battleships, 15 cruisers, 44 destroyers, and 15 submarines to go up against America's 3 carriers, 8 cruisers, 18 destroyers, and 19 submarines. The Americans, though, had the incalculable advantage of knowing the enemy's intentions in advance. U.S. intelligence had broken the Japanese navy code and deciphered key radio transmissions. In the ensuing Battle of Midway, carrier-based U.S. bombers attacked the Japanese fleet when it was still five hundred miles from its goal, sank all four heavy carriers and one heavy cruiser, and forced the rest of the fleet to retire. Midway would go down as a turning point in the war in the Pacific, but the Japanese garrisons remained on Attu and Kiska, a thorn in the side of U.S. military strategists, and a lingering embarrassment.

Minnie Dole had imagined the 10th would be a defensive force, fighting a guerrilla action as the Finns had done, repulsing a Nazi invasion of the northern United States. But by late 1942, with German and Japanese expansion contained and, in fact, shrinking, that scenario didn't seen likely. Where then might the 10th be used? Rumors bounced off the mountain walls at Camp Hale like echoes. Actually, no decision had yet been made about where and how to deploy the mountaineers. A lightly armored mountain division didn't fit into the actions in North Africa or the planned opening of a western front in France. More to the point, this new division was not nearly ready to fight. Myriad questions still needed answering. How, in a vertical world, would tactical theory change from flatland fighting? How do you move men and artillery in large numbers over the snow? How will they eat and sleep and stay warm? How to attack, and how to defend? How will it all work?

The early experiments on Rainier had provided some answers, but those had been relatively small groups of, in most cases, already snow-savvy men. So, in February 1943, commanders at Camp Hale ordered the first large-scale maneuvers into the winter backcountry. Some said that the troops were still too green, but the Army needed a baseline, some way to evaluate its equipment and training to that point. A full battalion—one thousand soldiers—plus a battalion of pack artillery would march five miles from near the top of Tennessee Pass to Homestake Lake at 11,300 feet. There they would camp and engage in a number of tactical "problems."

Problems of a very practical and debilitating sort began the instant the order came to march. Many of the thousand were new recruits who had not had time to acclimate to Hale's altitude, and now they were being asked to go higher still. Under the crushing weight of their rucksacks—ninety pounds and more—they staggered up the snow-packed trail. Mortar men and machine gunners carried loads of up to 125 pounds each and suffered commensurately. Some of these men had not yet been taught how to wax their skis for climbing or how to use their plush climbing skins. For every two feet up the trail, they slipped back one. Frustration grew. Sweat poured down necks and into eyes cursing a blazing sun in an otherwise cold, blue Rocky Mountain sky.

Nor were the humans the only sufferers. Hundreds of mules, on whom pack howitzers and other supplies had been loaded, wallowed up to their bellies in the soft snow. When the mules couldn't make the grade, their burdens were unloaded onto sleds, and these were hauled by teams of sweating soldiers on snowshoes.

When the long, white line finally stopped near the shore of Homestake Lake, the perspiration froze. For the next eight days, the daytime temperature hovered around zero. At night it dropped to 30 below. One morning, Cpl. Bob Parker, a young ski racer from St. Lawrence University, reached in a pocket for his glasses, to read a note he was to deliver to battalion headquarters. The metal frames shattered into tiny pieces in his hands while the lenses fell to the snow. A radio message from the nearby town of Eagle put the morning low that day at minus 48 degrees Fahrenheit.

Tents were set up in orderly rows, but tents alone could not warm the frozen troops. Men with some experience, including the native Scandinavians in the outfit, knew to warm themselves from the inside out with hot drinks. They melted snow on their camp stoves and mixed up coffee and hot chocolate. The rawest recruits had not even been taught how to work the ingenious little gasoline-powered stoves that Bestor Robinson and the Quartermaster General's office had developed. These men ate their first-night rations cold.

For the next few days, the medics had their hands full. Men had to be sent down for altitude sickness—headaches, nausea, difficulty breathing—and for simple exhaustion. Frostbite was epidemic. In all, 260 men were treated for frozen extremities. More than a few pulled off their boots and socks and stood around freezing their feet on purpose to earn a trip back down to the relative luxuries of coal stoves and warm beds. Companies dwindled to just a few men. The "enemy detail," which consisted of seasoned 87th skiers, never went into action. There was no way the battalion could have mounted a concerted response.

Clearly, the 10th had a long way to go. Still, there were successes; assignments were carried out, lessons learned. Bob Parker, for one, had a grand time on the Homestake "raid." Fit from months on Rainier's summer glaciers, Parker and a squad from E Company skied up the snowbound east ridge of Homestake Peak right on the Continental Divide at 13,205 feet, "looking for enemy." A Norwegian American in the group, Birger Torrisen, gave a clinic in the art of ski waxing, specifically the use of tacky klister wax when climbing. He went the whole way up without resorting to climbing skins. And then on the way down, he sliced graceful telemark turns in the deep snow, cold powder hanging in the air behind him like a contrail. Parker and the other young Americans followed, awestruck. "Nobody froze," he said later, sizing up the exercise. "Nobody got hurt. We delivered our report: No enemy. It was a fantastic learning experience."

The Scandinavians had other tricks to teach. Tummy warming, for example. They knew that if you needed to warm dangerously cold toes, you took your boots off and put your feet up against another soldier's belly, inside his sweater. Two could play this game, and in fact it worked best when performed symbiotically. They also knew how to build fires right on the snow and keep them fueled with dead tree limbs. These men knew what to do with their breakfast ration of bacon: They slathered their hands and faces with the grease to protect exposed skin against frostbite.

Right away, the experienced snow campers abandoned their waterproof pyramid tents and dug snow caves instead. These were the same tents that had been rejected by the men on Rainier, the ones that caused interior "snowstorms." The Army's double-goose-down sleeping bags kept a man comfortable even at these brutal temperatures, but only as long as they stayed dry, and with four men snoring, there was enough trapped moisture inside the tents to turn feathers to mush. Snow caves were both warmer and more commodious. Body heat kept temperatures inside right around freezing. Properly ventilated, there was no condensation, and a cave could be sculpted to fit any number of occupants, complete with sleeping shelves, kitchen alcoves, and storage areas. These cave dwellers used their tents only to cover the entrances to their underground igloos.

Harry Poschman, an experienced snow camper in the mountains of Southern California, remembers visiting one such snow cave at Homestake on his daily tour of the various machine-gun squads. "This was the greatest. Five men lived in comfort without snowflakes to disturb their sleep. They invited me in with an air of smugness and handed me a cup of hot chocolate. Yes, the ski troops were finally getting better."

Harry and the other ski instructors from the Mountain Training Group practiced their slalom technique on the slopes above the lake. In his memoir, *The Birth and Death of the 10th Mountain,* he wrote: "Soon we were joined by others who understood this mountain life, and we conducted the first Upper Camp Hale Winter Olympics—unofficial of course. This went on until 9 P.M., when it was moonlight." This is the life, Harry thought. This was what he had had in mind when he joined the mountain troops. The cold didn't bother him. "One day Corporal Brelsford and I skied back to Camp Hale, a distance of sixteen miles round trip, just to get a couple of quarts of ice cream."

The Army organized various mountain-warfare experiments during the two weeks at Homestake. One involved resupply techniques. Mules still couldn't negotiate the deep snow, so they had the Air Corps drop food in by parachute. Some of the packages flew well out of range over distant ridgelines or disappeared in the fluffy snow, but one drop did land enticingly nearby on the east face of Homestake Peak. A platoon was ordered out on skis to pick it up, then quickly ordered back; the slope in question was about to become an artillery target. In yet another experiment, the division's artillery commander, Col. David Ruffner, decided to fire his howitzers at the peak, to see if he could artificially trigger an avalanche—to harness the mountain itself as a weapon.

The concept was not new. Devastating snow and rock avalanches figure in the histories of alpine warfare as far back as Hannibal's crossing from Gaul into the Po River valley in 218 B.C. That summer Celtic tribesmen rolled big rocks down from the heights on Hannibal's twenty thousand foot soldiers and thirty-eight elephants. In World War I, a third of all combatant deaths in the Italian Alps were caused by avalanches. (Another third died of cold-related injuries, and the final third were killed in actual combat, mostly in summer.) Over the two winters of 1915–16 and 1916–17, sixty thousand men perished in snow slides, nine thousand in one week at Christmas 1916, when thirteen feet of snow fell above treeline. Avalanches swept away fixed ropes, communications lines, even iron ladders bolted to the rock. Whole companies were buried without a trace. Bodies of the swept-away are still melting out of Tyrolean glaciers today.

There is no evidence that either the Austrian Jaegers or the Italian Alpini used artillery to purposely set off avalanches on one another; big snowfalls and natural slide cycles at high altitudes were deadly enough. But what if, from a distance, one could bring tons of snow crashing down on an unwary enemy? Colonel Ruffner was about to find out. Most of the battalion plus a gaggle of high-ranking officers stood on the moraine at the far end of the lake in anticipation.

The guns were fired from well behind the bivouac camp. Shells screamed overhead and burst one after another just below the cornices lining Homestake's summit. Suddenly, the whole wall of snow fell. The avalanche gained momentum and volume until it completely obscured the front of the mountain. Millions of tons of snow plunged into Homestake Lake, shattering the ice on its surface. Poschman describes it: "The tremendous weight forced the water toward our shore, and the lake leaped into the air like a geyser." Parker remembers the incident somewhat differently. He doesn't recall there was much water in the lake, but that "a wafer of ice, six feet thick, was pushed right up on shore to within a few feet of the brass. We infantry thought this was the greatest show." It might have been a tragic accident too. But Colonel Ruffner got lucky, and nobody was hurt. The name, Homestake Lake, was subsequently changed, and to this day appears on the map as Slide Lake.

The drama at Homestake—experiment or fiasco, depending on your point of view—became known around Hale, particularly among those who *didn't* participate, as "the retreat from Moscow." Minnie Dole, who had watched the whole thing as a civilian observer, criticized the Camp Hale brass in a scathing report to Washington. Dole would retain strong paternal feelings for the 10th throughout the war, and his opinions had clout. At least one officer in charge of the Homestake maneuvers was relieved of his duties soon after.

Minnie proffered a number of general criticisms, some of which couldn't have sat well with Army traditionalists. He suggested, for example, that the staff "is rank happy, with rank at the top and brains at the bottom." (Sgt. Paul Petzoldt, the renowned Tetons climber and guide, put it just as bluntly, if more in tune with his Wyoming cowboy roots. "Here come all these West Point officers," he groused, "and they didn't know a snowball from a spittoon.") Dole knew that the wealth of experience in the 10th lay mainly with enlisted men and noncommissioned officers (Pfeifer and Prager, for example, never got beyond the rank of sergeant; Peter Gabriel was a lowly corporal), and he argued for a system of ideas flowing up the ranks as well as down—a heretical notion. In fact, such a system already existed, informally, from the beginning at Mount Rainier, even if it didn't result in recognition or promotion for the dogfaces with the proper wax on their skis and bacon grease on their cheeks.

Harry Poschman was right; the ski troops were getting better. But it was a circuitous route to competency they took at Camp Hale, a trip made more difficult by the bureaucracy's inability to hear lessons from its underling experts. In that sense, Homestake Lake was a classic snafu—infantryman-speak for "situation normal all fucked up."

CHAPTER 5:

"Too Beautiful a Place to Die"

Harry Poschman wasn't one of the Ivy League guys who gave the 87th its elite reputation. He wasn't a college man at all. When the crash of 1929 wiped out the family business (a Buick dealership in Pennsylvania), Harry dropped out of high school and moved to Southern California to work in his uncle's industrial laundry. He never did finish school. But he developed a passion for skiing as profound as that of any eastern Brahmin.

Most winters, there was snow within an hour's drive of the beach, in the mountains east of San Diego. To the majority of coastal dwellers, this anomaly of weather and high elevation nearby seemed irrelevant. To Harry and a handful of friends, it was a miracle, and it fed their passion for the new sport. There were no established ski areas yet, no Peckett's-on-Sugar-Hill with Austrian instructors to show the way. So Harry and his crew started from scratch. They founded the San Diego Ski Club. Members pooled together $15 to buy a Model A Ford, which they stripped down and used to power a rope tow at Cuyamaca Lake, 5,000 feet up in the Cleveland National Forest. Harry skied every weekend. He became the local style master, and for two years running in the mid-1930s he aced the slalom course at Cuyamaca to claim the county championship.

When he wasn't racing or working on his Arlberg technique, Harry taught himself the tricks of winter camping—in tents he sewed himself out of parachute cloth—on the slopes of San Gorgonio Mountain high above Palm Springs. With climbing skins and a sleeping bag and a miniature camp stove, Harry realized a freedom he'd never imagined before; if it weren't for the laundry job, he'd never have to leave this peaceful, snowy domain.

When, in 1939, Minnie Dole started the National Ski Patrol System, Harry and a bunch of his ski-club mates took the required courses and set up a member patrol of their own. Harry always took his vacations in the winter so he could ride the Union Pacific train north to Sun Valley to ski with the famous expatriate Europeans, with Sigi Engl, Friedl Pfeifer, and Otto Lang.

By the time Pearl Harbor interrupted this idyll, Harry was twenty-nine. His body was lean and fit, but his broad forehead already sported a widow's peak, and his eyebrows drooped with a kind of hound-dog resignation. Harry answered the draft call soon after the December 7 "day of infamy," but bureaucracy and basic training as a machine gunner kept him from a timely meeting with what he called "the real mountain troops on Mount Rainier." Letters from Washington "made it sound worth the effort . . . the big mountain up north where the snow lay deep covering the first stories of their luxurious barracks . . . Paradise, they called it." Camp

Hale, where he did join the troops a few months later, was not paradise, but it was good to Harry through the winter of 1942–43. With his stylish Arlberg turns and obvious experience, he was made a ski instructor, and he even had fourteen other instructors under his command. They lived in rustic one-story barracks right at the base of Cooper Hill, where the Army had erected what was then the world's longest T-bar. Cooper was a pleasant three miles from Camp Hale proper, and so Harry managed to avoid much of the odious duty heaped on enlisted men, things like marching drill and KP. Instead, he and his fellow instructors taught skiing by day to the steady stream of new recruits and drank beer in the evenings, from a secret keg hidden in the rafters. It was good duty, but it was about to end.

On June 11, 1943, the 87th Regiment received orders to pack up and leave Camp Hale for Fort Ord, California, one of the biggest military staging areas on the West Coast. The newer 86th and 85th Regiments would stay behind. The average soldier was told nothing about the mission; all but a few top officers were kept in the dark. The men assumed that Fort Ord would be just a stopover, but they could only guess about their ultimate destination. With a mixture of excitement and apprehension, Cpl. Harry Poschman got his gear together and trundled aboard the waiting trains with everyone else.

Fort Ord teemed with soldiers when the 87th arrived two days later. The camp, on Monterey Bay just north of the old Spanish mission town, looked out over sand dunes to the blue Pacific. It was warm and sunny, not unlike San Diego, and Harry thought that if they couldn't be skiing, this wasn't a bad second choice. "Too bad there had to be a war going on out there somewhere."

The first clue as to their planned deployment was the judo. In the Fort Ord gym after breakfast, instructors introduced the mountain men to the ancient Japanese martial art. Harry and a Greek-

67

American friend named John Vasos drew a petite, blond instructor who said, "Soldier, rush up to me and throw a punch at my face." Vasos demurred, "Aw, lady, I don't want to hurt you."

"Do as I say, soldier." Vasos charged, punched, and landed on his back with the sound of a small thunderclap.

"Next." Poschman was next in line and "watched, amazed, as the ceiling went spinning by." Each man took his punishment in turn, three times in three different maneuvers. The instructor explained that in a real hand-to-hand fight with a Japanese soldier, without a mat to cushion your fall, "you would go down and stay down." A voice from the back of the room chirped, "If ever I get that close to a Jap, I'm not going to rassle him. I'm going to shoot him." To the ski troops, it all seemed surreal. Big Vasos the Greek screwed his face up in contempt and predicted, "This outfit will never go into combat."

Next came endless rounds of immunizations, for the Asian diseases of the Pacific combat area, Harry assumed. The day after the shots the men became stiff and sore, and their food would not stay down. So many men came down with fevers that there was talk of fifth-column treachery within the ranks.

But the fevers cooled, and soon enough the regiment found itself in a new kind of training, colder and wetter than the ski drills had been. First the men scrambled down rope nets from the Monterey pier into landing craft bobbing on a chilly ocean swell. Then they repeated the drill down the side of a big, gray ship anchored offshore. This time the packed landing craft surged ashore, and everyone got soaked charging imaginary defenders in the dunes. Amphibious landings? Judo? Surely the 87th was headed somewhere in the Pacific theater. Some men hurried to marry their sweethearts on weekend leave in San Francisco, and Harry thought blackly to himself, "Who would want to make widows out of such sweet young things?" Meanwhile, he pictured himself flying down a white-powder mountain and wondered if he'd ever have a chance to do that again. He realized how far out of his element he was here, and how much stranger things might still become. He marveled to Vasos, "I signed up to be a skier, not a fighter," but Vasos the Greek just repeated his mantra: "This outfit will never go to war."

U.S. military planners decided early in 1943 that the Aleutian Islands that had been invaded, Åttu and Kiska, had to be reclaimed, for American morale as much as for the islands' strategic value. In fact, they were of little strategic importance. The main Japanese forces were engaged elsewhere; the islands were an unlikely staging ground for an attack on the North American continent. And besides, the U.S. Navy had committed a number of destroyers and other ships to a blockade of the islands, to prevent any resupply or reinforcement from Japan. It was nevertheless decided to send troops to roust the invaders. This proved to be an expensive choice.

The recapture started with Attu, the farther out and less heavily defended of the two, in May 1943. Planners thought it would take between three and five days to clear out the twenty-six hundred dug-in Japanese. After preparatory shelling by air and sea, twelve hundred troops of the 7th Infantry Division landed unopposed on Attu's still-snowy shore. The 7th had been training for duty in North Africa. The marshy Aleutian tundra quickly soaked through the men's desert boots, as it all but swallowed up the division's vehicles. Rain and wind penetrated their khaki jackets. Men couldn't keep their feet warm; there were thousands of cases of frostbite and what in World War I was known as "trench foot" from prolonged cold and wet.

The Japanese, it turned out, had retreated to the high ridges, where they waited for the Americans to come to them. Two and a half weeks later, the last eight hundred Japanese troops charged down Engineer Hill in a final desperate counterattack. They very nearly succeeded in reaching U.S. artillery positions (and turning the guns around on the Americans) before they were stopped. Unwilling to surrender, the remaining five hundred enemy soldiers blew themselves up with hand grenades held to their chests.

All 2,600 Japanese soldiers died, along with 549 Americans. In addition, 1,148 Americans were wounded, and 2,100 were taken out of action by the severe weather. Bitter lessons not to be repeated on Kiska. For that campaign, the Army would marshal an even more formidable force—spearheaded by its newly created mountain troops.

On July 27, three thousand men of the 87th boarded a rusting, thirty-six-year-old, German-built troop ship in San Francisco harbor and steamed north. Destination—for the dogfaces anyway—still unknown. Life aboard the renamed USS *Grant* consisted of "a little sleep, a little swearing at the squawk box, a big craps game, and a big rush for the seasick tube," according to Harry Poschman. Conditions were so cramped belowdecks, one soldier bet Harry he could touch twenty bunks with a six-foot pole. Harry took the bet, guessing he could do better than that. Standing in the middle of the cabin and using his rifle as an extension of his arm, Harry tapped the metal frames of forty-two bunks, sardined from floor to ceiling, without moving his feet.

The squawk box roared to life at any hour of the day or night: "Now hear this! Now hear this! . . ." The men came to see it as an instrument of torture, and after a time, a version of the boy crying wolf. One black night Harry and a fellow machine gunner stood watch on deck when the squawk box shattered the peace. "Now hear this! Now hear this! Torpedo wake off the port bow."

"We strained our eyes and ears, and nervously thumbed the trigger bar on the old 20-mm antiaircraft guns."

"Now hear this! Torpedo wake off the stern." The voice both droned and cackled. The night was so impenetrably dark, Harry couldn't even see the *Grant*'s wake. "Pierpont and I discussed the situation and concluded the guy was a damned liar, just trying to keep us awake. We went back to sleep." And the ship forged ahead into the ever-colder sea with its cargo of guns and equipment and thousands of scared young men.

The USS *Grant* was not alone out there. The Pacific Command had assembled a formidable armada, Aleutian Task Force 9. One hundred ships carried 35,000 men toward the certain dislodging of 6,000 Japanese from Kiska. American soil (even though few Americans had heard of it, way out in the Bering Sea, four thousand miles west-northwest of Seattle—only five hundred miles from Russia's Kamchatka Peninsula). It would be the largest amphibious landing in the Pacific theater to that point in the war. Besides the 87th Regiment, the force included the U.S. 7th Division; the 17th Infantry Regiment; 5,000 men from the Royal Canadian Army's Pacific Command; another 5,000 from the 53rd Combat Team of the Alaska Defense Command; 2,500 men of the 1st Special Service Force (a combined U.S.-Canadian force known as "The Devil's Brigade"); and various artillery, engineer, and other support units.

North and west the task force steamed along the string of islands that reached, like a frigid necklace, across the Bering Sea. Most days fog restricted visibility to a few hundred yards, but one morning Harry awoke, as he wrote in his memoir, to "the most marvelous sight." "Islands, beautiful and green rising up to great heights, looking like the fiords of Norway, were on the horizon." Unimak. Unalaska. Umnak. Adak. After a brief stop in Adak Harbor, during which the 87th experienced its first walk on the tundra ("more like a stumble on a mattress"), the task force headed for Kiska and an invasion scheduled for August 15.

Chief of Staff General Marshall, who authorized the Aleutian campaign, told Minnie Dole after the Attu debacle, "I should have sent alpine troops to Attu." The Aleutians were hardly the Alps, but they *were* alpine: treeless, snowy (even in summer), and devoid of flat ground. Weather was the enemy here as much as the Japanese. Just the kind of place for which the mountain division was being trained and equipped. Like Attu, Kiska bolted steeply out of the wind-swept ocean, a fifteen-mile-long fist of an island with the snow-capped Kiska volcano rising to 4,000 feet at the north end. The only good harbor tucked into a notch on the southeast shore. Task Force 9 would storm the opposite coast on the assumption that it was less heavily defended. The brass wanted the 87th to spearhead the landing, to climb the hillsides inland from the rocky beach and clear out local opposition so that the main force could then come ashore. What they didn't tell the men—for obvious reasons—was that they expected 80 percent casualties among all units on Kiska, worse for the first companies to land.

American planes from the airfield on Adak, 250 miles to the east, had pounded the island for nearly a year, but they were not in the air on August 15 because of the fog. American warships, including the battleships *Pennsylvania* and *Tennessee*, did blast the island's ridgelines, however, as the armada approached Kiska's western shore. The night of the 14th, the men went to bed at 7:00 P.M., and were roused at midnight for sandwiches and coffee. Personal items were left behind in order to carry more ammunition. "We were limited to three days' food and no blankets," Harry Poschman remembered. "If we did not take the island in three days, we would all be dead." Then it was over the side in the dark, down the rope nets into the landing barges, secure your pack, and wait.

The shivering set in almost immediately. Whether from the cold or nerves, the men couldn't tell. No amount of training could have prepared them for this, their first battle test. They had been briefed again and again onboard ship about how important Kiska was and how tricky and dangerous—how skilled in the arts of murder—the defending Japanese were likely to be, every one of them ready to die for the emperor. Rumor pegged the number of enemy soldiers thought still to be on the island at anywhere from 4,500 to 30,000. Imaginations ran wild. Would they defend the beaches or wait, as they had done on Attu, to fight on the high ground? Everyone was afraid. Some reacted with an agitated desire to move, to get going. Others sat numbly in the boats.

There had been other bits of news, just as troubling as the casualty estimates, that the brass had chosen not to tell them. For nearly two weeks Japanese Radio Kiska had been silent. There had been no return fire when, in good visibility, American planes bombed and strafed the island. Similarly, there had been no fire on the U.S. warships from coastal batteries. A photo mission on August 2 showed Japanese trucks bunched together at Kiska Harbor rather than being dispersed, as they should have been for protection. Still, spotters for one air strike reported light flak. Some fliers said they had seen tracer bullets, and one pilot insisted he had strafed a fleeing Japanese soldier, who fell flat. Conflicting evidence notwithstanding, the high command decided that the enemy were simply hiding, as they had been on Attu, in caves and bunkers along the high ground, waiting to annihilate the Americans when they set foot on shore.

Also kept from the landing forces that morning was the fact that a company of Rangers had gone ashore during the night to spy out Japanese positions. They'd been ordered to radio back on what they found, but in the fog and diffuse moonlight they saw nothing, continuing across the island all the way to the eastern shore without sending a single message. When at dawn the first elements of the 87th hit the rocky landing zones, it was assumed the Rangers hadn't reported because they were locked in battle somewhere over the ridge.

In the gray light, Harry drew the "lucky" first position—first out of his barge as the ramp went down. Fortunately, the sea was glassy, the swell almost nonexistent. Harry timed his leap, painfully conscious that the load he was carrying would take him straight to the bottom if he jumped too soon. In addition to his own gear, Harry lugged an extra forty pounds of mortar shells ashore, which he dumped at the high-tide line. On his packboard he'd strapped a poncho, food, ammunition, a rain suit, a belt with a canteen, a bayonet, a shovel, and other small items. His machine-gun squad split the weight of their shared gear, including the gun itself, the range finder, and the aiming circle, and each man topped off his load with the nine-pound Springfield rifle, binoculars, and map case. No one actually weighed the burden, but the total probably approached the infamous ninety-pound rucksacks of song.

In spite of the weight, the first companies of the 87th made good progress up the spongy, tangled, boot-sucking tundra. Much to their relief, the climbers received no fire from above, though one overeager American soldier behind them did squeeze off a long burst of tracers up one of the ravines. By mid-morning, H Company had reached the island's spine, 1,800 vertical feet above the beach, and dug in. Through breaks in the fog, Harry caught glimpses of the volcano still higher to the north. From the ridge, he could see both coasts of the narrow island, a deeply wrinkled carpet of green flung over its rocky bones. Japan was out there somewhere, only about eight hundred miles to the southwest. Closer in, "little boats continued to skitter back and forth from land to ship looking like water bugs on a still pond, and huge battlewagons appeared and disappeared in the fog." The place did have a kind of austere beauty. Not the towering, icy presence of a Mount Rainier. Or the fine, crisp air of Colorado. But it was beautiful just the same. And at this moment, eerily quiet. Hard to imagine that the sharp folds in the landscape before him concealed other soldiers whose job it was to kill or be killed. Harry decided it was "too beautiful a place to die."

Then the williwaws hit. Sudden horizontal rain blew in from the Bering Sea. The wind shrieked so a man couldn't hear shouting from the next foxhole. The ponchos and rain suits they'd been issued worked for only a few minutes; then the water, like needles, pierced every seam until the men were soaked through. They'd never experienced anything like this in training, not even at 14,000 feet on Rainier. Then, just as swiftly as it had arrived, the wind stopped. Beginning in mid-afternoon, the williwaws came and went every couple of hours, replaced between times by swirling fog and mist.

As dark approached, I and K Companies sent patrols out along the meandering, intersecting ridgelines—standard procedure to scout for opposing patrols and to create a buffer zone out ahead of the line. Men in the line took turns peering into the fog and trying to sleep. When they were aboard ship, a system of passwords had been instituted to prevent enemy soldiers from infiltrating Allied positions. Soldiers approaching the line knew to call out "That thing," to which the countersign was "Long limb." In theory no enemy combatant, including possible German advisors, could correctly pronounce "That thing." And at the same time, no Japanese infiltrator, trying to impersonate a friendly guard, could convincingly pronounce "Long limb."

Occasionally, someone would hear something over the scream of the williwaw. Harry's partner got spooked by a sound and banged on Harry's tin hat with a rock. "Japs in the vicinity!" he rasped. "The trouble was," Harry remembers, "as I saw it, the noise was coming from behind us instead of down where the Japs should have been." Then it got worse. "A hysterical voice cried out, 'Give the password or I will fire.' If there was a password, the wind blew it away. The man with the hysterical voice fired. The pretty tracers streaked through the fog making blue and red pyrotechnics just like the Fourth of July."

A nightmare Fourth of July. In the fog and tricky terrain, patrols bumped into one another or else circled back unwittingly to their own lines. Unable to see or hear above the roar of the wind, these inexperienced soldiers became truly blind with a fear that rose up in their throats and choked off reason. Someone opened fire, and then—of course—someone fired back. Tracers lit shadowy figures on the next ridge. More firing. And now the sounds seemed to be coming from all directions, from down in the gully behind, from up ahead, from all around. Panicky fingers pulled back hard on the triggers of their M-1s so that whole clips of bullets fired off in seconds. Smoke and mist, shouts of anger and of pain—were the wounded calling out in English or Japanese?—only added to the chaos.

One K Company lieutenant, Roger Eddy, scion of a prominent Connecticut skiing family, told author Hal Burton in *The Ski Troops*, "There was a lot of rifle fire. Every time a helmet poked up through the fog, everyone let go, and a lot of people simply fired because they thought they saw Japs in the murk. We were all scared stiff, we were green, and everybody expected to die."

Eventually the fighting died down, and as dawn neared, scouts walked out on the ridges to assess the damage. Very soon the night's awful truth came clear: There were no Japanese among the dead and wounded. Fear and fog had cost them seventeen of their own men. Three times that many had been wounded. "We felt as if we'd been on an all-night drunk," said Eddy. "We were exhausted, disgusted, and ashamed. And we knew we'd done all the killing ourselves."

And still, top brass insisted the island's defenders must be there somewhere, holed up in caves or inside the crater of the volcano, waiting. To suggestions that the Japanese had somehow escaped the island without their knowing, the Navy reacted with incredulity. No one could have slipped through the American naval blockade in either direction, they said. Not without our knowing.

So, the anxiety remained, compounded now by the horror of

friendly fire, and the men of the 87th, along with the infantry regiments that followed them ashore, began their second day on Kiska patrolling to the far corners of the island, and waiting.

Bob Parker's I&R (Intelligence and Reconnaissance) platoon had been one of the first to scale the island backbone on the 15th. They saw and heard the shooting that night but, fortunately, had not been involved in the mistaken firefight. Next morning, half the platoon was ordered to stay on the ridge while the other half, eight men, were to work their way down to Kiska Harbor, to ascertain if there were any Japanese there. Down the soaking tundra they scrambled, as inconspicuously as they could, down and across intervening ridgebacks, four miles to the harbor.

Parker was, in some ways, Harry Poschman's opposite. Raised the second of three sons at Parker Farms in central Massachusetts, young Robert had New England roots that predated the Revolutionary War. Five Parkers died at the Battle of Lexington. Relatives were Civil War heroes and founders of Howard University. Great Uncle Howard was the man to whom Cochise surrendered in 1872. He later became superintendent of West Point. Parker men, when called upon, became citizen soldiers. So, after one year at St. Lawrence University, where he ran track and raced on the ski team, Bob quit school and joined the newly formed 87th Mountain Infantry Regiment. He arrived at Fort Lewis just after the storied May climb of Mount Rainier.

Unlike Harry Poschman, Bob Parker didn't regret missing out on Paradise. It wasn't in his nature. With a keen intelligence and the self-confidence that comes from being a natural athlete—the kid who jumped thirty feet off canal bridges in upstate New York and had to be dragged off the local ski hill for supper hours after the light had gone—Parker loved every minute of training and volunteered for I&R school knowing that he would probably see the war from a forward observation post, way out on the point.

Now, approaching the edge of the Japanese encampment at the harbor, he felt "thrilled and terrified at the same time." As he moved from one hiding place to another, however, the terror soon passed. The patrol found scores of bombed-out buildings; the Air Corps had done its job in spite of the fog. They found a harbor littered with sunken barges. They even found a camouflaged launch ramp and a small fleet of miniature submarines. But no Japanese soldiers. All of the subs had been scuttled on their cradles, gaping holes blown in their sides. It was clear no one had occupied the place for some time.

Mission accomplished—and much relieved—the squad set about, in true 87th tradition, to make the most of the situation. There may have been a war on, but there were always opportunities, especially in the wild. Sure enough, one of the men, a Scandinavian American, called out to the others, "At least we can have some salmon." There on a gravel bar where one of Kiska's ice-cold streams entered the harbor, hundreds of spawning salmon thrashed in the shallows. The Scandinavian had already jumped into the calf-deep water and was tossing fish, the firm ones, onto the beach. Someone grabbed a knife and started filleting. Someone else built a fire on the hard sand with boards from a bombed-out building. They nailed the fillets to planks stuck in the sand beside the fire, and when the fish were done, ate the roasted pink flesh with their hands—"plank salmon" they called it with mock culinary seriousness. After weeks of shipboard food and Army C rations, this was a feast of indescribable sweetness, not unlike the one they'd had when Tap Tapley shot that blue grouse on maneuvers in Colorado. When they had eaten all they could hold, they built up the bonfire, took off their wet boots, and leaned back against the long, northern evening.

Meanwhile, elsewhere on the island, patrols explored the elaborate tunnel systems in which the occupying forces had lived and from which they had departed in a hurry. Meals were found half-eaten, and board games on tables abandoned mid-play. There were huge bunkers filled with rice and saki, and some rooms with colorful, silk kimonos. There was an underground hospital, a Shinto shrine, and even a Japanese victory garden with vegetables growing in the volcanic soil. The patrols found two mongrel dogs, the only living remnants of occupation, and one Japanese soldier, dead of natural causes apparently and left underground as the others fled.

Sometime in June the Japanese high command had decided to pull out of Kiska. Their war now was in defending their gains in the South Pacific. The first six hundred men had been evacuated over the course of a month by the miniature submarines. Then on July 28 the Tokyo Express had arrived. A force of light cruisers and destroyers slipped through the fog, and the blockade of American destroyers, into Kiska Harbor. In something less than an hour the remaining fifty-two hundred men of the garrison were hustled aboard. Then the whole force disappeared back out into the North Pacific. It was a stunning feat of organization and stealth, not on the order of the rescue at Dunkirk perhaps, but stunning nonetheless, and profoundly embarrassing to the U.S. Navy.

Perhaps out of embarrassment, or a desperation for certitude, Allied commanders on Kiska waited eight days to declare that there were definitely no Japanese fighters on the island. By this time, the men of H Company had already figured out how to make their own rice wine and how to build walls of boulders to keep their tents from blowing away in the williwaws.

When the official word finally came, John Vasos nodded his head in satisfaction and said, sighing dramatically, "This outfit will never go into combat."

Leaving Kiska would be no easy task, though. First the Army had to bring in a replacement force to hold the island against any future threat. But more difficult than that was the matter of finding transport back to the mainland. The summer of 1943 had seen a dramatic buildup of U.S. forces around the world, and now there simply weren't enough spare seaworthy ships. U.S. war planners had decided to attack Japan from the south and southeast (and not by way of the Aleutian chain or from mainland Asia), and so there had been a tremendous massing of resources in the South Pacific. Then there was the ongoing sea traffic to and from England in preparation for the Normandy landings the following spring.

In May 1943 the British Eighth and U.S. First Armies finally defeated the wily "Desert Fox," General Rommel, in Tunisia and accepted the surrender of Germany's Afrika Korps. In July, the Allies invaded Sicily, and by September the British Eighth Army had hopped across to the boot toe of Italy. Mussolini's Fascist regime was toppled from within, and the new government of Pietro Badoglio began secret surrender negotiations with the Allies. On September 9, the U.S. Fifth Army, under General Mark Clark, landed at Salerno, south of Naples, and began the slow, bloody drive north, from one defensive line to another, against German soldiers who fought desperately and well, despite the loss of their Italian allies. In fact, Hitler had ordered all his armies to stand their ground, never surrender, even in tactically hopeless situations. "Germany shall either be a world power," he proclaimed apocalyptically, his dream of European dominion shrinking with each passing month, "or be not at all."

In short, the Navy and the merchant marine were busy, and the retreat from Kiska became a relatively low priority, leaving some men waiting there for months. Harry Poschman was lucky. He and members of the 2nd Battalion landed one of the first rides off the island on the freighter *John B. Floyd*. "The fun started immediately," Harry remembered of the shipboard celebrations. "Out came Peter [Wick's] accordion and Steve [Knowlton's] bass fiddle. The party was on."

Out came the war souvenirs too—the Japanese machine guns, grenades, shells, pistols, and bullets. The good ship *John B. Floyd* was, according to Harry, "in mortal danger of going to the bottom as the result of an internal explosion." Fortunately, that didn't happen, and "the guys laughed and sang and gambled" all the way to Seattle.

The first stop en route was at Dutch Harbor, Alaska, where the men of the 87th "were treated like heroes," Harry wrote, "for we had chased the Japs from the Western Hemisphere. The lights came on and the people were no longer afraid. Show girls welcomed us. Gorgeous dolls they were, too. We must have looked like a ragtag army to them, dirty and smelly, straight from the land of mud and mildew. A few of the lucky guys got kissed."

In Seattle, it was the same thing, a hero's welcome. The blackout had been lifted; the soldiers got fresh-water showers, new clothes, and new shoes; pretty girls flocked to the dock. But it all came with a hollow echo, for the soldiers knew they hadn't done anything, really. Worse, nearly a hundred of their comrades had died "liberating" Kiska. Twenty-three men of the 87th were killed—seventeen by friendly fire on the first awful night and six more in booby-trapped tunnels or by exploding mines. Fifty-five ski troopers were injured.

Bob Parker's unit didn't start back until December. Resourceful and self-reliant as they were, after three months even they began to feel tortured, by boredom and by the knowledge that both the war, out there, and winter skiing at home, were going on without them. They were finally picked up by a wooden, side-wheeler paddleboat, *The Denali*, a craft designed for the calm waters of the Inland Passage. "We bobbed like a cockle shell" on forty-foot seas in the Gulf of Alaska, Parker remembers. Two Liberty ships broke in half during that storm, but *The Denali* made land at last in one piece.

And Kiska was left to the blue foxes and the puffins and the sea lions. Almost. One group of 87th men never did sail for home; they stayed in the Aleutians for the duration of the war as part of the North Pacific Combat School, or NPCS, which taught "muskeg" combat techniques on the off chance that American troops would invade Japanese outposts in the Kuril Islands. The Austrian down-hiller Toni Matt was one of the NPCS guys. As was Horace Quick, a former National Park Service ranger and survival expert who had been the model for the famous *Saturday Evening Post* cover. Most notorious perhaps was Ernest "Tap" Tapley, who was part Pas-samaquoddy Indian and who grew up trapping, foraging, and skiing in western Massachusetts. On Unalaska Island, where the NPCS was based, Tapley was out messing around with bow-and-arrow one day when an American P-38 fighter plane crashed close by. The plane's pilot, who had parachuted safely to the ground, joked that Tapley had brought his aircraft down with an arrow. Tapley claimed he was just hunting rabbits. Tapley's friends in the mountain troops, some of whom had seen him bring down a full-grown cow elk with a perfectly thrown knife, weren't so sure.

CHAPTER 6:

Sport Imitates War

W hile the 87th Regiment battled what one of the men called "optical Aleutians" on Kiska, nineteen-year-old Pvt. Burdell S. "Bud" Winter was ducking live machine-gun fire outside Camp Hale, Colorado.

The newly designated 10th Light (Alpine) Division refocused training that summer of 1943 from snow to rock. As always in the high Rockies, snow lingered in shady couloirs throughout the summer, but down in camp, the ground was dry and a bright sun warmed the B and C Street rocks just east of the barracks. Climbing classes ran every weekday there and on a granite outcropping at the confluence of the Eagle River and Homestake Creek. Early on, camp commanders decided that the instructors' group should stage a demonstration. Not just a demonstration of movement and rope-handling skills, but a full-on, dramatic exhibition simulating combat conditions. A scenario was devised to inspire as well as instruct new recruits. There would be good guys and bad guys. A squad of armed climbers—the good guys—supported by machine-gun fire would attack a fortified "enemy" position at the top of a cliff.

The attack group was to be led by Tacoma, Washington, climber Chuck Hampton (who wrote about the episode in a privately published memoir), and the defenders by the irrepressible, jug-eared Winter, an Eagle Scout and a high school skiing and pole-vaulting star from Schenectady, New York. The attackers would be climbing unroped, so the route had to be just right: difficult enough to look dramatic but easy enough so the climbers wouldn't be likely to fall. Once the perfect site was located, the climbers spent half a day cleaning the route of loose rock and practicing their moves until they'd memorized every hand and foot hold.

The defenders dug a trench along the top of the cliff to protect themselves from the live fire. There they would lie, detonating quarter sticks of dynamite to simulate grenade explosions until the attackers surged over the top. Also in the trench with them would be a life-sized dummy—an old uniform stuffed with rags—that could be tossed off the cliff during the ensuing hand-to-hand fighting.

They recruited a machine-gun crew from a heavy weapons company and ran through the scene a couple of times for practice. Hampton and his squad got to know the crag so well, they fairly flew up the route. At that point, their platoon leader, David Brower, warned, "Listen, you guys. Don't make it look too easy. You *can* fall off there, you know."

Brower did know. This was the same David Brower who had edited the Sierra Club's *Manual of Ski Mountaineering* and was in the process of writing the Army's new field manual for mountain operations. A passable skier, Brower's real expertise was on rock, where his skills were world class. The shy, beanpole, piano-playing drop-out from Berkeley was a stalwart, along with Hampton and Winter, of the Mountain Training Group, most of whom were already adept skiers and climbers when they joined the Army. The super competent John Woodward served as the MTG's first commanding officer; the second CO was the ubiquitous renaissance man John Jay. There were never more than 150 of them in the teaching group, each man hand-picked, including obvious choices Friedl Pfeifer and Walter Prager, Rainier guide Peter Gabriel, as well as young hotshots like Bud Winter, and, when they got back to Colorado from Kiska, the likes of Bob Parker and Harry Poschman.

The day of the demo came. Bud Winter and his defenders slid into their trench. Chuck Hampton and the attackers hid in the bushes at the base. The audience, a battalion of infantrymen, spread out on the ground well back of the machine gun.

With a burst of machine-gun fire ricocheting off the cliff, the performance was on. The attackers scrambled across the talus slope at the foot of the wall and then swarmed up the rock, the machine gunner adjusting his fire so that bullets struck the hill behind Winter's dugout. Just below the cliff top, Hampton writes, "I threw a stick of wood over and waited until one of Bud's quarter sticks of dynamite exploded loudly."

With that, the machine gun stopped firing; we charged up and over to engage in a bit of friendly wrestling with Bud and his defenders. Andy Black, one of our attackers, took on Nate Morrell in hand-to-hand combat that culminated in a bayonet thrust and a blood-curdling shriek as the dummy was hurled from the cliff. It was all very realistic. So realistic that John Woodward told me later some senior officers had been alarmed when the dummy was finally thrown from the cliff top. He told them it was what happened to soldiers who didn't follow orders.

The exhibition lasted four or five shows, most or them performed on warm summer evenings. The audiences loved it—they regarded the show as shirtsleeve burlesque. Each time at the conclusion, as Hampton remembered, "the demonstration team stood at the top and acknowledged the accolades with formal bows." During what turned out to be the final demo climb, phosphorus-filled tracer bullets from the machine gun ignited dry grass on the hill behind the defenders' trench and started a wildfire that swept instantly, it seemed, into summer-dry brush and aspen trees. While the fire raced uphill, the performers, including the dummy, retreated back down the rocks. There was nothing to do but let the fire burn, which it did until winter's first snow finally doused the smoldering. For weeks during the fall, smoke from the fire settled over Camp Hale and mixed with the ever-present coal haze to exacerbate the Pando hack.

These men trying to create a mountain division were improvising as they went; there was no blueprint to follow. David Brower felt the live-fire exhibition was of dubious value compared to the MTG's hands-on daytime instruction in the tying of knots, the proper placement of pitons in the rock for protection, and the crucial protocols involved in belaying a man, or in this case whole squads of men, safely up or down a vertical face.

Brower's pragmatism was rooted in the mountaineer's need to return alive to climb another day: Getting to the top is optional; coming home is not. But climbing was also his obsession, his "moral equivalent of war," to use the philosopher William James's phrase, and some of that passion found its way into the 10th's training. The years leading up to World War II had seen a radical shift in alpinism, as equipment improved and the list of the world's great unclimbed peaks shrank. Climbers tackled harder and harder routes. Bestor Robinson hammered iron pitons into cracks in the rock and introduced aid climbing to Yosemite's granite walls in

1934. Brower himself used "extreme" climbing techniques in his first ascent of New Mexico's Shiprock Peak with Robinson and two others in 1939. Europe's last unclimbed walls were being knocked off one by one, until the last great "problem" in the Alps, the north face of the Eiger, was finally conquered in 1938. The traditional "romanticist philosophy of mountaineering," wrote the historian John Keegan, "which laid stress on its spiritual value to man through the harmony it engendered between him and nature" had been largely replaced by a desire to "push to the limits of what is physically and psychologically possible."

"Mountaineering," Keegan surmised in *The Face of Battle*, "has become in our time a sort of military operation in which sport imitates war." For evidence, he had but to paraphrase the literature on the Eiger's many attempts, tales of climbers "crouching, shivering, day after day in tiny, filthy holes hacked with infinite labor, short of food, depressed by the death of comrades, expecting at any moment to be swept away by avalanche. . . ."

Dave Brower never lost his sense of harmony, his joy and wonder at the places climbing took him, but he nevertheless utilized the military terminology his sport had adopted. Writing in *For Earth's Sake: The Life and Times of David Brower*, he discussed a failed attempt to scale British Columbia's Mount Waddington in 1935. He talked of "assault teams" and "support teams" and of "pushing forward on two fronts." He and his partners planned a "ten-day attack on the peak" but were repulsed ultimately by "barrages" of stones and ice from above: "Waddington had deployed [its] defensive weapons."

So, the climbing instruction at Camp Hale, by the very nature of the sport, dovetailed with the military objectives. Where skiing (the other half of a mountaineer's skill set) was essentially an individual sport, climbing was fundamentally cooperative. Share a rope with another man on a vertical cliff, and you will perforce develop "mutual dependence and comradeship." That from the Austrian Heinrich Harrer, one of the pioneers on the Eiger Nordwand. A climber functions best, Harrer wrote in *The White Spider*, when there is a "sense of mutual reliance . . . subordinating his personal well-being to the common weal." One would be hard pressed to find a better description of the Army's formula for success: replacing the individual's goals with an overarching loyalty to the squad, the platoon, the company, the battalion.

Not that all of the climbing at Hale was deadly serious. Even Dave Brower was not above a little fun. Twice a month, with his fellow instructors Dick Emerson and Leo Healy, he would put on a falling demonstration, or rather a demonstration of how to hold a piton fall:

> Leo would climb up a thirty-five-foot cliff to a carabiner through which the rope ran back down to Dick. He would then gather in about twenty feet of slack and jump, relying upon Dick to stop his fall, pulleywise, from below. Mere stopping of the fall became so routine that I would place an X on the cliff and have Dick stop Leo so precisely that his feet would strike the mark—which was three feet off the ground. My part in the demonstration was to give the lecture—and to insist that the mark be at least three feet high.

Before the war, no one would have been crazy enough to try this falling stunt. That's because the hemp ropes climbers used had very little stretch to them, very little give before the rope simply snapped. Climbers used their ropes for protection against a possible fall but rarely tested the ability of their cords to hold a fall. With the arrival of the war, traditional sources of hemp (Italy and the Philippines) went away. An alternative material had to be found, and not just for the mountain division but for the Navy and Air Corps as well.

The answer came in the form of a new petroleum-based fiber called Perlon. The original patent was, ironically, German. But the American company DuPont had a cross-licensing agreement and had already begun manufacturing what it called "nylon." Before 10th Mountain climbers got hold of nylon rope, it was already in use by the Army Air Corps for parachute cords and glider towropes. Then 10th climbers were asked to test the new ropes, which could be formulated with varying degrees of stretchiness. When an early prototype arrived at the offices of the Quartermaster General, Bob Bates, a well-known climber who had been with Paul Petzoldt on K2 (the world's second-highest peak) in 1938, tied one end to his desk and the other around his middle and proceeded to rappel out the window. The stretchy rope let him down farther than he had intended to go, and he ended with his legs dangling outside the window of the floor below. A secretary in that office screamed, certain that someone had hanged himself.

The Army eventually got the stretch right and shipped thousands of 120-foot, olive-drab, nylon climbing ropes to Camp Hale for the safe training—and amusement—of the mountain troops. Nylon not only reduced the sudden impact when stopping a fall, it turned out to be much stronger than hemp, more abrasion resistant and far more supple, easier to handle and coil. Though the 10th's equipment wing, the Mountain and Winter Warfare Board, couldn't exactly take credit for inventing it, the nylon rope did in fact presage a revolutionary new era for rock climbers.

Bud Winter, young as he was, turned out to be very adept with the ropes. He got so excited when he passed his climbing instructor's test, he wrote home immediately: "Dad, passed my test with the fifth highest mark in the troop. Friedl and I had the same mark: 44 out of a possible 50!"

Everything about the 10th thrilled Bud: "The camp and the

trip to the camp are the most beautiful things I have ever seen in my life. We traveled up the Arkansas River between 1,000-foot cliffs and saw the world's highest suspension bridge [at Royal Gorge], 1,300 feet high! . . Dad, Toni Matt and Herb Schneider (Hannes Schneider's son) have just joined our troop. What a ski team!"

He wrote home with observations on everything from the wild-flowers to the famous skiers in the MTG:

Guess I have been boring you talking [about] how swell our troop is. Found out yesterday that 15 out of 40 men in my barracks have won United States winter sports records, and eight of them hold world records. . . .

Hiked twenty miles to Tennessee Pass and over Chicago Ridge, over 13,000 feet. From the top we could see the second and third highest peaks in the U.S.: Mt. Elbert (14,431) [actually 14,433 feet] and Mt. Massive (14,415) [actually 14, 421 feet]. . . . There are more wild flowers above timberline in these mountains than you have ever seen before. The columbine are deep purple and white. They look just like orchids. . . .

This morning we gave a demonstration of an assault on a cliff. I was one of the enemy and had to light and throw sticks of dynamite while they shot over my head with machine gun tracers. I'm not kidding: I was scared.

Chuck Hampton remembered Bud as having "a personality just like a puppy. He was friendly with all his fellow soldiers, relentlessly cheerful and optimistic, trusting of everyone and everything and . . . without a mean bone in his body. . . . He had two obsessions in life. One of these was skiing, the other was fly-fishing . . . As far as we know, he was the only man in the entire division who had brought his fly-fishing outfit to the war."

"I've had some excellent trout fishing," Bud wrote home. "Sure love it out here!"

When he could, Bud liked to fish for native cutthroats in the ice-blue lakes at timberline. And when he couldn't go high, he took his fly rod a couple of blocks to the Eagle River where it ran through camp, still chock full of brookies in spite of its ruler-straight course.

To read Winter's letters is to hear only his congenitally upbeat *Field & Stream* version of the ski army. Most men of the 10th were also well aware of the wider war that summer and fall of 1943.

In the Pacific, in accordance with the U.S. strategy of moving up deliberately from the south, Gen. Douglas MacArthur's armies took the Solomon Islands one by one, attacked the crucial Japanese naval base at Rabaul, and, with Australian units, advanced up the coast of New Guinea toward Japanese-held positions there.

In Europe, following the Allied victory in North Africa, only one front remained active, that on the east. Stalin pleaded with Churchill and Roosevelt to open a second, western front to relieve some of the pressure on his people, but the long-planned-for invasion of western Europe still was not ready.

The great strategic disadvantage Hitler faced in 1943 was the immense breadth of his conquests. German armies were spread out over thousands of miles, from Moscow to Stalingrad, from Athens to Paris. Occupying forces battled resistance movements in Greece, France, Norway, Yugoslavia, the Soviet Union, and Poland. Additional resources were tied up carrying out the Reich's genocidal policies against the Gypsies, Jews, and Slavs within the conquered lands. Hitler knew the Allies would attempt an invasion in the west, but he didn't know when or where. Defense of the vast empire turned out to be much more problematic than the initial expansion.

Meanwhile, the buildup for the cross-channel Normandy invasion continued as men and materiel poured into southern England. In the interim, at Churchill's insistence, the Allies instigated "more modest operations" against Europe's "soft underbelly," moving into Sicily on July 10, 1943, and then, in early September, onto the Italian mainland. German General Field Marshall Albert Kesselring had only eight weak divisions with which to defend southern Italy. In theory, he also had the Italian army in reserve, but the Germans felt the Italians had proven to be ineffectual fighters, and the Italian surrender (negotiated in secret by Marshal Badoglio and Gen. Dwight Eisenhower) on September 8 took them out of the fight. (As per the deal with Eisenhower, Badoglio would complete the official about-face and declare war on Germany on October 3.)

Kesselring chose not to confront the British Eighth Army landings on the toe and heel of the Italian "boot." But he did contest, effectively if temporarily, Gen. Mark Clark's U.S. Fifth Army landings at Salerno just south of Naples. Then he pulled back to a defensive line (this one was called the Gustav Line), from coast to coast across the mountainous spine of the country, in the first of a series of protective moves, designed not to win the war, but simply to hold on to as much territory as possible for as long as possible. Hitler had apparently resolved to preside over the downfall of the German nation, and Kesselring, a good soldier to the end, would use his limited resources and the rugged Italian geography brilliantly to slow the Allied advance, to delay the inevitable, for nearly two more years.

As the 10th began its second winter at Hale, the winter of 1943–44, Bob Parker returned from Kiska and rejoined his I&R platoon. They studied map reading, radio operation, and uniform and aircraft identification. Before Kiska, ironically, they had learned to identify only German uniforms and aircraft. After Kiska, they studied both German and Japanese livery.

Harry Poschman came back to his first love, teaching skiing with the MTG up on Tennessee Pass. The Cooper Hill T-bar dragged skiers a mile and a half up the Continental Divide to 11,700 feet. The terrain wasn't very steep on Cooper's rounded shoulder, but the snow stayed good and cold up so high. And Harry could practice his elegant Arlberg turns, of which he was so proud. "It was nothing but a damn ski club," he says, with much fondness.

Every day, soldiers from the newer regiments trucked up from camp with their white-painted skis, their square-toed, leather mountain boots with the white spats-like gaiters to keep the snow out, their bamboo ski poles (manufactured for the war effort by the Orvis fly rod company) with baskets as big as phonograph records, and they lined up and got their lessons. Harry taught the classic Arlberg progression: walking, sidestepping, kick turn, snowplow, snowplow turn, sideslipping, traversing, and finally the stem turn and skidded stem christie. At the end of six weeks each set of skiers took a proficiency test. Most passed; many caught the bug, became experts, and bonded in spirit, and in song, with the early 87th skiers.

When you were in, you got to sing the 87th Glee Club songs, like "Oola and Sven."

Oola had a cousin from the wild and wooly West.
While Oola liked the skiing, Sven liked snowshoeing the best.
They got into the mountain troops and put it to a test.
And everywhere they went they gave their war whoop.

Chorus:
Oh, give me skis and some poles and klister.
And let me ski way up on Alta Vista.
You can take your snowshoes and burn 'em, sister.
And everywhere I go I'll give my war whoop.

PETER SHELTON

Everyone was keen to see how it would all turn out.
The Winter Warfare Board was standing anxiously about.
And even Axis agents had been sent up there to scout.
And everyone was waiting for the war whoop.

(Chorus)

The colonel pulled the trigger and they started out to race.
Sven got an early start and set a most terrific pace.
But Oola whipped right by him with a sneer upon his face.
And when he reached the top he gave his war whoop.

(Chorus)

Two seconds later Oola finished in a mighty schuss.
A-passing on the way poor Sven a-lying on his puss.
The moral of this story is that snowshoes have no use.
And poor old Sven no longer gives his war whoop.

(Chorus)

The Eighty-Seventh had a heavy weapons company.
They spent six weeks at Paradise and never learned to ski.
The reason for this tragedy as you can plainly see
Is everywhere they went they wore their snowshoes.

Oh, give them skis and some poles and klister.
And let them ski way up on Alta Vista.
They can take their snowshoes and burn 'em, sister.
And everywhere they go they'll give their war whoop.

While most of the MTG was busy in Colorado that winter of 1943–44, some members of the elite training outfit were detached elsewhere, to the Upper Peninsula of Michigan, for example, to teach courses in winter survival to regular infantry divisions. And the Army sent MTG stalwarts, including David Brower and Peter Gabriel, to establish a climbing school across the country at Seneca Rocks, West Virginia, where upwards of ten thousand flatland infantry from five different divisions got at least a basic introduction—a week's worth—of rock work with the experts.

One of the strangest and most fondly remembered of the detached assignments sent 10th men up to the Canadian Rockies for two months, July and August 1942, on the Columbia Icefields. This was a secret mission to test new over-the-snow vehicles. The Studebaker Corporation had a contract with the Army to build such a vehicle, and the mountain troops' job was to build the camps, keep the engineers and their prototypes from falling into crevasses on the glacier, and ski as much as possible on their days off.

The engineers tested ten to fifteen different designs, settling finally on a small, tracked, mini-tank-like thing that became known as the Weasel. Weasels saw limited action on Kiska, where tracked machines proved better than trucks with wheels in the deep mud. At Camp Hale, where the brass hoped the Weasel would serve as a kind of go-anywhere snow jeep, reviews were mixed. They went well enough on the snow-packed roads, but in deep, unconsolidated powder, they bogged down and dug themselves into ever-deeper holes. They also had a tendency to throw off their tracks, as a mule occasionally throws a shoe. Bob Parker complained that one of the prime skills his I&R team had to learn was how to muscle the track back onto a derailed Weasel. Weasels were popular with their drivers during winter's coldest snaps, though: Without removing a glove or lighting a match, these men could heat their C rations on the engine manifold.

Things were much more low-tech for infantry learning the basics in Michigan. There an MTG detachment trained elements of the 76th Division in snowshoeing, cross-country skiing, and winter survival. They slept in lean-tos on frozen lakes and tromped around for weeks at a time through logged-over forests in sub-zero weather. The land was almost dead flat, so there was no downhill skiing. For fun, the instructors went skijoring. They strapped on skis, wrapped a length of telephone cable around a car bumper, held on to the cable, and toured the countryside around the iron-ore town of Watersmeet. You could skijor behind the car of a willing friend, or you could hitch a ride behind an unsuspecting driver. The roads were all snow covered, except for the bridges. When they saw a bridge coming, the skiers just leaned back on their heels and tore across. They'd get new skis when they returned to Colorado.

If you were lucky, you went skijoring with Albert Gronberg, a large and often angry Finn who had fought in the Russo-Finnish war. When the Russians finally won that mismatch, Gronberg escaped to Norway, then shipped out to the United States. On the way across, a Nazi U-boat sank his ship, and he floated for twenty-four hours in the North Atlantic before being picked up by an Allied freighter. Soon after landing in New York, he was drafted and eventually found his way to the MTG.

There were a lot of Finnish immigrants in and around Watersmeet. You could tell their houses by the saunas in the back-yard. When it was lunchtime on a skijoring adventure, Gronberg would let go of the tow cable at the nearest Finnish home and walk right in, inevitably to a warm welcome. There was little news coming out of Finland at the time, and Gronberg, as one of the last people to leave the country, was like a walking newspaper. After sharing what stories he could, Gronberg (and any mates that happened to be along) invariably tucked into a generous, home-cooked meal.

Soon after this detachment's return to Camp Hale, in February

1944, a group of the MTG's more ambitious skiers decided to ski over the Continental Divide to Aspen. As the crow flies, it wasn't that far, maybe thirty miles, but the actual distance over the snow would be twice that and require a snow camping trek of at least four days and three nights.

Camp Hale soldiers had been making the four-hour drive the long way around to Aspen—down the Eagle River to Dotsero, down the Colorado River to Glenwood Springs, then up the Roaring Fork River to the ruined silver town—with some regularity on their weekends off. The old place was just one step above ghost-town status, but there was skiing there. In the mid-1930s, a group of eastern investors had seen the potential for European-style skiing in the high country nearby. Their grand plans were permanently interrupted by the war, but their Swiss advisor, André Roch, convinced townspeople to cut a trail down the face of Aspen Mountain into the heart of town. The resulting Roch Run hosted the national championships down-hill in 1941, and it provided a world-class descent of nearly 3,000 vertical feet to those soldiers willing to hike for it. The only lift in Aspen in those days was the dime-a-ride "boat tow," a tippy, twelve-person sled hauled up a short beginner slope by an old mine cable.

Chuck Hampton notes in his memoir that an unusual number of 10th troopers (unusual for a regular Army division) "spent precious weekends skiing and climbing instead of or in addition to pursuing the more common military sports of pub crawling and chasing women." Aspen appealed to the real skiers in the division; there was but one bar there, and a terrible paucity of young women.

The MTG group, thirty-some men headed by then Capt. John Jay, hoped to make the trip overland. It was to be both a reconnaissance training and a "pleasure exertion," as one soldier wrote in the *Camp Hale Ski-Zette*. Under heavy loads (they carried ten days' food in case of bad weather, and the despised impermeable, four-man tents), they set out in fourteen inches of fresh snow. Breaking trail knee-deep required so much effort that they had to rotate leaders every ten to fifteen minutes. Hampton remembers that the ever-eager Bud Winter "seemed to actually enjoy the work." "Aware of Bud's propensity for trying to please everyone, we were more than happy to oblige, allowing him double shifts and even going so far as to compliment him on how rugged he was."

Bud wrote home: "I have acquired the name 'rugged Winters' from the trip. I guess I was in a little better condition and tired some of the other fellows out when I was trail breaking."

The mountaineers crossed three passes higher than 13,000 feet and enjoyed downhill runs of up to six miles "without stopping—in new powder!" Winter wrote. "It was beautiful." The only problems seemed to be melting enough snow morning and evening to stay hydrated in the dry, high-elevation air, and breaking apart the infamous D ration chocolate bar, which had been specially formulated not to melt in the tropics. In Colorado in the winter, it was hard enough to break your teeth. Mostly, the dehydrated food worked out fine. The men boiled up stews of rice, dried meatloaf, tomato powder, cheese, and condiments. For breakfast they cooked a mixture of rolled oats, bits of fruit, raisins, dates, sugar, and powdered milk and drank cups of instant Nescafé.

On the final climb before the descent to Aspen, Captain Jay and Sgt. Paul Petzoldt of the 10th Medics disagreed about the stability of a particular slope. Jay thought it would be fine to zigzag directly up the face. Petzoldt argued that the intense sun of the previous three days had created potentially dangerous avalanche conditions and announced finally that he would be skirting around the suspect slope. Six men joined him for the end-around, while "the rest of us," Hampton wrote, "not choosing to spend the remaining years of our military careers on John Jay's skunk list, meekly followed him."

There weren't many men in the world who knew more about avalanches than Petzoldt, though the actual science of snow was in its infancy then. Even the experts relied heavily on experience and intuition, and Petzoldt, by the time he joined the 10th at age thirty-four, had had plenty of each. A polar opposite to the intellectual, self-deprecating David Brower (the other "famous" American climber in the division), Petzoldt was an expansive, bear-like man, with berry thickets for eyebrows. Fabulous stories—most of them true—were forever being attached to his legend. The first was that he had scaled the 13,770-foot Grand Teton in Wyoming, a serious rock climb even today, at age sixteen, in his cowboy boots. In 1938, he joined the first American expedition to K2, in the Karakoram Range on what is now the border of China and Pakistan. Petzoldt's group didn't succeed in reaching the top—an Italian group made the first ascent in 1954—but Paul did establish an American altitude mark of 26,700 feet and set a record for the longest stay above 20,000 feet. Legend has it the preternaturally fit Petzoldt could have summited, without supplemental oxygen, had the team planned a little better. He even brought back the world's first color photographs from those altitudes.

In the 10th, Petzoldt shared invaluable lessons on dressing for the cold. (Winter daytime temperatures in Jackson Hole, where he ran the nation's first guiding and mountaineering school, rarely popped up above zero and often stayed down in the minus-20-degree range.) He told the ski troops: Keep a wool layer next to your skin—never cotton; cotton fiber absorbs water, but wool helps wick the moisture away from the skin—and keep a second pair of socks on your torso sandwiched between underwear and sweater, where body heat will help to dry them out. Cold feet were a greater threat to a maneuvering army (witness Attu) than was the enemy.

He also worked to develop the 10th's standard operating procedure for mountain rescues, along the way devising a rescue sled from existing body baskets set on skis. At Hale, he orchestrated scores of actual evacuations of frostbite and hypothermia cases and of one person with a burst appendix on maneuvers in below zero weather. Summers, Petzoldt designed a "zipline" procedure for getting lots of troops down a cliff in a hurry. Soldiers clipped onto a fixed line and jumped—like paratroopers jumping out of an airplane—sliding at high speed down the rope to the ground. Petzoldt was quite proud of the fact that among hundreds of "zipliners" there were "lots of bruises but not a single broken bone."

Captain Jay, an Easterner, had nonetheless spent many days in avalanche terrain, on Mount Rainier and in the course of his film work, and he doubtless felt secure in his decision to lead the troop directly up the steep snow slope. He probably didn't tell his followers about the time he had led a detachment in the high country above Ashcroft for the express purpose of studying avalanches. On the way up, a corporal in the squad triggered a slide and rode it all the way to the valley floor. When the snow stopped moving, only the corporal's head was showing above the surface. Jay had been so intent on capturing the slide on film that he failed to notice a sympathetic release, which swept his skis out from under him and left the camera staring at the sky. Both men were unhurt.

Bud Winter might have heard that story about his CO. He certainly had several of his own to tell. The most dramatic probably was the time he joined another detached group trying to summit Mount Democrat, one of Colorado's 54 "fourteeners," in the Mosquito Range east of Camp Hale. The climbing party had to cross a number of very steep snow gullies to gain the summit ridge. Each couloir was filled with four to five feet of wind-blown snow and another ten inches of hard wind slab on top of that. The question was, Would the wind slab hold their weight? Staff Sgt. Bill Hackett kicked at the hard slab and decided it was safe to proceed. Two steps later the whole thing let go, and Hackett found himself prone on a moving block of snow.

Sgt. Skip Finn later wrote in the 10th's newspaper, the *Blizzard*:

No one could have possibly thought faster than Bud Winter did. He was just behind Sgt. Hackett but was standing below a rock which prevented the snow around him from avalanching. With his left hand he grabbed the rock, threw himself on the snow and reached out with his right ski pole to Sgt. Hackett. "Grab the pole!" he yelled. Hackett did. He was just able to grasp the part below the snow ring and hold on to it while the snow went out from under him, tumbling 2,500 feet down the couloir.

A lot of skiers had encounters with moving snow during the two winters at Hale, most of them rather less exciting than Hackett's. And remarkably, no one was seriously hurt in a slide. Both parties on the way to Aspen made it safely to the saddle. Hampton figured the larger group with John Jay in the lead "had simply been lucky." Petzoldt's team, with farther to go, took a little longer to gain the ridge. "So respected was Petzoldt," Hampton remembered, "that when he reached the top, knowing glances and shoulder shrugs were exchanged but nothing further was said about the dispute."

Typically upbeat, Bud Winter reported simply, "Paul Petzoldt was along. He was the man who climbed on the K2 expedition. He wants some of us to come on another expedition after the war."

That afternoon the troops skied right to the center of town over Aspen's empty streets. Laurence Elisha, proprietor of the Hotel Jerome, the only working hotel during those "quiet years," offered the tired crew showers and beds for the night. And he put two bottles of Seagram's Seven Crown on the bar and said, "Help yourselves." Chuck Hampton peered through the dim light at the furnishings: "The still elegant and ornately carved woodwork, the carpets . . . [were] showing signs of their antiquity. The bar was some forty feet long, complete with a brass rail to rest your foot on." High on the wall, a life-sized painting of a gossamer nude gazed languidly at no one and everyone, and over in one corner, a green cloth covered a card table. "The only thing missing was a bunch of trail worn cowboys or dirt-stained miners bellied up to the bar."

Laurence Elisha was a mountaineer too. He knew what the guys had achieved in skiing over from Pando. He appreciated their enthusiasm for skiing in general and for his mountains in particular. He enjoyed being around their vitality and their innocence. And he knew that sooner or later they would surely be asked to put themselves in harm's way.

Elisha had a standing deal with the ski troops: A dollar a day got you a bed at the Jerome and a steak dinner. Scores of soldiers took him up on the offer whenever they could wrangle a weekend pass from Hale. There wasn't much else to do, frankly. Leadville was still off-limits. You could go to Denver (a four-and-a-half hour drive in good weather), and many did for the parties and the warm hospitality of local families (and bartenders) who felt duty-bound to keep the troopers' spirits high. The big event on Denver weekends—besides mixing punch in the bathtub at the Brown Palace Hotel—was the subsequent, impromptu rope demonstration; lightheaded troopers couldn't resist rappelling down the hotel's atrium walls.

On Aspen weekends, they'd pile into somebody's car on Friday, at 5:00 P.M. sharp, drive three or four hours to the Jerome, bounce up early for skiing both Saturday and Sunday, and straggle back to camp in time for reveille Monday morning. In Aspen they had to get up early in order to catch the truck to the Midnight Mine. Bob Parker remembers greeting the driver and another miner in the semi-dark. The skiers would throw their skis and packs in the back "among the cables and shovels and other mine equipment" and then clamber in on top of the mess for the cold ride up Castle Creek.

The Midnight was on the back side of Aspen Mountain, one of the few silver mines still in operation. A ride with the mine crew gained you 2,000 vertical feet on the way to the top of Roch Run. The final thousand-foot climb with skins on "revived our circulation and our spirits." On the ridge they removed their skins and "glided north taking in the glorious scenery across the Roaring Fork Valley." "This was why each one of us had joined the ski troops," remembers Parker, "fresh powder snow, and the mountain world all to ourselves."

They'd stop for lunch—sandwiches provided by Mrs. Elisha, Laurence's wife, Svea—someplace where they could see the naked, timberline cirques of the Elk Range—Highland, Castle, Mount Hayden—the ones that had so charmed André Roch. Then it was down the vertiginous Roch Run to town. "Some of us New Englanders," Parker remembered, "never having skied a mountain this imposing, experienced the same gut-tightening feeling we had felt before our first ride on a big roller coaster." The empty streets of Aspen looked like a checkerboard below them. Only the Jerome, the Wheeler Opera House, and a few pioneer buildings stood out against the white.

At the bottom, "feeling like heroes," the men took a couple of runs on the boat tow before sliding back to the Jerome and one (or two) Aspen Cruds, Laurence Elisha's infamous whiskey-spiked milkshakes.

Aspen unfurled like a dream, and no one was smitten harder than the Austrian champion Friedl Pfeifer was. In his autobiography *Nice Goin': My Life On Skis*, he wrote about first glimpsing Aspen: "I was filled more with the beauty than I was proud of our accomplishment [in hiking over]. The mountain peaks looming over the town made me feel like I was returning to St. Anton." Pfeifer imagined Aspen resurrected after the war as a "skiing community," much as his bucolic hometown had revived, thanks to ski sport, in the 1920s and 1930s. On one visit, Friedl dropped in on a meeting of the Aspen town council and promised that if he survived the war, he'd be back to help with the transformation. The city fathers, most of whom still hoped that mining would stage a comeback, weren't sure what to make of this wiry foreigner with the slicked-back hair and visionary glint in his eye.

By the spring of 1944 the three regiments of the 10th were filled. Camp Hale bustled with nine thousand infantry soldiers, thousands more in artillery and supply, and at least five thousand Missouri mules to haul the material of war. In the end, Minnie Dole and the NSPS had been able to supply at most seven thousand volunteers to the division. The rest had come through the draft. The men in the early battalions had been training for two and a half years—sometimes, as John Woodward recalled, "feeling guilty for doin' the things we loved." Everyone was fit and hard from the training, and it was time to erase the "debacle" of Homestake, to test the troops in division-wide maneuvers—D-Series.

Almost the entire division participated, for three sometimes hellish weeks in March and April 1944. Bob Parker missed all but the first days. His I&R platoon was once again sent up to Homestake Peak. "Some of us couldn't get enough. We were practicing our slalom right up until dark. I caught a tip between two little spruce trees and broke my ankle." He spent the night in a sleeping bag on a bed of fir boughs "without so much as an aspirin." Next day a team of medics tobogganed him three miles down to the nearest Weasel, which carried him the rest of the way back to camp. "So I missed the second part of D-Series, the storm part."

A massive late-winter storm blew into the central Rockies on Easter Sunday. It was accompanied by high winds and followed by unseasonably cold temperatures. Still, the various companies continued to patrol, dig in, move, dig in again. They'd crawl, fully clothed, into their sleeping bags only to be rousted scant minutes or hours later to saddle up and move again. Since the maneuvers were tactical, no fires were allowed, and at night no smoking lest the glow of a single cigarette give away an outfit's location. "Enemy" forces waited in ambush to capture unwary platoons, which maneuvered, in turn, to outflank and capture them.

Everything was done to make this mock combat as real as possible, right down to the gruff interrogation of prisoners. Pvt. Harris Dusenbery was captured in one exercise and pinned to the ground by a ski pole to the chest. In his book, *Ski the High Trail*, he recalls that for the first time the Army seemed to be "preparing the individual soldier for death." There was a very real aura of desperation around the games, a code of "kill or be killed" that had not been present in training.

Dusenbery brought age and a philosophical bent to his observations. He could have stayed out of the military. He was twenty-nine and a self-described pacifist, with a wife and child in Portland, Oregon, when he enlisted in 1943. "To my mind the war was a conflict between tyranny and democracy, between discipline and freedom. My desire for freedom was stronger than my desire for peace, and so, temperamentally unfit as I was, I went to war."

He also thought that joining with the mountain troops would be safer than combat with flatland infantry. "It was my theory that I would be fighting the altitude and the snow and so would be fighting my human enemies to a lesser extent. . . . Alpine terrain is familiar and comforting. I feel at home there." Better to be swept away by an avalanche, he thought, or gently freeze to death on a mountainside than to be raked by machine-gun fire or blown away in an artillery barrage. "I can accept nature on her own terms. . . . It is the wrath of man I fear."

No doubt many in the 10th felt the same way. If this was a war that had to be fought and won, then why not discharge that duty in one's beloved mountains? D-Series planners did their best to quash that love, or at least to take the element of play completely out of it. And by all accounts they succeeded in pushing Minnie's ski troops to their limit. What that did was give this disparate bunch a common bond; it made them brothers, not just in song or in the shared adventures of mountaineering, but now brothers in misery too. And out of that misery, Dusenbery thinks, "We gained something that the Army calls morale. . . . We who went through the experience had an elan that could have been acquired in no other way."

After three weeks of scrambling the ridgelines at 12,000 and 13,000 feet, of eyelashes frozen shut, of numb fingers and toes and nights buried in the snow like ptarmigan, the 10th was officially deemed fit and tough and ready for war. But, would there be a war left for the 10th to fight? In April and May 1944 Soviet armies made steady gains on the eastern front. The British finally turned the tide against the Japanese in Burma, and American bombers in the Pacific hit the Japanese home islands for the first time. On June 5, elements of the American Fifth and the British Eighth Armies entered Rome on their slow and costly advance up the boot of Italy. The British Home Fleet had been conducting operations off the Norwegian coast for a month—part of a series of deceptions leading finally to the Normandy landings on June 6. That day Operation Overlord put 156,000 American, British, and Canadian troops on the French beaches. The long-awaited invasion of Hitler's "Fortress Europe" had begun.

As for the 10th, their orders came through on June 7, 1944. Without explanation, they were to pack up en masse and relocate to Camp Swift, Texas. Bastrop, Texas, thirty miles east of Austin. Elevation: 300 feet. Terrain: flat as a pancake. Temperature in the shade: 90 to 110 degrees Fahrenheit. Morale in the alpine division plummeted. And Harry Poschman's friend, Vasos the Greek, now wearing the mantle of soothsayer, pronounced again: "This outfit will never go to war."

CHAPTER 7:

Not Too Swift

T he fact was, the Army had no mission for the mountain troops. Observers from Army Ground Forces noted in their April 1944 report that the D-Series maneuvers had gone well, that the light division had proved its ability to operate at extremes of altitude and weather. But the writers remained skeptical of the 10th's organization and specialized equipment, its lack of motorized transport, and its relatively light firepower. Of course, these things were precisely the point of a light division, that it could move swiftly—lightly encumbered—in remote, possibly snowy, roadless places.

But that wasn't what the Army believed it needed in the spring of 1944. When Chief of Staff George Marshall offered the 10th to various theater commanders, they all declined, citing the division's comparatively small size, its specialized training and its light armament. General Eisenhower, by then the Supreme Allied Comman-der in Europe, passed the question on to his chief of staff, Gen. Walter Bedell Smith, who reportedly took one look at the 10th's table of organization and said, "All those mules? Hell no!"

In late April, Minnie Dole went to see General Marshall to plead for a combat-zone assignment for the ski troops. Marshall hedged, saying only that because there was just one light infantry division (the only other light divisions, by definition, were the air-borne 82d and 101st) and because transportation had become so scarce, it didn't make sense to send the 10th to one theater of war if the need might subsequently prove greater in some other theater of war. The 10th would just have to wait in reserve until the right opportunity presented itself.

The stated reason for the move to Texas was to acclimate the 10th to hot weather and low elevation so that it could participate in large-scale maneuvers in Louisiana in September, maneuvers that never took place because so few Army divisions remained stateside. The real purpose of the relocation was to beef up the 10th so that it could fight alongside regular heavy infantry divisions wherever they might be in action. General Marshall wasn't ready to give up on the mountain troops; their special skills might yet prove useful. But he did want to bring their manpower and firepower up to the levels of a full division. And that meant reorganization.

To the dismay of the 10th's senior mountaineers, the Mountain Training Group was disbanded and its men distributed among the various companies, about five instructors to each company. At least two thousand additional officers and men were added to the infantry regiments, and heavy weapons companies were added to all battalions. These included the much more powerful .50-caliber machine guns (the 10th had trained with .30-caliber) and mortar platoons using larger, 81-mm ammunition. The outfit's mule-borne 75-mm howitzers were augmented with motorized 105-mm and 155-mm artillery. New men—transfers mostly—expanded the ranks of the 10th's medical, engineer, and signal (communications) battalions. In the heat and the flat terrain of southeast Texas, the 87th's regimental motto—*Vires montesque vincimus* (We conquer men and mountains)—seemed like a cruel joke. Many of the Camp Hale veterans felt betrayed.

Of the experience at Camp Swift, Harry Poschman wrote in his memoir, "If it can be said the 10th Mountain died, this is where it started. . . . Whole new companies were formed consisting of men not familiar with the ski troops and their special training." With the dissolution of the MTG—there being nothing for the elite mountaineers to teach—Harry was reassigned first to a standard rifle company, then to a heavy weapons company in the 85th Regiment. Morale hit rock bottom. Many of the original Hale guys scrambled to transfer out, and some of them succeeded. When a call went out in July to replace the paratroopers depleted at Normandy, so many men volunteered from the 10th that division commanders were forced to bar further transfers.

Nineteen-year-old Robert Woody had only been at Hale a couple of months before the move to Swift, but he had developed a real connection to the place, to the mountains and the skiing, to the *idea* of being mountain troops. He slept "good and heavy" on pine bough beds, learned from the grizzled Paul Petzoldt how to evacuate wounded down a rock face, and even turned down a chance to "escort a college girl to a couple of dances at the service club . . . in order to go skiing with the boys."

Woody hated Swift, the comedown it represented—the insult even—and the reality of its stultifying summer days. Letter home, June 27:

The day before yesterday we fired the carbine. During the afternoon I was in the pits; on a given whistle signal I'd hold up my target. . . . There was no air circulating and the rays of the sun made the small six-by-three hole just like a bread oven. I could write notes on the wall with my sweaty finger. The floor was a graveyard of horrid bugs dead and living. . . . The bullets would sing over your head and kick dirt onto your sweaty back. . . . Flies, gnats, mosquitoes made a meal out of you. Believe me I don't wanta know nothing about holding targets again.

The humid plains around Bastrop swarmed with insects and just about every poisonous snake native to North America. A man in Bob Parker's platoon woke up one morning "with a copperhead curled up in the warmth of the guy's stomach, inside his sleeping bag."

Paul Petzoldt, so unflappable at high elevation, on vertical rock and snow, had a deathly fear of snakes. The night he arrived at Swift his new unit was assigned a nighttime field problem. The men were told to dig foxholes and wait for a mock attack. "Don't move until I give the command," said their officer. Petzoldt lay in his hole listening to noises in the oak trees and seeing what he thought were eyes glinting in the branches above him. He tried to sleep and might have dozed off briefly when something soft and wiggling fell onto his lap.

At that moment, the attack began. "Enemy" soldiers ran at them banging on pots and yelling "Yankee, you die!" Petzoldt bolted upright swiping desperately at the squirming thing on his uniform front. The officer yelled, "Get down! Not yet! Not yet!" But Petzoldt had had enough. He stalked off and the next day pulled some strings with division command and had himself transferred to Officer Candidate School at Fort Benning, Georgia, where he remained as an instructor for the duration of the war.

Not everyone wanted to get out. Bud Winter did, in fact, leave for three months to OCS, but he returned to Texas a second lieutenant in November. And Winter's sunny disposition continued in spite of the gloom that infected many of his comrades. "Dear Fred," he wrote to his brother from Camp Swift. "Last week I had one day off to go to town and I really had a wonderful time. I got a date with a nice little co-ed from Texas University. She was really a swell kid. Austin is really a nice town to go to."

Bob Parker never seriously entertained the idea of transferring, not even after an incident that could have killed him. He and his I&R mates had figured out a way to sleep up off the ground away from Swift's various crawling things. One of the guys in the platoon had been a fisherman before the war, and he taught them how to weave fishnet hammocks out of laundry cord. Parker felt pretty smug and secure one morning at reveille as he climbed down from his suspended bed to dress for chow. Most of his clothes had spent the night in the hammock with him, safely above the forest floor. Only a few items—his helmet and helmet liner, for instance—had to be left on the ground. (Because of the heat, the men were not always required to wear their steel helmets, but they did have to wear the lighter helmet liner into the mess hall.) Parker donned the liner, felt a searing pain at his temple, and immediately blacked out.

Shocked, his buddies stood staring at the scorpion and at Parker lying on the ground. They finally recovered their wits enough to carry him to the base hospital. The scorpion had stung Parker right on the temporal artery. He remained unconscious for about twelve minutes but eventually came to, apparently fine, but with "the worst headache" he'd ever had. "It lasted two days."

Midway through the summer of 1944 Bob Woody contracted poison oak on his legs and face, a debilitating case, but it meant he got to spend what he described as "five delicious weeks" in the camp infirmary. "With Epsom salt baths [and] Texas University girls coming to the hospital to teach us archery," it certainly beat bedding with the snakes and enduring forced marches in the heat.

As Woody wrote in *Charlie Red One, Over and Out*, his self-published memoir of the war years, the hospital also exposed him to a different world. The food servers at the hospital mess were actually prisoners from the defeated German Afrika Korps.

They were prisoners in body [only]. Their souls were still with the Korps and German supremacy. They did not look at you. They looked through you. They slapped servings in your tray with clear disdain. Fuck 'em, I thought. Then one day as I left the mess I just happened to be singing in Latin: *Adeste, fideles, / Laeti triumphates, / Venite, venite in Bethlehem.* One of the prisoners came over to me. "I know that song," he said. "We sang it at home." There was no disdain in his voice or eyes.

The next ward over from Woody's was the VD ward. "A lot of those guys were in bad shape, hunched and shaking. . . . Made a believer out of you." Everyone in the division was made to sit through what they called the "Mickey Mouse" movies over and over. "It began with the War Department musical fanfare," Woody recalled.

Then a familiar, gray-haired Hollywood actor, who always played chairman-of-the-board types, comes on in the uniform of a medical officer. "As an officer of the Medical Corps of the United States Army, it is my duty to inform you of certain pertinent facts regarding your body. Most men know less about their bodies than they do their own cars." He'd pull down a chart and with a pointer begin: "This is the chest, the abdomen and the testicles—commonly known as the balls. . . ."

Woody was a buzz-cut, 137-pound, fresh-out-of-high-school virgin. His mates in C Company, 85th Regiment had given him the nickname "Cherry." But he laughed along with everyone else at the movie's misplaced sincerity. And like everyone else, he accepted the condoms and the prophylactic kits the first sergeant handed out with each weekend pass, "whether [the men] had grizzled faces or fuzz faces."

Week after blazing week crawled by. The soldiers suffered through longer and longer conditioning hikes. David Brower, newly arrived from the dismantled Seneca Rocks climbing school, and out of shape after an eleven-day furlough to visit his pregnant wife in Berkeley, actually fell asleep while leading a platoon on a twenty-four-hour march—"fell asleep while walking." "I think I usually avoid hallucinations," he wrote in *For Earth's Sake*, "That night I had enough for all time."

New men arrived daily until the 10th reached its full compliment of over fourteen thousand soldiers. Heat exhaustion, which had crippled up to two-thirds of the ski troops when they first arrived from Camp Hale, became less and less common. Their bodies were adapting. Now they trained with air cover, something they hadn't done at Hale. They trained with the heavier weapons. This was different work, a different life. Even their spare time was altered to the new environment. Where once they might have skied into an old silver mining town, now when they had a night off, they went to Austin, where the girls' wide taffeta dresses swished against their pressed A uniforms on the dance floor. Still, to remind themselves of their mountain heritage, they sometimes brought climbing ropes downtown and practiced rappelling off Austin's tallest building, a six-story hotel.

Then, in early November 1944, the Army declared the alpine division officially reorganized and gave it a new name, the 10th Mountain Division. Each man was issued a cloth tab with the word MOUNTAIN embroidered on it. These were to be sewn above the shoulder patch they already wore—a blue powderkeg with crossed red bayonets on it, signifying the Roman numeral ten. The MOUN-

TAIN tab put the 10th in the same league with other elite outfits, the ones who wore RANGER or AIRBORNE above their division patches.

This was definitely a morale booster. But the 10th still didn't know for what it was being readied. The most persistent rumor whispered Burma. Up near Bob Woody's company headquarters stood an obvious clue: a big relief map of Burma, which showed how mountainous the Burmese terrain really was. Woody figured it made sense: "We still had the mule pack. Mules were being used in Burma. Yup, we would be fighting under the famed General 'Vinegar Joe' Stilwell in what was called the China-Burma-India Theater of Operations." But he also understood that the map might be a decoy planted by his leaders. "If there were leaks to the enemy," he figured, "let the leaks say the 10th was going to southeast Asia."

There was still no word when, after Thanksgiving, the division got a new commander, a genuine war hero and old friend of Chief of Staff Marshall's, one Brig. Gen. George Price Hays. (Hays replaced Gen. Lloyd Jones, who had fallen seriously ill.) He was a man of spare frame, born in China to Presbyterian missionary parents, wiry and weather beaten, with the direct gaze and relaxed stance—one Westerner in the division thought—of a cowhand. Permanent smile lines around his eyes and mouth balanced a deep worry crease between his dark brows. The headline in the *Blizzard* announcing his arrival read: "Gen. Hays, Hero of Two Wars, Wins Battles—and Keeps Casualty List Short." The officers and men liked him right away.

Hays had won the congressional Medal of Honor as an artillery forward observer during the second battle of the Marne. (The medal citation states matter-of-factly that "seven times he had horses shot from under him" as he raced from the front lines to his own artillery positions again and again to keep the lines of communication open.) He owned two Silver Stars for gallantry, the French Croix de Guerre, the Legion of Honor, and a Purple Heart. He had just returned to the States after commanding the artillery for the U.S. 2d Division at Normandy. Fresh from combat, he gathered the 10th's senior officers and noncoms (noncommissioned officers—sergeants, for example) together at Swift and delivered a surprising talk. Lt. Col. Robert Works recalled in *Soldiers on Skis*, "He gave a picture of war which most people hadn't heard—that war was an exciting thing. He said we would look back on it as one of the greatest things that ever happened to us."

Hays told the group—and his words quickly filtered down to the men in the line companies: "We are going to have good times and bad times in our combat overseas, and as far as possible it will be my policy to . . . have as good a time as possible as long as we accomplish our mission."

The general didn't know a lot about the mountain troops and what they were trained to do. But he could tell right away that they were a special group suffering a crisis of identity and purpose. Minnie Dole, still the division's mother hen, wrote Hays in an introductory letter from Connecticut: "Many men have spent three, and some four, years with the outfit with no apparent prospect of combat. The result is that they have felt they are the forgotten division and the Army's bastard child." (Burton, *The Ski Troops*.)

Hays's solution was to push the troops harder. Always fair and considerate of the men, he nevertheless sensed that to come together as a unit, they needed more discipline, more rigor. Hays became the shot in the arm the division sorely needed. One sergeant wrote home with enthusiasm typical of the infantrymen's feelings about their new leader:

Mother, he is the answer to the prayers of us all. . . . Yesterday he actually came right out onto the field with us, and secretly every damn one of us cocked our helmets a little to the same angle he had his. He talked to us and told us to have fun at the front and keep a smile on our faces and give the enemy ten bullets for every one he fires at us. This guy doesn't know what he has done for this outfit, but we will do our damndest to show him when the hot stuff comes. (Whitlock, *Soldiers on Skis*.)

The general knew, of course, where his division was headed. But he was not at liberty to share that knowledge. In late November 1944 orders came for the 86th Regiment to move out by train to Camp Patrick Henry, Virginia, hard by the military port at Hampton Roads on Chesapeake Bay. The 85th and 87th Regiments left Swift for the same destination just before Christmas, and the division artillery battalions followed days later.

When the order came to board ship at last (December 11 for the 86th, January 4, 1945, for the other regiments), the mountain troops left port without their mountain equipment—their skis and mountain boots, their white anoraks and down sleeping bags. They had instead been issued standard infantry khaki and rubber shoepacs. A concerned senior officer wrote to Minnie Dole, and Dole fired off a letter of complaint to General Marshall's office. To Dole's surprise, the answer came not from official Washington but from General Hays himself. Hays explained in no uncertain terms that he was now commander of the division and responsible for its welfare, and he concluded, "I shall brook no interference whatsoever."

In one swift stroke, Hays ended Minnie Dole's informal, but very real, influence over decisions affecting the 10th Mountain Division. It had to have been a blow; Minnie had worked so hard, become so immersed in "his" ski troops. He would have gone overseas with them had the Army let him. But in the end, he took the rebuff well. "After all," he philosophized, "Hays is the commander. He's the one that will take them into battle, not me."

CHAPTER 8:

The Winter Line

The 86th Regiment sailed first, on the USS *Argentina*. The 85th and 87th followed three weeks later aboard the USS *West Point*, a converted luxury liner known before the war as the *America*. Built for the North Atlantic passenger trade, the *West Point* was the biggest and fastest troop ship in the fleet—faster, it was said, than any German U-boat. Inevitably though, rumors flew about what might be stalking her below the surface. One of Harry Poschman's shipmates, seasick and miserable belowdecks, complained to one of the *West Point*'s merchant seamen. "It's okay, soldier," came the laconic reply, "you'll be off this ship in a week. Less than that if we get torpedoed."

Poschman's platoon was assigned to a "good stateroom, way up high in first class." This was definitely an improvement over the old USS *Grant* on the way up to Kiska. "The only trouble," he wrote, "was that twenty of us were packed into what was once a deluxe cabin for two. Somebody with authority dropped in to say we were given this fine room because it was near the mess hall and we would have the privilege of KP for the entire voyage." The worst part was that the guys on KP didn't get to see any of the USO shows with their look-but-don't-touch female entertainers.

Bob Woody, crammed into a rather less luxurious troop hold, heard music one night. "Top side, a band was playing. I climbed up some pipes and lo, there were WACs—enlisted women—dancing with officers. Ahhhh, how those officers could bend the rules. I joined the dancing and was promptly escorted down the deck stairs by MPs with a warning not to return." The often-informal, egalitarian relationship between officers and men that had characterized the division in the mountains (and would reassert itself in the stress of combat) had been at least temporarily revoked.

Fine weather brought calm seas for most of the voyage. Men lounged on deck, gambled in their bunks, smoked endlessly. (Cigarettes were only five cents a pack in the ship's store.) Or else they leaned on a rail and stared into the waves: to the east beyond the bow toward what might be coming, or back west to what they'd left behind. Medic Nate Morell says, "The big topic was: Were you afraid to die? Or how you might die."

The slower *Argentina* crossed the pond with an escort of destroyers and occasional sub-spotting aircraft. The *West Point* sped across alone, picking up a convoy only when she entered the Mediterranean Sea through the Straits of Gibraltar. It was just before Gibraltar that the veil of secrecy finally lifted, and the men learned their destination: Italy.

Italy, Winston Churchill's "soft underbelly of Europe," had in the sixteen months since the landing at Salerno, proved to be anything but soft. In part this was due to the Allies' unwillingness to commit a truly overwhelming force there; the way to Germany and to Hitler's ultimate destruction lay to the north—across France and the Low Countries—not up through the hundreds of miles of tortuously folded countryside that characterized the Italian peninsula. And secondly, General Kesselring's defensive strategy used that convoluted terrain to brilliant advantage, stymieing the Allied advance most notably at the Gustav Line south of Rome.

At the center of that line stood Monte Cassino crowned by its hilltop, sixth-century Benedictine monastery. Three times over the winter of 1944 Allied forces—British, American, Polish, French, and New Zealand troops—tried and failed to dislodge the tenacious Germans occupying the heights. On January 22, in an attempt to bypass Cassino, Gen. Mark Clark put fifty thousand men and five thousand vehicles of his U.S. Fifth Army ashore at Anzio, just thirty-three miles from Rome. But Kesselring's counterattack bottled up the Americans there. Meanwhile, Allied bombers flattened the ancient abbey on the hill, but the rubble turned out to provide even better cover for the defenders, and more difficult going for Allied tanks and foot soldiers. Finally, in May, British Field Marshal Sir Harold Alexander shifted his Eighth Army over from the Adriatic to join Clark in a redoubled effort against Cassino. This time, the Gustav Line was breached and Monte Cassino itself fell to a Polish battalion. At the same time the Americans broke out of Anzio, joined the combined armies moving north, and marched, unopposed, into Rome on June 5, 1944.

But Kesselring was not routed, as expected. Instead he led an orderly retreat to yet another string of mountainside fortifications south of Florence, the Arno River Line, and after that to the Gothic Line in the Northern Apennine Mountains, the last range of hills before the Po River valley. The Po was Italy's breadbasket, one of the last and most productive sources of food and munitions for a far-flung German army increasingly short of both. Berlin wanted desperately to hold the Allies south of the valley, and Kesselring had the advantage of the high ground—of superior observation and prepared positions.

Through the fall of 1944, the British on the east and the Americans on the west managed to shoulder the Gothic Line north but a few kilometers. There was no breakthrough anywhere along the front, which stretched from near Pisa on the Ligurian Sea to Ravenna on the Adriatic. The Allies might have made faster progress but for two rather major handicaps, attention and priority. First, the world's attention shifted to Normandy; D-Day was June 6, the day after Rome's liberation. And then in August, the Allies launched Operation Dragoon, to open a second front on France's Mediterranean coast, which drained away several crack divisions from Clark's Fifth Army. The fighting in Italy ceased being news. What with Mussolini's overthrow, the negotiated surrender of Italian forces, and now the liberation of Rome, much of the world assumed the war in Italy was over. Alexander and Clark would just have to do the best they could with the limited resources they had. The first snows blanketed the Northern Apennines in November. Movement of men and machines became nearly impossible. As winter set in, the two sides hunkered down, wary and exhausted, across what Allied maps now called the Winter Line.

Official strategy in Italy now was simply to occupy as many German divisions as possible, in order to keep them from being reassigned to the fight in France or to the rapidly deteriorating eastern front. But Mark Clark didn't like the idea of his soldiers sitting pat; he wanted to force the issue as soon as better weather allowed. His goal was to capture the industrial and railroad center of Bologna, at the edge of the Po River valley, and he was hoping the fresh troops of the 10th Mountain Division would help him get there. He had a particular assignment in mind for the 10th—the last U.S. division to enter the war in Europe—one that had frustrated several earlier attempts.

Three times in November 1944, Fifth Army battalions, including soldiers of the Brazilian Expeditionary Force (BEF) and the U.S. 92d Division (one of two "all-Negro" divisions), had tried and failed to take Monte Belvedere near the center of the Winter Line. Belvedere was not a particularly imposing peak; taller and craggier summits, up to 7,000 feet high and crusted with early snow, could be seen to the northwest. Belvedere stood only 3,800 feet high, a three-mile-long humpback of a mountain with a patchwork of fields and orchards, stone barns, and chestnut woods nearly to its summit. It looked unremarkable, even benign. But Belvedere was the military key to Highway 64, one of only two roads from Florence over the mountains to Bologna, and thus crucial to Clark's plans. From Belvedere's ridgeline, artillery observers with the German LI Mountain Corps could direct fire onto any movement approaching the highway. Further progress to the north required that the Allies take and hold Monte Belvedere. The hope was that the 10th, with its mountain training, its esprit, and its very high level of fitness, could do what no one else had yet managed: to dislodge Belvedere's defenders.

On board ship, the ski troops got their first glimpse of Italy as the island of Capri slid by to starboard. Then, growing on the horizon, came the broad cone of Mount Vesuvius, still smoking following its March 1944 eruption. That blast—from the same volcano that had buried the cities of Pompeii and Herculaneum several feet deep in ash and debris in A.D. 79—had raised the overall height of the mountain 500 feet to just about 4,000 feet above the wide crescent of the Bay of Naples. The water in the harbor was green and clear, and staring down into it one could conjure thoughts of romance and holiday. But a broader glance revealed a naval graveyard. Ships of all descriptions lay twisted half in and half out of the water. The waterfront had been blasted to rubble by both Allied and Luftwaffe bombers, and the ancient city of Naples stood in tatters, its human inhabitants dressed in rags, scrounging scraps from GI food lines. Suddenly, to the men of the 10th, the war was very real.

On disembarking, the soldiers were immediately accosted by prostitutes. "They were hungry," Bob Woody remembered. "Little boys would come up to you with their filthy faces and say, '*Fichi, fichi*. Wanna fuck my sister?' One girl kissed my shirt collar—big red lipstick marks. Newc [Eldredge] and I said, 'We're too tired.' Meaning, *we're scared*. A lot of guys had no compunctions. No money changed hands; these people had nothing to buy. The standard medium of exchange was a pack of cigarettes."

Dave Brower, a smoker like most of the men, noticed that a cigarette butt would no sooner hit the ground than a flurry of barefoot beggars, like pigeons in more prosperous times, would flutter in to claim it. "For the first time, for most of us," he wrote, "we were now foreigners."

The ebullient Bud Winter, while not oblivious to the squalor and sadness of Italy, focused instead on his fly-fishing. He'd brought along his rod and reel, and now he wrote home to his mother, asking her to send, at her earliest convenience, "some trout hooks and line."

The 10th's three regiments stayed only briefly in Naples before shipping out again, either by coastal boat or by train, to Livorno and then Pisa just south of the Winter Line. Woody and a few others climbed the famous Leaning Tower and rang the bells. Afterward, Woody found the bell ringing "irreverent and disturbing." It was about this time that a company of 86th men walked into a minefield near the regimental staging area at Quercianella. One man was wounded when he stepped on a "bouncing betty," an antipersonnel mine that jumps up to waist height when detonated and sprays shrapnel in all directions. Heeding the cries for help, several medics left the safety of nearby railroad tracks and were themselves killed trying to reach the wounded man. Adding to the melee, a chaplain rushed too hurriedly to help and was also killed by the buried mines. The 10th Mountain had been bloodied for the first time since Kiska.

There was no time to stop to mourn the dead. The regiments were quickly off to the Apennine foothills, to little towns called Pieve and Bagni di Lucca and Vidiciatico. They traveled by night in lumbering six-by-six trucks or on foot over rutted dirt roads and ancient stone tracks too narrow even for the versatile army jeep. The men stopped under cover during the day and moved out again in the dark. The arrival of a mountain division to the front was supposed to be a secret; the troops had even been ordered to cut off their division patches in order not to tip off the Germans. But despite the stealth tactics, the Germans seemed to know as much about the 10th's identity and whereabouts as did the average dogface. David Brower remembered that when his battalion stole into the town of Vidiciatico, a German loudspeaker on Riva Ridge bellowed, in English: "Welcome, men of the 10th Mountain Division." Later, when the 85th Regiment settled in discreetly near the base of Monte Belvedere, German artillery rained down on the Americans propaganda leaflets that read: "Welcome, men of the 10th Mountain Division. It's a long way from Camp Hale to Mount Belvedere . . ." How did they know? And what did it bode that the enemy apparently knew so much about its untested adversaries?

The mountains here reminded no one of Rainier's lofty, glacier-draped cone or of the strings of alpine ridgelines surrounding Camp Hale. These mountains looked more like New England's Appalachians—rounded by eons of erosion and heavily wooded except where generations of Italians had carved out field and orchard. The villages' ancient stone buildings huddled on rocky outcrops, as if to take the least possible space from the fields below. Some had been fortresses from medieval times, and some were de facto fortresses now, first for retreating German soldiers, then for the Americans. Walls that had stood for centuries sported gaping, dark holes. Terracotta roof tiles and pale, limestone wall blocks spilled unnaturally into the narrow streets thanks to shelling by both sides.

The luckier men of the 10th got to sleep in barns or schools with hay for bedding and a roof, or at least part of a roof, over their heads. The really lucky guys, like Bob Woody, befriended locals and spent time in their homes. In a letter to his brother, Woody described the village of Pieve:

> Remember those books on fairyland? This is fairyland.... At the village fountain, I met Dora Pellegrini, a 36-year-old mother of two. . . . She invited me to her home where I met her husband Giuseppe, a handsome dark-haired man with mustache. Giuseppe was in the Italian Alpini but when "Mussolini finiti" he took off for home, to his wife and two babies. . . . They gave me hot soup—and grappa. The grappa burned a ring down my throat. Giuseppe threw some into the fire and laughed as it exploded. . . . I gave them some of my rations, chocolate and cigarettes.

By January 20, 1945, all three 10th Mountain regiments were in place and sending patrols into the line. Both sides ran patrols, mostly at night. The two armies were sizing each other up, like heavyweights in the ring, circling and jabbing through the early rounds of what promised to be a long fight. Many times patrols never even saw the opposition. Bob Parker remembered one night when his reconnaissance team crept up to spy on the fortified town of Corona on Belvedere's western flank. They worked their way through the woods to within a few feet of the old town's stone walls, so close that Parker could hear the German guards talking quietly and smell the smoke from their cigarettes.

Most patrols hiked on foot through the crusty thin snow—probing, listening, cutting the enemy's communications wire wherever they came across it, hoping to bring back a prisoner or two for questioning. Where deeper snow and more distant objectives required it, patrols went out on skis. But these were rare. John Jennings figured he participated in six night ski patrols for his 87th company through January. The last one, to the farm on the ridgeline, provided their biggest scare by far. The vast majority of 10th men never saw a ski in Italy.

By the end of January, beginning of February, the weather eliminated any need for the 10th's skis. Continuing warm and dry conditions quickly melted the snow on all but the true north exposures, and those were typically held by the defending Germans. Roads turned to mud, and the soldiers not fortunate enough to have billeting inside a building of some kind found themselves camped in deep muck. Nighttime temperatures still dropped below freezing, but during the day, a blazing sun warmed the air into the forties and fifties. In these conditions, the standard-issue olive-drab uniform—equipment initially resented by the mountain troops—was definitely superior to the whites they had hoped to be wearing. It looked as if Italy might be experiencing a very early spring.

While patrols continued to probe at night—and the rest of the division tried simply to give away as little as possible during the day—the generals were plotting the new Allied offensive, code-named Operation Encore. General Hays studied the terrain with new eyes and saw something that had escaped previous planners. Not only was Belvedere itself well defended, but the existence of a tall, unusually steep, perpendicular ridge to the west made it all but impregnable. Hays figured that the Germans atop what came to be known as Riva Ridge had been the real culprits in the previous failures on Belvedere. They not only had a perfect stadium-like view of Allied comings and goings, they could direct devastating fire in *behind* any approach to Belvedere's south slope. Reconnaissance flights proved the existence of observation posts on the ridge and of elements of the 4th (Edelweiss) Mountain Battalion and a battalion of the German 232d Infantry Division garrisoned nearby. Hays determined that the 10th needed to neutralize Riva Ridge before a fourth attempt on Belvedere could succeed.

Riva looked, at first, like an insurmountable wall. Striated like a many-layered cake by horizontal rock bands, the cliff was actually a series of connected high points, three and a half miles long, from Monte Mancinello (4,770 feet) on the south, across Monte Serrasiccia and Monte Capel Buso, to Pizzo di Campiano (3,175 feet) at the north end. (For simplicity's sake, the Army shortened the so-called Mancinello-Campiano Ridge to Riva Ridge.) Riva's east face bolted 1,500 feet seemingly straight up from the Dardagna River at its base. But the pitch was not uniformly steep. The metamorphic rock had shattered and eroded into a series of gullies and ramps. There were routes that an experienced hiker could negotiate with relative ease. But there were also slabs of vertical rock and deep ravines hidden from the sun where ice and snow remained. The warmup in the weather meant that water from melting snow poured down the face during the day and froze in a thin glaze overnight. The backside of the escarpment, the German side, sloped gradually to the northwest, over still-snowy benches toward the town of Fanano. Several companies of seasoned German mountain troops were garrisoned there, but only a handful of defenders, forty to fifty men, occupied the spine of the ridge at any one time. The German command evidently felt that the eastern precipice was simply too much for the Americans to attempt.

General Hays asked Lt. Colonel Clarence E. "Tommy" Tomlinson, commander of the 86th Regiment, if his men could climb Riva. Tomlinson, who had served most recently in the South Pacific and was no mountaineer himself, scanned the serrated ridge with binoculars and reported back with skepticism: "It looks pretty steep, sir." Hays replied, "Nonsense. You're supposed to be elite mountain troops. I don't take that. You get out there and find a way."

Still doubtful, Tomlinson sent patrols across the Dardagna torrent with orders to scout routes up Riva. The first week, patrols on skis probed unsuccessfully for a way up the cliff; the snow was going fast. Then a squad from B Company, 86th, climbed, without skis, to the northernmost section of the ridge, to Pizzo di Campiano. Nearing the crest at daybreak, the B Company men dropped into a crawl and peered over the top. A vicious burst of barking took their breath away; they'd been discovered by a guard dog. When three German soldiers popped up out of a dugout to investigate, the American staff sergeant in charge told them in English, "Hands up!" One of the soldiers went for his weapon instead, and the patrol shot him dead. At that point a hidden machine gun opened up on the interlopers, who turned tail and dashed back down the mountain with bullets zinging off the rocks around them. They made it safely down and were congratulated on achieving their mission. The trail they found was designated Route 1.

Over the next weeks, patrols established four more routes up Riva. The climbers did not go unobserved and had to duck occasional pot shots from above. But the Germans on top appeared to regard the few Americans scrambling on the face as relatively harmless; their conviction that no large-scale force would attempt the climb remained intact.

On two of the routes, 10th mountaineers attached fixed ropes to the rock so that troops burdened with rifles and ammunition could haul themselves up the steeper ledges. The ropes—of the new olive-drab nylon—could not be seen from above. To secure them, climbers looped sections around trees and roots or, when there were none, used piton hammers to drive anchors into the rock. The sound of steel on steel would surely have sent a signal to the Germans, so the mountaineers wrapped their hammers in thick cloth to deaden the sound. The anchors were then fitted with snap rings (now called carabiners) and the rope passed through, as one would do on an assault of Half Dome in Yosemite (there was that overlap of military and mountaineering language) or an attempt on the Matterhorn. The sport Dave Brower and others had taught so enthusiastically in training was now being employed with deadly intent.

While a handful of top climbers fixed the routes, most of the 1st Battalion, 86th Regiment, was sent back behind the lines for intensive rock-climbing and marksmanship training in a quarry near the town of Lucca. Although 70 percent of these men had been with the regiment at Hale, General Hays wanted to make sure all of the soldiers were fit to climb, that they all felt a mountaineer's esprit. Battalion commander Lt. Col. Henry Hampton wrote later: "The 30 percent not trained at Camp Hale were fairly good in movement over rough terrain as they were young and desired to be as good as the rest of the mountaineers. Of course, if we had to use skis and snowshoes, it would have been a different story. Skiers and snowshoers are not trained in two weeks." The 1st Battalion men would have to be comfortable with the rock and rope, and with each other, because they were going to make the climb at night.

That was the plan. Hays figured the Germans would never anticipate an assault up Riva's "unclimbable" east face, at night, by inexperienced troops, and he was counting heavily on the element of surprise. The plan called for the 1st Battalion (Companies A, B, C, and D) plus F Company from the 2d Battalion—about eight hundred men—to scale Riva on the night of February 18 in preparation for a dawn attack. The rest of the division—the 85th and

87th Regiments and the 3d Battalion of the 86th (upwards of twelve thousand men, including reserves)—would attack Monte Belvedere on the night of the 19th.

Then on Friday, February 16, two days before the attack, the general did something unusual. He sat down with the men of his division, not just the officers but the dogfaces too, and told them exactly what to expect. "He said," Dan Kennerly wrote in his diary (excerpted in *Good Times and Bad Times*): "'I have never before talked to men of your level about the details of a coming campaign. But I'm trusting you to carry this off.'" He said there would be no artillery or aerial bombardment prior to jump-off because it would ruin the element of surprise. Companies would move up the mountain in silence with fixed bayonets and no ammunition in their rifles. Again, to enhance the surprise. The general didn't want any premature firing, and he didn't want companies (echoes of Kiska) mistakenly shooting each other in the dark. Load weapons only at daybreak, he told the anxious faces around him. "You must move forward," Kennerly remembers him saying. "Never get pinned down. Move forward. There will be no order to turn back. Any order to turn back will be a false order. Shoot the enemy. Bayonet him. Brain him with your rifle. To the victor will go the spoils. Take trophies—anything: pistols, cameras, watches. Send them home for the grandchildren to see. You're going to go there, and you're going to do damn well. Good luck."

At least one GI reported later that in spite of their inevitable nerves, "the feeling of affection for Hays ran so high, we would have followed him to hell."

CHAPTER 9:

Riva Ridge

Through the night of February 17, the men who would climb Riva Ridge hiked the fourteen miles from their training area in Lucca to one of five tiny villages at the base of Riva's east wall. Each village housed an assault company, one company for each of the designated climbing routes. From north to south along the Dardagna River, now bellowing with snowmelt, eight hundred 10th Mountain Division soldiers piled into farmhouses and outbuildings in Pianacci, Ca di Julio, Farne (the battalion command post), Migliante, and Poggioforato. On their way through Regimental Headquarters at La Ca, the riflemen received double the normal issue of ammunition—ninety-six rounds—and extra K rations. It had been decided they would go without blankets or extra clothing to make room for the added firepower.

Throughout the next day, the men stayed in their hiding places at the foot of the cliff, marking time, breaking down and cleaning their weapons. They talked, they argued, they grew understandably restless. Some tried to sleep. Some withdrew into silence, while others became more voluble in their anxiety. This was it: They were about to confront an enemy demonized for years in the media as ruthless killing machines—some had even called them Supermen. The mountaineers knew themselves to be all-too human. Just kids, most of them. Still innocent of killing, of the real stuff of war. Would they perform bravely? Or wither in fear? Would it hurt awfully to be shot? Would there be time to feel anything? They were about to find out.

Jump-off time was set for 7:30 P.M. the night of the 18th. Sgt. Jacques Parker, who was with the advance party that would lead C Company up Route 3 to Monte Serrasiccia, remembers a moment just before the order came to move out. "Our group was in the attic of one of these homes, and we all knelt together. We had people of various faiths, including this big Austrian who lost part of his family to the Nazis. We all just knelt up there. Nothing was said. . . . Even though we all thought we were so tough, we knew it was going to be rough on the mountain."

Harry Poschman, who was lying in the dark a few miles away at the base of Monte Belvedere, wrote of the feeling: "Nothing to do but wait, and write letters home, or where? Some of these boys are scared. It's the night before, and I don't mean Christmas. I can't imagine a man saying, 'I'm going to get killed tomorrow,' but some did. Not knowing what to expect I don't expect anything; just sort of blank."

The Riva columns moved out on time into an artificial moon-glow created by banks of searchlights aimed up into the clouds from miles behind the lines. The lights had a dual purpose—in theory— to blind the enemy high on the ridgelines and, second, to provide just enough light so that Allied forces could maneuver in visibility

This somewhat romanticized 1943 *Post* cover served as an unofficial recruiting poster for the ski troops.

The 10th Mountain Division shoulder patch: a blue powder keg with red crossed bayonets indicating the roman numeral ten. The MOUNTAIN tab put the 10th in the "elite" league with Army Ranger and Airborne divisions.

Insurance man Minnie Dole *(center)*, the 10th's founding father (and mother hen) with Roger Langley and Paul Lafferty at Camp Hale, Colorado, 1943.

The 87th Mountain Infantry Regiment trained for one winter at Paradise Lodge, Mount Rainier, Washington, 1941–42.

Lt. John Jay, a fixture on the ski-film lecture circuit, became the 10th's unofficial documentarian. Mount Rainier, 1942. (Charles C. Bradley)

Swiss mountaineer and Dartmouth College ski coach Walter Prager demonstrates rappelling technique on Mount Rainer, 1942. (U.S. Army Signal Corps)

Burdell S. "Bud" Winter, of Schenectady, New York, one of the most enthusiastic members of the Mountain Training Group, ca. 1943–44.

World-record holder Torger Tokle jumped 289 feet before becoming the 10th's most famous enlisted man. Aspen, 1944.

Instant city at 9,250 feet.
Camp Hale, Colorado.
1942–44. (Winston Pote)

MTG ski instructor
Cpl. Harry Poschman shows
off his Arlberg turns at Cooper
Hill, Camp Hale, 1944.
(Courtesy of Harry Poschman)

Hugh Evans dries his socks and felt
insoles on maneuvers above Camp Hale,
April 1944.

Former world champion and Sun Valley instructor Friedl Pfeifer rides the Aspen boat tow. (Courtesy of Heritage Aspen)

Front page of the *Blizzard*, the division newspaper, featuring a sketch by Sgt. Jacques Parker of the Riva Ridge assault, February 1945. (Courtesy of Jacques Parker)

Aerial tramway built by 126th Engineer Battalion to evacuate wounded and resupply troops attacking Riva Ridge, February 1945. (U.S. Army Signal Corps)

The 10th reinforcements move up Monte Belvedere. Riva Ridge in background left; Belvedere summit on right. February 1945. (U.S. Army Signal Corps)

Congresswoman Clare Boothe Luce visits the mountain troops in Italy. General George Hays at left. (Roy O. Bingham)

The 10th troops pinned down by sniper fire on the road to Castel d'Aiano, March 1945. (U.S. Army Signal Corps)

Sgt. Walter Prager finds a moment to write home prior to the Spring Push, April 1945. (Richard A. Rocker)

Highway tunnels on Lake Garda saw some of the last, grim fighting in northern Italy, late April 1945. (Richard A. Rocker)

"The Pianist." David Brower in the Po River valley following the liberation of Verona. (Wilbur G. Vaughan)

approximating that from a partial moon. The lights had been standard operating procedure for weeks, but this night some in the columns making their way up the rock worried that the light could betray their advance. The climbers were extraordinarily exposed and vulnerable, veritable ducks in a shooting gallery. A single enemy machine gun from on high could wipe out a column of men working single file up any one of the narrow trails. Maj. John Hay, a commander with the 3d Battalion, which huddled in reserve at the bottom of the ridge that night, said of the German advantage, "A dozen men, each with a handful of rocks, could have defended those positions."

But then a dense fog rolled in during the night, blanketing the top of the ridge and obscuring the climbers from above. It also blocked the light from the searchlights, and at least one column lost touch with its lead group. But actually nothing could have been better for the element of surprise.

The night was cold, not bitter, but below freezing. Meltwater on the rock turned to glaze ice. Only the lead climbers had been issued the fine, stiff-soled mountain boots developed at Camp Hale. The rest struggled with the standard-issue, Army pac shoe, which had a soft leather upper and a rubber sole that deformed and gripped poorly. But thanks to the support from fixed ropes, and perhaps the comforting cloak provided by the fog, the columns progressed deliberately, if haltingly, upward. The line stopped, as highway traffic does, when its lead elements slowed to negotiate a tricky patch of water ice, for example, or to make a move up a particularly steep section. For the most part, this wasn't technical climbing; the trails angled through steep, but not vertical, rock and brush. (One route was mellow enough for mules to navigate.) The trick was not to stumble, to use the many exposed roots and saplings for handholds, to stay focused and patient. The fog demanded special care. At times the climbers could see only five or six feet ahead. When the line moved forward again, each man turned and tapped the man behind. In the gauzy quiet, the distances, the void both above and below, seemed endless.

One by one, still in darkness and pretty much on schedule, the companies crested the ridge. Much of the terrain on top was barren of snow, rocky and wind-scoured with only a few saplings for cover. In some places remnant snow cornices allowed the climbers to dig in. With one exception, there was no resistance, no German defenders to be seen or heard in the mist. That exception came at the far north end of Riva (Route 1), where a detached platoon from A Company under the command of Lt. James Loose apparently woke the crew of a German observation post. Loose's men had no choice but to scramble up a scree field to their objective, and the clatter of rolling rock invoked a hail of grenades from the other side of the ridge. "Fortunately," Loose told Flint Whitlock in *Soldiers on Skis*, "they thought we were further down than we were," and the grenades exploded harmlessly below. Once on top, Loose organized his men into a tight defensive perimeter and waited. "The Germans backed off and let us alone for a while. We found out later that they thought we were a lost patrol so they were just going to let us sit there and chop us up when they were ready. Which was one of the biggest mistakes they ever made."

Jacques Parker and his lead climbers on Serrasiccia (Route 3) crept over the top about midnight, moving as quietly as they could, and found—nobody. They did come upon a small hut just back from the edge, hastily built of wood with a stovepipe sticking out of the roof. "We didn't know if anybody was in there or not, so we dropped a grenade down the chimney. It blew the door off, and we crept up and peered in. Nobody there. Just a couple of girly magazines and some benches for the guys to sit and rest."

Here and everywhere else along the ridge, the enemy had apparently withdrawn for the night, secure in the assumption that no significant force could or would climb Riva's sharp side. The German observers had a network of fortified dugouts down the relatively gentle hillside to the west, and the defenders had all—all but the crew James Loose encountered—retired in complacency. The dogs, too, had retired. Later, when it was all over, General Hays joked about the 10th's luck: "They must have sent the dogs back to Bavaria on furlough." With the coast clear, Jacques Parker turned around and descended his climbing route to fetch the rest of C Company.

As dawn neared, the Americans dug in, each company on its particular section of ridge. Now they were the defenders. Perimeters were established. Weapons squads set up their machine guns on the flanks; mortar men deployed to the rear. Wherever possible, companies sent patrols out along the scarp to establish contact with one another. Signal Corps men strung communication wire on the ground between the various positions and back down to Battalion HQ. Everyone preferred phone communication to the radios, which functioned erratically, although the phone wire was vulnerable to sabotage and to random artillery hits. All the while, the obfuscating fog concealed the 86th's movements from the enemy. "It was sort of supernatural," remembers Lt. Howard Koch of C Company. "Somebody was watching over us, we all felt." But sooner or later the Germans would have to discover the intruders.

About 11:00 A.M. on the 19th, a wind came up, and the fog lifted. At noon, A Company on Monte Mancinello (Route 4) engaged an enemy patrol of about a dozen men, killing six and taking the rest prisoner. An hour later on Serrasiccia, C Company watched as a patrol of forty Germans approached from the west, from the garrison town of Fanano. Some of the Germans spotted figures moving around on the ridge and, assuming them to be their own troops, waved in greeting. The Americans waved back and waited for the Germans to get closer. Howard Koch recalled, "If we had been more combat wise, we would have let them get in really close. We pulled the trigger a little too early." The enemy platoon melted back into the woods.

Now the battle for Riva Ridge was truly on. The Germans finally realized what had happened and organized counterattacks on Riva's most critical high points, the ones nearest to Belvedere (Routes 1, 2, and 3). During the night of the 19th, German patrols sneaked up to the ridge in the gaps between American positions. (Distances along the ridge were too great for one battalion to fill.) The Germans infiltrated in two places—between James Loose's detached platoon on Pizzo di Campiano and his distant B Company neighbors on Capel Buso, and again between B Company and C Company on Serrasiccia. They cut the communications wire the signal teams had laid, and killed and wounded several men on C Company's far right perimeter, before digging in themselves just off the summit.

By this time automatic-weapons fire no longer surprised the men of the 86th. Occasional firefights erupted all along Riva's crest, and more firing echoed from across the river on Monte Belvedere, where the principal attack had just begun. C Company's Lt. John McCown heard the gunshots on his right flank but couldn't send anyone out to investigate until morning. At daybreak he and a squad of nine, including Jacques Parker, went to see what had happened. McCown was one of the division's best climbers, a member of the American Alpine Club and, with Dave Brower, a lead instructor at the Assault Climbing School in West Virginia. He and Jacques Parker together had done much of the reconnaissance for Route 3. He was also a bit of an anachronism, a gentleman soldier who wore his father's World War I pearl-handled officer's revolver on his hip.

After organizing evacuation of the casualties, McCown and his squad moved down a grassy knoll to the west in search of the German infiltrators. Quite unexpectedly, several enemy soldiers rose from their hiding places and raised their hands as if to surrender. McCown continued forward, when suddenly the "surrendering" Germans dropped to the ground and a hail of bullets erupted from unseen gun placements. The squad was cut down where it stood. McCown and two other soldiers were killed. Six Americans fell to the snow wounded by the treachery. The wounded didn't dare move for fear of being shot again, and the Germans opened fire every time U.S. medics tried to scramble down to tend to them.

In retaliation, the company commander, Capt. Worth McClure, ordered artillery fire on the Nazi position and readied two platoons from C Company to storm down and retake the ground lost. A short time later, shells screamed in over the ridge from the battery near Vidiciatico. The ground around the Germans erupted in geysers of mud and steel. The barrage lasted only a few minutes—long enough to scatter what was left of the enemy patrol. At last the C Company wounded could be treated and the dead removed. One of the men made sure to save McCown's revolver so that it could be returned to his father.

Six Germans were captured in the retaliatory attack. One of them, Jacques Parker remembers, "was a real diehard," an SS lieutenant, shot in the gut. Some prisoners, their war over at last, tried to make friends with the Americans, or at least behaved submissively. But this guy remained obdurate, "even tried to cut [the] communication wire with the heel of his boot." What to do with the man? Sending him down to La Ca via the trail would take hours and require an escort of at least two men, and Captain McClure needed all the soldiers he could muster up on the ridge. Besides, when asked, regimental HQ said they didn't particularly want to interview the SS lieutenant.

One of the men said, "I'll take him down." Parker and the rest understood what was about to happen, and they accepted the harsh expediency of it. It wasn't by the rules, but emotions were running high—good men had been grievously tricked and gunned down—and Riva was far from secure. From a short way down the trail, they heard a single rifle shot. Apparently, the soldier had ordered his prisoner to march over an outcrop, and when the man hesitated, shot him for disobeying an order. If C Company men dwelt on the moral ambiguities involved, they kept it to themselves. A decision had been made that placed the welfare of the group ahead of ethical niceties. It was a harsh lesson, delivered for the first time on Riva's knife edge. There would be others, they knew, before their war was over. And none of them would be immune.

The episode with the prisoner only underscored what the men of the 86th already knew—that their "impossible" climb up Riva had put an enormous distance between them and their support in the valley below. From the planning stages, it was recognized that two of the toughest challenges on Riva would be figuring out methods both to resupply the troops up top and to evacuate the wounded. The easiest of the five climbing routes, Route 2 to Cappel Buso, soon teemed with mule trains, though not with the 10th's big Missouri mules. They hadn't made the crossing to Italy; they'd been sent to Burma instead. But General Hays did secure the services of hundreds of smaller Italian mules capably driven by loyal Alpini. And the mules did yeoman's duty, hauling ammunition, food, and water up Route 2. On all the other climbing routes, though, as the Germans counterattacked and supplies ran low, exhausted human porters struggled over rock and ice—often two and three times a day—with sixty-pound loads.

The problem of evacuation remained, however. Stretcher-bearers took six to twelve hours to haul a man safely down the 1,500 vertical feet to aid stations at the base of the cliff. In some cases, sadly, that wasn't fast enough. The alternative was to erect an aerial tramway, which, fortunately, the 10th's engineers came prepared to do. Back at Camp Hale, the Army had decided to develop a portable tram for use in mountainous terrain. The people most familiar with aerial systems at that time were mining engineers. Mines throughout the Rockies and Sierras had long used cable trams to haul machinery up and bring ore down to the mills. Could the engineers build a tramway that could be broken down and transported in crates weighing no more than 250 pounds each? And then be reassembled again in a hurry?

A young mine engineer named Robert Heron, who would go on to design and build some of the first chairlifts at Colorado ski resorts, came up with an ingenious, modular design, powered by a Piper Cub aircraft engine. It was a jig-back tram: One car went up while the opposite car came down. The same concept—much less refined—ran the Boat Tow on Aspen Mountain. When they got to Camp Swift, members of the 126th Engineer Battalion practiced taking the whole thing apart and putting it back together two or three times until they shaved their record down to just a couple of hours.

That first morning on Riva, as soon as the assault companies reported topping out on the ridge, engineers began hauling cable up the Capel Buso route. The going was not as easy or as smooth as it had been on the flat ground at Swift. There was the racing Dardagna to cross, and there were mines buried in an orchard partway up the route. A few Germans, caught away from their units on the sharp eastern contours of Riva, fired on the tram builders. A couple of engineers were wounded by mines. But they persevered, and by the afternoon of the 21st, they had a working tram that covered two-thirds of the vertical to Capel Buso. The fourteen-minute ride cut the total time needed to bring wounded down from the top to about two hours. Many of the fifty casualties evacuated this way probably owed their lives to the engineers.

Meanwhile, the tram also shuttled tons of food, water, and

ammunition to the 86th companies holding on tenaciously against counterattacks by the German 4th Mountain Battalion. The position hardest hit was that of Lieutenant Loose and his A Company platoon. (Asked later to explain why the regimental brains had charged a mere platoon with taking the most important objective on the ridge—the one closest to Monte Belvedere—Loose replied: "The Army made a mistake.")

Not only was Loose's platoon outnumbered, it was cut off by a knife-edge ridge from the resupply at Capel Buso. The lieutenant and his men improvised brilliantly while running dangerously low on ammunition and, in the end, having only snow to melt in their mouths for sustenance. The Germans counterattacked six times over two days. The forty-man platoon fought back by anticipating the enemy's next angle of attack, by throwing his grenades back from where they came, and with stealth raids of their own down behind the lines. On the first morning, Loose led a patrol through the fog to an elaborate German dugout with sod walls, a window and a door, and a wire clothesline strung to a nearby tree. Loose's bazooka man fired a round through the window, killing four. Three more were captured along with a briefcase of documents, one mortar, several machine guns, and some much-needed food. The men also found a portable record player. Among the recordings were an Al Jolson LP and a recording of "Lilli Marlene," a popular German song that was often broadcast over Nazi propaganda radio. Loose's men took the player and the record back to their perimeter, where they played the song over and over to torment any German soldiers within hearing range.

By the second night, Loose's men were out of hand grenades and desperately low on ammunition. The counterattacking Germans, sensing an opportunity, crept ever closer. With no options left, Lieutenant Loose called down to his supporting field artillery and requested defensive fire practically on his own position. "Do you realize what you're asking?" came the reply. "I do," Loose said, "but if we don't get artillery in tight, you'll have nothing left to support."

Loose ordered his men to burrow deep in their foxholes while the gunners dialed back their coordinates to within twenty-five yards of the perimeter. At 2:00 A.M. a torrent of shells smashed into the advancing Germans, ending the threat, for the moment. Twenty-four hours later, down to six rounds of machine-gun ammo and "so hungry I couldn't see straight," Loose and A Platoon were finally relieved by the battalion commander himself, Col. Henry Hampton. James Loose and six of his men would each be awarded the Silver Star for "gallantry in action."

Counterattacks of diminishing strength continued for the next few days and nights, but for all intents and purposes, Riva Ridge was secure. Considering the risk, casualties had been miniscule: seventeen American dead and something over fifty wounded. Over a hundred German troops were taken prisoner; uncounted scores lay dead in the northside snow. No longer could the enemy direct fire onto Belvedere's south face, and as a bonus, the Americans on the ridge could now pinpoint artillery targets on Belvedere's back side, which greatly improved prospects for the massive night attack by the 85th and 87th Regiments that jumped off just before midnight on the 19th. The 10th's special training had proved its worth. Along with a daring plan, some spectacular weather luck, and a defending force stunned by the audacity of the attack, the mountain troops, "Minnie's ski troops," had pulled off the most successful alpine assault in U.S. military history.

But almost no one back home heard about it. As it happened, February 19 was the day three divisions of Marines landed on Iwo Jima against twenty thousand fanatic, dug-in Japanese. Iwo Jima was just a speck in the western Pacific, but it had airfields and it would be crucial to American bombing missions targeting the main islands of Japan. The famous photo of Marines raising the flag on Mount Suribachi justifiably dominated the nation's front pages.

Minnie Dole heard the news about Riva, several days after the fact, by way of a confidential phone call from a staff officer in Washington. And then, with some digging, he was able to find a couple of censored newspaper stories. Censored, because the Northern Apennines fighting was far from over. It was just beginning.

CHAPTER 10:

Belvedere

T ime deals out many kinds of hours," David Brower wrote in *Remount Blue*, a combat history of his 3d Battalion, 86th Mountain Regiment:

There is the microscopic one that passes without the knowing of the fond couple parked on the hill. There is the short hour by which a newsman's deadline measures its approach. Hours are from moderate to long, depending on one's interest in a task, attenuated if you are on time and someone else is late, interminable if you're pacing the maternity hospital lobby. But how to describe the kind of hours the soldier gets when he is waiting for the jump-off, the hours that he divides into minutes and again into seconds that he cannot squander?

Brower's battalion, which had been in reserve the night before, when the 1st Battalion climbed Riva, now waited in the dark at the foot of the Belvedere-Gorgolesco massif. The plan was for the 87th Regiment to attack up Belvedere's left flank (facing north) beginning at 11:00 P.M. (Bob Parker would lead a column up the same route he had scouted two days before to the village of Corona.) At the same time, one battalion of the 85th would move straight up toward Belvedere's summit, and a second battalion, further right, would climb to the saddle separating Belvedere from its slightly lower sister peak, Monte Gorgolesco. The 86th Regiment's 3d Battalion—Brower's group—would then secure Gorgolesco's right flank.

As General Hays had said, all of this was to be accomplished at night, without artillery preparation and without loaded rifles; he was counting once again on the element of surprise. Soldiers worried that this was foolish; hadn't the enemy been sufficiently alerted by the previous night's attack on Riva Ridge? Nevertheless, the orders read: No arms are to be used before daylight; the aim is to slip past the German positions if possible and gain the high ground behind them; positions that cannot be bypassed are to be eliminated with bayonets, knives, and grenades; if we don't fire our weapons, the defenders will not know where we are or what our strength is; artillery and air support will come only after daybreak and after initial objectives have been taken.

"Man alive," said Dan Kennerly when Sgt. Harry Poschman read the orders. "We are to make an assault with five battalions against the strongest German positions in Italy and not a goddamn loaded gun in the entire outfit. That's a large order, Sarge. I hope the general knows what he's doing."

While Brower and his battalion waited, Poschman and his machine-gun squad shouldered their loads and started up the hill behind C Company, 85th Regiment. They had been hiding all day in haystacks and hedgerows and rubble-strewn stone buildings, and now, as word came that the Riva climbers were holding firm against sporadic counterattacks, they moved across the line of departure. "This is it, men!" Harry thought about the line his officers had used at Camp Hale to simulate drama, and how the dogfaces had snickered under their breath every time. "This is it, men!" Now the phrase was devoid of humor. And Harry thought about Vassos the Greek, who had been wrong after all.

It was exactly 11:00 P.M. Boots crunched through freezing mud and what little snow remained on Belvedere's south slopes. The moon peeked over the mountain's flank and added to the incandescence provided by the searchlights. Together they threw enough light on the snow patches to make them glow. Trees cast multiple shadows. More than once, Harry thought he saw them move.

Harry's squad of eight men was in charge of one water-cooled, .30-caliber heavy machine gun. One soldier carried the gun itself while another lugged its tripod. A third carried the bezel, a solid brass ring on which the gun could spin 360 degrees and which showed compass bearings and range-finder distances. The rest of the squad struggled with packboards loaded with boxes of ammunition. Everyone carried his own rifle and pocketfuls of hand grenades. An extra soldier had been assigned to carry antifreeze for the gun's water jacket. That's what kept the barrel from burning out while firing twenty rounds per second. (When machine-gun squads did, inevitably, run out of antifreeze, the men would urinate into the water jacket to keep their gun operational.)

Belvedere's fields and woods were not tilted nearly so steeply as Riva's rock, but the way was long and folded, riddled with streams and ditches, with sharp ravines and bombed-out wagon roads. Here and there lay the ghostly remains of U.S. tanks—abandoned on the November attempts to capture Belvedere, attempts that were forced back by heavy and accurate German artillery. Through the night the columns advanced, haltingly, gaining altitude, listening to the odd explosion, the occasional firecracker sound of small-arms fire and wondering if this was it, if they'd been found out. It was only a matter of when. Then the night grew still again and they trudged on. Harry's platoon followed in support of C Company, a rifle company spearheading the attack on the saddle. The machine guns could not fire on the move; their job would be defensive, to protect C Company's perimeter once the company gained the ridge. When the line moved forward, the men sweated under their huge loads. When the line stopped, as it did all too often, the sweat froze.

It must have been about 6:00 A.M., Harry thought, when a ripping sound broke the silence. It sounded "like somebody tearing a big piece of canvas." The ripping sound was followed by "the flutter of a wounded bird. The wounded bird landed with a terrific flash and a big bang. Somebody screamed, and somebody called for a medic." The assault had been discovered, the battle begun.

The wounded bird had been a mortar round; the fluttering-wing sound was the sound it made as it fell. (Artillery cannon fire high-velocity, flat-trajectory rounds over many miles—shells that shriek or whine overhead. The portable, short-barrel mortar tube lobs shells at high angles over relatively short distances. The resulting explosions can be equally devastating.) More German mortars crashed into the earth. Harry told his boys to dig in even if they were to be stopped only a few minutes. Any depression, no matter how shallow, into which a man could flatten himself was safer than standing exposed. Harry hugged the earth as it heaved with each explosion. He wanted to become the earth. He imagined himself crawling up completely inside the protection of his helmet. A ridiculous fantasy, he knew, but it turned out to be a common one.

The mortar barrage lasted but a short eternity. The squad ahead got up and started forward, and Harry's squad staggered to their feet and followed. They hurried along the edge of a wood and then, beyond it, onto an open slope lit by faint daylight. Now the enemy opened up with machine guns. Harry could see neither where the bullets were coming from nor where they were landing, so he just kept going into what seemed like a wall of noise. Mortar shells landed in the trees the men had just left, shattering tree limbs and sending deadly wood splinters flying. Incoming artillery shells split the air above before exploding, their jagged fragments spinning, buzzing through the dawn like angry hornets. Spent shrapnel lost momentum and smacked the dirt with a dull thud. Dan Kennerly noticed that each piece of flying metal had a different pitch, probably because the shards were different sizes. "Some actually harmonize with others . . . musical shrapnel, a deadly melody." When a shell exploded close by a man, even if he escaped the whirling fragments, the concussion forced blood to ooze from his ears and nose. Small-caliber stuff—from rifles and machine pistols—whizzed about with a high-pitched zing.

Harry had his men running forward spaced a good ten yards apart, as he had been taught. From somewhere up ahead another German machine gun burst to life, and this time Harry could see the bullets striking a patch of snow and advancing right for them. But then the bullets stopped. Out of ammo? Jammed? Or maybe, Harry thought, one of our guys got the gunner. He hoped it was the last. But just in case, he signaled his men to drop into a ravine on their right. A soldier on the far side of the gully saw them and shouted across, "No! It's mined!"

It turned out that the 1st and 2d Squads of Harry's platoon had tangled with the minefield, fatally, just minutes before. Kennerly had watched as two men ahead of him went down, caught in trip wires, then four more. "An aid man, I think it's Rosey, goes to help.

As he sits down beside Haak, the ground under him explodes. He sat on a mine."

Mines had not been much of a factor on Riva. The terrain was mostly too steep and rocky. And luck had played a part: The 10th men later learned that hard snow crusts had, in places, allowed them to walk right over the top of several minefields. But Belvedere was a different story; the terrain was gentler, the soil easier to dig. The Germans had had months to prepare their defensive strongholds, and they had mined all logical approaches to the ridge. Huge antitank mines had been buried in the farm roads. But it was the antipersonnel mines—the trip wires and "bouncing bettys" and *Schuh* mines—that could so suddenly and terrifyingly disable an otherwise strong push. These mines sometimes killed soldiers outright, but they had a crueler and more practical purpose—to wound, and thus to cause the enemy to lose two or more combatants, the actual casualty plus the men who came to his aid. The *Schuh* mine was so named because it contained only enough explosive to mangle the foot of a soldier unlucky enough to step on it. Engineers were trained to detect and disarm mines, and the 10th's engineers performed this ticklish operation countless times in Italy. But not on Belvedere that first night, in the dark, when speed and surprise were paramount.

Harry's squad avoided this particular carnage and moved on up the rib toward the ridge. Nearing the top, through smoke and dust and the deafening noise, Harry could see lots of men running around. He felt "blown out mentally and physically" after seven hours of climbing, and the scene before him looked like nothing so much as chaos. "Most of us could not put the pieces together." A rifle squad, ten men, lay dead in a shallow depression, mowed down by German machine-gun fire. "Even the trees were cut down about eighteen inches above the ground" as if by a ragged chainsaw.

Harry's platoon sergeant ran up and told him where to set up his gun. Harry couldn't believe his eyes; the man had a bullet hole in the front of his helmet. "He ran along with me saying, 'The damn thing went in at a slight angle, skidded around the inside of my helmet, and dropped down the back of my neck.' The bullet burned his neck. He was mad."

Now that they'd reached the Belvedere-Gorgolesco ridge, the machine guns would be critical in holding it against the inevitable counterattacks. Harry and his men dug furiously, one hole for the gun, others for themselves. The digging was strangely comforting. They had trained to do this. But the setting, the lethal chaos, was entirely foreign. "This is a meat grinder," Harry thought to himself. "And I'm in it." Off to one side a lifeless face stared up at him as he worked.

Theirs seemed to be the only gun out of three in the platoon to have survived the minefield. The company commander, Capt. Richard Johnson, hustled by and told Harry to "fire at anything you can find." Harry hunted for targets with his binoculars. "Across the meadow ahead to a low ridge I searched again and again. Finally, I found him—a German machine-gun nest firing directly at us. The rounds were wild, buzzing like bees. I told Churney to fire. He lifted up on the trigger. Nothing happened. He worked the bolt fast and triggered again. Still no fire.

"I heard Johnson yell, 'Get that gun going!' I ran to the gun and told the crew to scatter, jerked out the bolt, and gave it a fast inspection." The bolt appeared to be okay. Harry reinserted it and tried again to fire. Nothing. He took a new bolt out of his pocket and jammed it into the gun. Still nothing. "I was numb with despair." Then a light came on: It must be the ammo. "I cleared the belt from the gun and flung it away, fed a fresh one and fired. The tracers ran true like a red-hot wire straight to the target. Eley and Demitroff laid down on the legs of the tripod while I fired the entire belt."

Within minutes, or seconds, Harry couldn't tell, the order came to get up and move again; 1st Battalion would charge to the right, from the saddle up to the summit of Gorgolesco. "Now we had to move fast, with the heavy loads, not because we wanted to, but to keep up with the hard pace set by the company commander. I had the boys pick up the gun by the legs and run with it about two hundred yards. There we stopped briefly, broke it down into lighter components, and continued on in the attack. It was a good move, as the artillery commenced hammering the spot we just vacated."

On they ran into a meadow and through a maze of berry bushes that grabbed at their clothes and tore their exposed skin. Thorns ripped Harry's face from forehead to chin. On the far side of the meadow, a new order came down: Unbuckle your chinstraps. A near miss—just the concussion from an artillery blast—could tear your head off. Great, Harry thought. "Now it's impossible to run without losing your tin hat. What a dilemma."

But the survivors got used to it, learned to run as if balancing books on their heads. One almost never saw a GI beyond his first combat with chinstraps buckled. Harry was growing wiser by the minute. "Running along I almost stepped on a German sniper. Fortunately for me he was dead. I would like to have had the scope sight on his rifle but was afraid the body was booby-trapped. That's where the expression comes from: Any booby can be trapped. The Germans were tricky and would go to great lengths to kill us. Not me. I'm going to ski the Alps this spring."

The shells rained down all around. Harry wrote in his memoir:

My boys all struggled along as best they could under the big loads. Occasionally I went back to help one, then another and another. . . . At the end of the column came the medic. We ran along together for a few yards. A shell landed between us and bounced away singing—a dud. I heard the breathless words, "I wish I . . . could . . . get out of this." I heard another shell and dove into a shallow depression. It landed between us and he was up in the air turning over like a leaf in the wind, then on the ground—a shapeless form."

General Hays's admonition passed in a nanosecond through Harry's mind: "You must continue to move forward. Never stop. If your buddy is wounded, don't stop to help him. Continue to move forward, always forward." "I was up and gone in a flash."

What was it that made the soldiers plow forward, against their most basic survival instincts, through hails of lead and smoke, through what John Keegan, in *The Face of Battle*, calls "automatic and inhuman lethality"? It wasn't the land itself; neither side fought for an Apennines home. And unlike in the animal kingdom, where fighting over territory is usually just ritualistic, on the battlefield, Keegan reminds us, "there is proprietorship which is fictive, and combat which is in earnest."

Why then, when the mind says no, does the body continue? Harry watched the walking wounded return down the path, almost always with relief on their faces. The men moving forward could be forgiven a bout of envy; the wounded had survived—not unscathed—but survived that which still threatened those advancing. And so the attack soldiered on, trusting in . . . what? Luck? Leadership? One's own sheer determination? Some power greater than all this? Keegan writes that "individuals fight for personal survival which [the individual realizes] is bound up with group survival, and out of fear of incurring by cowardly conduct the group's contempt."

Patriotism rarely played a role. Dan Kennerly wrote in his diary: "I don't recall thinking of patriotism at any time during the day. My only thought of duty was to myself and my comrades." On the first morning of the attack up Gorgolesco, Hugh Evans, a twenty-year-old staff sergeant with C Company, 85th Regiment, came upon his friend and platoon leader, Bob Fischer, lying face-up in the arms of another friend, Mac MacKenzie. Fischer's chest was riddled with holes from a machine-gun burst.

> Seeing that he had a sucking wound, and not being able to think of anything but to put an air-tight bandage on the wound, I ripped the back out of Mac's pile jacket and began to make such a bandage. Before I had finished, I looked at Bob's eyes and saw that he had died. . . . Mac said he kept saying, "Oh god. Please not now. Please not now!" Bob was maybe a couple of months older than I . . . and the first person I had seen die.

Evans's eyes filled with tears of rage, and the young man whose tenor voice lent a sweet harmony to 10th singalongs became a *Berserker*—a Viking term for a warrior who fights outside of himself, with a controlled fury. Evans and a couple of other soldiers crawled to within a few yards of the offending machine-gun nest:

> [We hurled grenades] at the points where we thought the Jerries were. All of us were so angry we didn't speak. Finally, I jumped over the last little rise and . . . landed on two dead Germans. For the next ten minutes I just kept moving, throwing grenades and firing my machine pistol.

By himself he took out a second machine gun, killing six more "Jerries" and taking twenty prisoners. "The last Germans, who got up and yelled '*Kamerad!*' I held with an empty gun." As it happened, these were the last two enemy strong points before the summit of Gorgolesco.

By the end of the first day (sundown on February 20), six battalions of the 10th Mountain Division (with three battalions in reserve) had control of nearly six miles of ridgeline from Riva on the west across the top of Belvedere to Gorgolesco on the east. The Americans occupied the high ground on Belvedere, but other Allied divisions had done so before. The trick now was to hold it against the inevitable counterattacks and the withering rain of artillery from guns miles away to the north. Those guns, indeed all of the German rear echelon, remained protected in the difficult, buckled hill country still separating the Allies from their ultimate objective, the Po River valley, twenty miles to the north. Belvedere was only the first step—a key one, but only one—in the drive to Bologna.

After Belvedere and Gorgolesco were captured, the 85th Regiment's 2d Battalion took off to the northeast toward the operation's final objective, Monte della Torraccia, the last in this chain of hills lording over Highway 64. Lt. Col. John Stone's men ran into hellish artillery fire in an exposed saddle on the way to the peak and were pinned down. The retreating Germans intended a bitter fight over della Torraccia and called in their most accurate artillery, the deadly 88s. Shells came down "like a New England hailstorm," vaporizing soldiers in their holes. Stone heard the orders to move forward and knew the danger in staying put, but he couldn't move. Every attempt to attack up the hill drew more devastating fire. His ranks were seriously depleted, his men low on ammunition, food, and water. The battalion remained in place and suffered dreadful losses. Two days later, the Third Battalion of the 86th moved through the 85th, and Stone was relieved of his command. Many of his men never accepted the justness of that verdict.

There had been bravery, sometimes foolish bravery, in those days, and there had been cowardice. The fear simply ate some men up. Pfc. John Jennings, the Dartmouth undergrad whose quiet competence on ski patrols before Riva had earned him a role with Headquarters, F Company, 87th Regiment, saw it happen the very first night, in the quiet before the attack was discovered. His unit was out in front with the company commander, charged with relaying information back on routes, enemy resistance, whatever they found. "We were just starting our assault on Belvedere—a couple of communications people, a captain, and a first sergeant. He just dropped the radio and took off. It was one of those big goddamn Infantry 300 radios on a packboard. Weighed about forty pounds. I picked it up and carried it for the rest of the war. Where he was during the rest of the war, I don't know. I never saw him again."

In the middle of the grisly battle for Gorgolesco, one of Harry Poschman's machine gunners decided he could take no more and shot himself in the calf with his .45 pistol. "Blew the bone right out the front. He said he was holstering his gun, but the guys told me no, he did it on purpose." Those who kept going understood the awful strain, and perhaps because of that understanding, voiced little condemnation.

A close sibling to bravery and fear—and a much more powerful force than either, to hear the men talk—was luck. Not a man in battle in the Northern Apennines didn't invoke luck's fickle nature, both good and bad. Hours before his C Company (85th Regiment) was to jump off on Belvedere, Robert Woody was told he would have to remain behind. "My wretched cough—deep and wracking—could give us away. I protested—feebly: 'I want to go.' [Peter] Wick and [Frank] Miller were adamant. Inwardly, I was glad their insistence was so strong. I was too young and dumb to fear lead and shrapnel; I thought myself immortal."

From a farmhouse behind the line of departure, Woody and another man, who had pneumonia, listened. And that sense of immortality evaporated. From Woody's memoir:

> Firing erupted in the darkness on the mountain and increased in crescendo. Their machine guns, rapid rate of fire. Ours, slower rate of fire. The silence had been broken, and we knew the shit had hit the fan.

Some artillery came in on us. It killed the battalion mail clerk, William Blaise. I had known him since junior high. The firing and explosions continued through the dawn and into the morning. But by mid-morning, the intensity of the rifle and machine-gun fire had ceased.

Later in the afternoon, the sun was out warm and bright. Roy Bingham walked in worn and wan. He had chosen to accompany C Company up the mountain. He told of the terrible things that he had seen and that had been done to the platoon by the Germans and by the platoon to the Germans. He said Capt. [Charles] Smith had either stepped on or had been hit by a mine. Medic Kurzinger had been killed by a mine. Walker had been killed. Fischer had been killed. But his buddy Evans, in great anger, had taken out a machine-gun nest.

His account went on. There had been killing of prisoners. We were not only red-blooded, but cold-blooded. Now the mules were coming down with bodies in the mattress bags tied over their backs like beef halves.

The following day, Woody climbed Gorgolesco to rejoin his unit. "I felt craven. I asked Thornton if there were bad feelings. 'Nah,' he said. 'The guys understand.'" Woody gave all his water away; the men, now defending the ridge, were parched.

Bud Winter, with M Company, 85th Regiment, on Belvedere, wrote to his brother about another kind of luck, the kind that ignores a man's health, his courage, and his skill:

Dear Fred.
I guess you have heard already that I did not duck soon enough. I got hit at three o-clock in the morning [February 20] by some shrapnel from a German 81mm mortar [two fragments in his chest]. . . . I am in bed, without a worry in

the world. The only thing[s] I do not like are the penicillin shots in my behind. . . . A Red Cross lady mailed my Purple Heart home for me. Please have "Lt. Burdell S. Winter" engraved on it with the year, 1945.

On March 3, he wrote again to say that he expected to be back with his mortar platoon the next day. "My wound isn't bothering me." And with typical Winter enthusiasm he added, "Found a couple of articles in *Yank* magazine which makes it look as if I won't have to worry about education expense. You don't have to worry about me studying when I get there. Since being over here, I realize how important an education is! You can be sure of one thing, though. I'm going to a co-ed college, and I'm going to make a name for myself in skiing."

Safe to say skiing intruded on very few reveries among the exhausted soldiers who made it through those first days. "It seemed a lifetime since we had any sleep," Harry Poschman wrote. "Actually, it was only three days." The 3d Battalion of the 86th finally took della Torraccia on February 24 and then held it despite numerous well-organized counterattacks. Dave Brower and his fellow 3d Battalion troopers came to think of "della Torraccia" only as the official, geographical name for the mountain on which so many of their friends had died. Among themselves they knew the mountain's facets by the events they'd witnessed there: "Purple Heart Ridge," "Honeycomb Hill," and "Dead Man's Gulch."

And then, except for scattered shelling from the other side, the front was again quiet. Harry Poschman recalled, only slightly sarcastically, that "the boys made themselves comfortable in luxurious, deep gun pits and foxholes, improvised cooking facilities, and ordered better food. The better food didn't come."

Prisoners streamed by toward the Allied rear, hands on their heads, number tags looped through buttonholes in their wool greatcoats. The 10th had taken more than four hundred prisoners in four days. Bob Parker watched one group of POWs march by his position and admired the footgear they wore. "In Italy we were never issued the mountain boots we'd had at Camp Hale. So I picked out this guy about my size. Poor guy, he'd been told that we indiscriminately shot prisoners. He was terrified. I told him, 'Sitzen sich! Schuhe heraus!' in my limited German.

"Now he was barefoot, and he *knew* he was going to be shot. I gave him my GI shoepacs and sent him on his way. His were beautiful leather—and a perfect fit! For the rest of the war I had a German sweater and German mountain boots."

Harry Poschman also scored a pair of superior German boots, but in the end he couldn't keep them:

> One day the boys got restless and went ahead of our line to explore. They found an abandoned bunker containing food, boots, and a body. I got the boots because they fit. . . . Those boots were the best footwear I ever owned. The edge nails—real tricounis—gave fine traction on any ground, just the opposite of our boots. They were waterproof and warm in the snow. That's what led to my undoing.
>
> Occasionally I had to get out and check gun duty and other things. I left tracks. One morning a rifleman came running to our platoon command post to say he had tracked a German right to our door. That ended my luxury footwear.

The unusually fine winter weather continued, and during the day the men of the 10th could bask in the sun without their clothes on. One balmy afternoon, battalion headquarters phoned to say a Red Cross doughnut girl was on her way up to the front lines with doughnuts and coffee. The girl turned out to be Debbie Bankart, the perky New Hampshire ski instructor who had taken John Jay's movies on the recruitment trail. Already in Italy when the 10th shipped over, she had asked to be transferred to the Northern Apennines. The men clutched whatever garments they could grab to cover their nakedness, helped themselves to pastries from Bankart's basket, and stood in wonderment at the beauty and absurdity of it all.

The respite—what Harry Poschman referred to as "the good life there on Gorgolesco"—turned out to be short-lived. The fall of Monte Belvedere—indeed the capture of all the hills from Riva on the left to della Torraccia on the right—had surprised not only the Germans but the Allied command as well. The untested 10th had exceeded even General Hays's expectations, and a critical salient, or wedge, had been driven into the Nazi defenses. Some in Allied command thought that the U.S. Fifth Army should exploit the 10th's gains before the Germans had a chance to reorganize, that the Fifth should push through immediately to the Po. But instead, the order came down for the 10th to attack again, in another "limited offensive" to extend by three or four miles Allied control of the hills overlooking the prized Highway 64. The offensive was expected to last just a couple of days. The all-out effort to reach Bologna and the Po, the so-called Spring Push, involving the entire U.S. Fifth and British Eighth Armies, remained stubbornly on-schedule for mid-April.

After a week of relative quiet, the "limited offensive" was set to begin March 3. All of the 10th's battalions had been returned to full strength using replacement soldiers, none of whom—with the exception of returning wounded like Bud Winter—had been with the mountain troops before. Jump-off was set for 6:30 A.M. The 86th Regiment, on the left side of the advance, circled around the base of della Torraccia and headed for Monte Terminale and a succession of smaller hills beyond it. In the center of the line, the 87th Regiment had as its objective the crossroads town of Castel d'Aiano, a medieval stone village utterly smashed to rubble by the competing big guns. The 85th would follow the 87th up to Castel d'A-iano and then veer right and secure the division's right flank from atop Monte della Spe.

Army histories say that all objectives were achieved by March 6, within the anticipated time frame. But this says nothing of the hard fighting during those four days, or of the losses suffered during the ensuing German artillery bombardment—some of the most inces-sant of the war in Italy—shelling that pounded ski troops for nearly two weeks after the ground had been "taken." Right off the bat, on the first morning, the 10th lost an icon.

On the left, A Company of the 86th ran into unexpectedly stiff resistance around the village of Iola at the base of Monte Termi-nale. A German machine gun on a forested ridge had three squads pinned down. Tech. Sgt. Torger Tokle, the man who had set world ski-jumping records (and had charmed his fellow trainees at Hale by leaping over supply counters in a single bound) volunteered to take his platoon bazooka man forward and rub out the offending gun. No sooner had the two men started out than an artillery shell landed directly on Art Tokola, the bazooka man. He had five bazooka rounds on him, which detonated in a fearsome blast, oblit-erating Tokola and riddling Tokle's body with shrapnel.

News of Tokle's death spread rapidly through the division and beyond. Newspaper accounts back home reported his death by name—such was his fame. The ski troops felt his loss viscerally. He had been the indomitable world champion, the confident Norwe-gian patriot with the troll cheeks and unfailing grin. If death could come for Torger, it could come for anyone.

That was the trouble with artillery; it was so lethal, so indefensi-ble, so random. One afternoon about a week into the "limited offensive," Bob Parker and his 87th reconnaissance platoon arrived at a place the soldiers had named Punchboard Hill for the terrific shelling it had received. A chestnut forest that had once blanketed the slopes had been blown to splinters. Not a single tree stood against the winter sky; the ground was a tangle of tree limbs and craters. Hardly a square yard of earth had been spared. (In fact, Fifth Army statisticians, who followed along behind the lines charting everything from casualties to tank kills, verified that Punchboard Hill, rising above the crucial road and bridge at Malandrone Pass, had received the most concentrated bombardment since Anzio.)

Parker and his boys were to set up an observation post on top of the hill. Company A's lieutenant suggested they wait until dark to set up the observation post. "Meanwhile," he said, "you guys better dig in—the Krauts always shell at supper time." Decades later, when he could finally write about the incident, Parker recalled:

> Our rocky clearing was a lousy place for foxholes—mostly shallow soil, shale, and hardpan. But I found a little bench where water had collected and soft soil built up. I began to dig.
>
> One thing we had learned in combat was the trajectories of German artillery. The 88s and 40mm ack-acks had flat trajectories. The rockets, and the shells of 105s and mortars—better suited to mountain warfare—arced high over a mountain then fell in a slanting dive, hitting the first projection they came to on the other side—a tree, a house, a man. As I dug my foxhole, I began to realize my little bench could be a perfect target for a high-angle 105.
>
> I dropped my shovel and looked around. The others were busy scratching out shallow foxholes farther up the slope. . . . I had already dug a deep, comfortable hole in the soft earth, with room for another alongside. With a faint sense that I was doing something wrong, I picked up shovel and pack, moved up the slope and started another hole in the tough shale.

Two more soldiers, Loren and Johnny, arrived from headquarters. One of them looked at Parker's first effort and asked, "Whose hole?" Parker continues:

I was sitting on the edge of my new foxhole, eating a K ration. "I dug it," I answered. "But I don't like the location. Sticks out of the slope too much." Loren said, "Looks okay to me. Johnny, you dig in next to me here, I'll take Parker's hole."

It was nearly dark when the lieutenant's voice drifted down to us. "Everybody dug in?" A muted chorus answered. Yep. Okay. *Si, Tenente* (that was Rossi). Friggin' A. Yes, Mother! (that was Bird Dog Patterson). The silence that followed was immediately shattered by the first German shell. The barrage was on schedule.

So we cowered in our holes, and our world was reduced to darkness, the scream of shells, ear-splitting explosions and the incessant shuddering of the ground beneath us. . . . Clearly, the Krauts didn't want the 10th Mountain Division breaking through that pass.

At last the shelling stopped. Again, the lieutenant's voice floated down. "Report in, guys. That was a nasty one!" One by one, the voices came out of the dark. Reynolds. Hawkinson. Rossi. Parker. Wilford. There was no answer from Loren and Johnny.

"Parker, you're the closest—check 'em out!" I crawled out of the foxhole and groped in the dark to the bench below, knowing what I'd find. The acrid smell of cordite, burned soil and flesh hit me with a wave of nausea.

"Parker, what happened?" The lieutenant now sounded close to panic. Swallowing my horror, I croaked a reply, "They're gone, sir. Direct hit."

I must have fainted then, or blacked out somehow. I awoke to the muted voices of the lieutenant and Sgt. Wilford, flashlights flickering, and shadowy men working around Loren and Johnny's foxholes. I helped to close the body bags, and carried a corner of one of them almost two miles to the nearest road.

Then Parker's brain or his body, or both, shut down in a kind of protective catatonia. Luckily, the officers present recognized that all was not right and arranged to transport the young corporal to the rear.

Bob Woody (C Company, 85th Regiment) and Harry Poschman (D Company, 85th Regiment) shared the hell of Monte della Spe—different companies, different foxholes, same hell. Their battalion drove the Germans off the hill on March 6, then endured ten days of shelling without once being relieved. Woody dug in with an Italian-American named Marsala. "We covered as much of the hole as possible with tree limbs and a topping of sandbags and soil to ward off tree bursts. The hole had the dimensions of a shallow grave—maybe three feet wide, three feet deep, and six feet long, just enough for two to cuddle and huddle in physical and psychological warmth."

Nights, the men could move around, maybe chase down a local chicken to relieve the monotony of canned rations. But by day, day after day, the shelling kept them in their holes. "The shelling did terrible things to the third platoon," Woody remembered. He saw a man with his head blown off, heard wounded soldiers beg to be shot. "Sometimes you did not know who had come and who had gone, for the bodies of the injured had already been removed by the time you got out of your hole. It was just, 'So-and-so got it.' And that was that."

In a letter to his brother on March 13, Woody wrote:

I nearly got mine the other night while digging a position about 30 yards in front of my present one. Someone must have heard us and dropped in a mortar shell—boom! All of a sudden I did a swan dive into the hole. Shrapnel got one guy in the ass and leg. A fragment went between my helmet and liner, ripped hell out of the liner. Wasn't my time though.

After a couple of days on della Spe, Harry Poschman's machine-gun squad was down to just three men. The fighting off of night-time counterattacks, the constant shelling, the blending of days into weeks, and the promise of relief that didn't come and didn't come—it all pushed Harry to the brink. Pressing himself into the very bottom of his hole during a round of shelling, he thought of Willie and Joe, quintessential cartoon dogfaces drawn by Sgt. Bill Mauldin (who served with the 45th Infantry Division in Italy) every week for the *Stars and Stripes.* Hugging the earth, one of the unshaven sad sacks says to the other: "Lower?! I can't git no lower, me buttons is holdin' me up."

That one, at least, made Harry smile. Another "Willie and Joe" rang only too true. In their hole on some blasted hill, wondering why they had been spared so far, Willie says: "I feel like a fugitive from the law of averages." Everyone on della Spe felt that way. The death and tedium wore Harry down, and he wrote bitterly, "It was obvious we were not the magnificent ski troopers who would charge the enemy on white skis and shoot him with a white rifle. We exchanged white for dirty brown, and we didn't do much charging, for it was only prudent to crawl on your belly. . . . It was apparent none of us would leave della Spe alive."

But Harry persevered, out of concern for his men and a stubborn anger. One day he got a phone call from battalion headquarters. The voice said he had won a raffle. The prize was a trip to

Rome. "Who are they kidding? I have three sick guys up here and you tell me I am going to Rome?. . . The voice continued, 'Put someone in charge of your squad and get your tail down here.' I went. I crawled, I ran, I felt like a deserter, ashamed. When I arrived at HQ, I asked what day it was. Someone said, 'March 13.' It was my birthday."

CHAPTER 11:

R&R

The last thing Bob Parker remembered was helping load the bodies of his comrades onto a jeep. After that, his mind went blank.

Concerned members of his 87th Headquarters Company could find nothing physically wrong with him. But mentally, he wasn't there, so they took him back to a farmhouse beyond the reach of German artillery and kept a close watch. His mates had to wake him up in the mornings, get him dressed, and get him down to meals. He remained cooperative and semifunctional but locked in a kind of walking catatonia. Parker's company commander could have sent him to the big military hospital in Livorno, where most cases of battle shock were treated. Parker himself is grateful he didn't.

"One day in the sun, on the terrace, I woke up. Five days with no memory. I guess that's the body's and the mind's way of protecting itself. Wiped out my conscious mind. . . . I'm really glad they kept me with the company, with the guys I knew. Some of the men sent to Livorno, cut off from people who knew them and meant the most to them—some of those men ended up permanently disoriented."

While Parker recovered, the rest of the 10th was relieved, in shifts, from the front lines. The salient had been enlarged, the German defenders pushed back another four miles. The hills ahead were smaller than the hills already won. From the top of Monte della Spe one could now see the vast plain of the Po. The valley remained at least fifteen miles distant, but the goal of forcing the Germans from their mountain strongholds and breaking through to the flat, fertile country beyond was at last in sight. Over a thousand Germans had been taken prisoner in the 10th's "limited offensive," and German Field Marshal Kesselring's strategic reserve, the 29th Panzer Division, had been badly mauled. But Allied headquarters in Caserta was not ready to push the offensive farther. Not yet. The massive Spring Push remained on schedule for mid-April.

In truth, the mountain troops were ready for some R&R—rest and recuperation. David Brower craved time to "sit back and feel muscles that you thought were relaxed loosen a little and slip back where they were before it all started. And then you can write letters again."

John Jennings took up his journal again on March 28, after a fighting break of more than a month. Early on, he had blithely described his writing as "scribbling," "a brief account of this GI cook's tour." Now, he needed desperately to make sense of what he'd seen. "So much has happened that I could never begin to write the small part even that I remember," he wrote in careful longhand at the rest center in Montecatini. "It is impossible to describe the utter fatigue of those first three days and nights of continuous driving and fighting . . . how thoroughly the Krauts dug their positions and how absolutely dead the dead are." And a little later, "One almost envied the dead and wounded all about, for now they were out of it, and away from the constant overburdening ache of complete weariness."

Harry Poschman, despite his guilt at leaving his buddies on della Spe, headed south toward Rome on his raffle week. (Somehow his name had been drawn out of a hat. Only a couple of soldiers from each battalion, maybe two out of a thousand, had won the prize.) On the way through the rest and supply town of Montecatini, he got a shower and new shoes. A supply sergeant pointed to a small mountain of shoes and told Harry to take his pick. Harry asked where he got all those combat boots. "I shouldn't have [asked]. Some were stained and torn. Most were in bad shape. I picked a couple that fit and later discovered they were different sizes. It was okay. I wasn't going to a ball."

And Rome in 1945 was no great shakes either. The Eternal City appeared decidedly mortal, hungry, and ragged. Black-market restaurants served the only food available—other than at Army mess halls—and that was expensive and often rancid. Harry and a friend bought a bottle of Chianti and some black-market cheese and picnicked on the marble steps below the monument to Vittorio Emmanuel.

Later, they walked to Saint Peter's. Pope Pius XII was speaking from his balcony. "I couldn't understand a word he said, but a nice Italian lady interpreted for me. Her little boy looked sad and hungry." The woman said her husband had left for the war five years before and she hadn't heard a word from him since. She asked Harry to come home with her, quick to insist that her parents and her other children were there, and she only wanted food. So Harry took her by an Army mess hall and "bought an armload of meals-to-go and sent them home happy." He wondered "how the American people would get on [in a war] . . . hoping they never are tested."

Harry was "too edgy" to enjoy Rome. The nightclubs "seemed like a good place to get killed," filled as they were with drunken, armed men. He couldn't stop thinking about his buddies and the hardship they continued to suffer "up on that terrible mountain." At the end of the week, he was happy to start back. Much to his relief, he learned that while he was gone, the battalion had been relieved at last and sent to Montecatini, down out of the mountains, for a well-deserved rest.

Before the war, Montecatini had been a famous spa on the road between Florence and Pisa. People came from all over Europe to take the waters and stroll the tree-lined thoroughfares. Wrought-iron balconies graced second-floor hotel rooms above a circular plaza. Now in the first blush of spring, the spear-like lombardy poplars showed nascent leaves. Daisies and violets peeped out of the ground. Horse-drawn carriages roamed the streets, and knots of American soldiers walked about in the sun. There was a strange normalcy behind the lines—almost as if there were no war—but always with a twist. Bob Woody wandered Montecatini as if he "had been given a shot of emotional Novocain." Harry Poschman's friend John Pierpont read a letter from home. It included snapshots of a daughter he had not yet met . . ."and my wife's thankfulness I had not been involved in combat." The irony was nearly too much; Pierpont had seen most of his machine-gun squad annihilated on the initial attack up Gorgolesco.

Mail could take weeks crossing the Atlantic, but the news-magazines were practically as current as they were in the States. With their weekly beer and PX rations, the men got *Time*, *Newsweek*, and *Reader's Digest*, in addition to the Army publications *Yank* and *Stars and Stripes*. The plates for the newsweeklies were flown over from New York to printers in Florence and distributed just a couple of days late. The 10th's own newspaper, The *Blizzard*, came off the presses every week in Florence too. How odd to read about one's exploits of just the week before. There were pictures, photographs and illustrations from the front. Jacques Parker, who had been with the 86th's Company A on the night climb up Riva Ridge, sent pencil-and-ink drawings of that encounter down the mountain rolled up inside empty mortar casings. Within days, they appeared on the front page of the *Blizzard*.

R&R gave the men a chance, after weeks of living in holes, to clean up. In combat, a man's helmet was his bathtub. During a lull in the action, he might build a fire under it, heat some water and shave, wash his socks, remove the worst of the grime. Back from the lines, in Montecatini and elsewhere, the Army set up portable showers, large enough to accommodate forty to fifty men at a time. Phil Lunday of the 126th Engineers remembered one such shower in his memoir *The Tram Builders*: "You take all your clothes off— they issued you all new clothes afterward—and they spray you, and you come out and here are forty to fifty men in their birthday suits. And one time I came out and there was this jeep with [Congresswoman] Clare Boothe Luce! [In an ascot and a natty Eisenhower jacket touring the Italian Front.] Looking at forty naked guys taking a bath!"

Invariably, long lines of soldiers waited for a chance at the showers. Just as there were long lines for beer, and chow, and for the movies and USO shows. Harry Poschman and John Pierpont stood in a Montecatini shower line for a few minutes one afternoon before Pierpont pointed toward a small hotel across the square and said, "Come on."

I followed. At the front door was a pink-cheeked boy with a gun. He even had on a necktie. We threw him a fancy salute and went up the stairs like we owned the place. Down the hall there were bathrooms with signs which read: PRIVATE BATH OF GENERAL HAYS and PRIVATE BATH OF GENERAL SO AND SO, and so on. John opened a door and said, "There is your private bath." I took it and he took the next one.

There were cakes of soap the size of a football and more hot water than I had seen since the States. I soaked and I lathered and I soaked some more, luxuriating in that big tub up to my chin. I even smoked one of the General's cigars.

A knock on the door about a half hour later said, "Let's get out of here." We departed after each taking another cigar. The pink-cheeked boy on guard snapped to attention as we left, and we walked quickly away laughing like a couple of simpletons.

Poschman and Pierpont enjoyed a minor celebrity for a couple of days thereafter. It wasn't that they disrespected General Hays; they, like most of the men, liked him personally. What they had done was pull one over on the "Rear Echelon Crows," the officers and enlisted men with jobs well behind the lines, who sported spiffy boots and creases in their uniform pants. There was little respect among the dogfaces for these men who, despite their importance to the American military machine, enjoyed a position of permanent safety and could not have imagined the brutalities experienced by the line companies.

Montecatini was just two hours west of Florence, and perhaps more than most divisions on R&R, the college-educated men of the 10th sought out the city's cultural offerings, which had been largely spared the ravages of artillery and bombing raids. They took guided tours, or they walked in small groups through the narrow, cobblestone streets. They crossed the Arno River on the seven-hundred-year-old Ponte Vecchio with its two-story shopping galleries. They stared at the thousands of Renaissance masterpieces in the Uffizi and Pitti galleries. They climbed the narrow stairs of The Duomo to the top of the great cathedral dome with its fine view of the city's red-tile roofs. In the evening, if they were so inclined, they could attend the Teatro Verdi for a performance of *La Traviata*.

To be sure, not all mountain troopers haunted the museums or avoided completely the ubiquitous fleshpots of the city. But the many who did seek out art lent credence to growing suspicions among other Fifth Army divisions that the 10th was an elite, maybe even an aesthete, bunch. The problem began with an admiring article—post-Belvedere and della Spe—in the March 16 issue of *Yank*. The writer stressed the division's high average IQ and mentioned several college associations by name. The words "elite" and "blue-blood" were used. And there may have been a reference to "yodeling as they attacked."

This all had unfortunate repercussions. The German propagandist Axis Sally seized on the characterization and in her radio broadcasts denigrated the 10th as mere "sports figures . . . sons of the wealthy." Soldiers from the 34th, 85th, 88th, and 91st Divisions— proud "ordinary infantry divisions" deployed alongside the 10th on the Winter Line—took umbrage as well. These were outfits with decidedly less refined bloodlines but a great deal more experience and heritage than the 10th had. Most traced their division histories to 1917 and the Great War. And in this conflict, they all claimed more battle time—much more—than the ski troops. The 34th had been fighting since the invasion at Algiers in 1942, and the others had slogged their way north through Salerno and Rome and Pisa. Now and then an "elite" mountain trooper would be challenged to a fight, where liquor and high spirits prevailed, on the streets of Florence. One particularly telling incident occurred in an army theater. In the middle of the movie, the show stopped and a message flashed on the screen directing men of the 10th Mountain Division to report immediately to their organizations. One 10th man started up the aisle—perhaps he swaggered a bit, the memory of Riva or della

Torraccia still fresh—and announced, "Well, guess we have to go take another hill." To which a soldier wearing the red bull patch of the 34th Division answered, "Yeah. That'll make two."

Of course, the reality was that the 10th, despite its unusual beginnings, was at this point of the fighting indistinguishable from any other infantry division. As Harry Poschman said, "We were just a damn ski club—until we got the shit shot out of us in Italy."

In early April, the 10th was sent back north into the line, replacing the 92d "Buffalo Division," which had stepped in while the mountain troops rested. An all-black division with all-white officers, the 92d had fought gallantly in Italy since August 1944, but was still subject to Jim Crow–type discrimination. Bob Woody remembers "bellying up to the bar in some little mountain village next to a black soldier. Nice kid. Pleasant conversation. But the next day the order came down not to fraternize."

The line was mostly quiet; the enemy lobbed in shells now and then for harassment only. The weather continued fine, and the living was easy, if not so refined as a weekend in Florence. For a few packs of cigarettes or cans of C rations, the men could trade with villagers for fresh milk and eggs. One lucky outfit enjoyed surprise meat when a German artillery shell killed a couple of rabbits and threw them on the roof of a nearby building.

There wasn't much to do. G Company of the 85th spent many happy hours watching a buxom young girl named Rita go about her chores on a farm called Tora. After a while, though, the men noticed that before every German mortar barrage, Rita would disappear into Tora's root cellar. Further investigation revealed that during the previous regime, Rita had taken a German lover. Now the theory was that Rita was sending him signals by hanging her wash out in a certain way.

John Jennings's squad spent a few happy days in a villa owned by a local Fascist leader and inhabited most recently by German officers.

One side of the building was almost completely blown away, but the interior proved a fruitful maze. From Jennings's pocket diary:

> In the cellar are great wine kegs (empty) and presses. Below this is another tunnel-like passageway, which came to play a big part in our otherwise humdrum existence. Led by a tip-off from a local Pisano (native on our side—at least they say so), a character named "Doc" Adams, a medic from White River Junction, Vermont, attacked the sub-cellar walls with a pick. Sure enough, before unbelieving eyes, he uncovered a hidden cache of wine bottles which glimmered enticingly in the shimmering candle light.

Over two days the boys from F Company of the 87th pulled one thousand bottles of wine (Jennings counted) from the vault—"all excellent."

During the day, Army radio piped broadcasts into just about every GI position. The soldiers heard how the war was winding down. Vienna had fallen to the Russians on March 8, and now the Soviet army was within hailing distance of Berlin. On March 26, Gen. George Patton and his Third Army had crossed the Rhine at Mannheim and now, on orders from General Eisenhower, was beginning his dash to the southeast, toward the Danube and Austria. Rumor had it, Hitler planned a final defense of the Alps, within a so-called Final Redoubt. High in the glacial mountains, he and a corps of elite troops could hold out for months, maybe years. But surely, went other rumors, the Alpine Redoubt was nothing but a figment of propaganda chief Josef Goebbels's imagination. Surely the crippled German armies, the ravaged and starving German cities, were within days of surrender. Maybe the war would end before the 10th would be called on to attack again. Maybe.

What the troops couldn't know was that secret negotiations for a surrender in Italy had been going on since December 1944. Without Hitler's knowledge, his generals on the southern front, Kesselring, Wolff, and von Vietinghoff, had met in Zurich with Allen Dulles of the Office of Strategic Services, who was in direct contact with FDR. Roosevelt supported what came to be known as Operation Sunrise, but the Soviets, also in on the negotiations, attempted to scuttle the deal. They apparently believed that Communist Yugoslav forces had a better chance of capturing Trieste, a long-contested city in northeastern Italy, if the Brits and Americans remained tied up in the Apennines. With the end game near, the future cold warriors maneuvered for advantage in a postwar Europe. And so a bizarre, behind-the-scenes minuet for an early peace in Italy went nowhere while the dancers continued to meet and engage.

Meanwhile, Hitler's threat of pulling back to an Alpine Redoubt had to be taken seriously. Bob Parker, ever philosophical, chalked it up to the "uncertainty of war."

> We *could* have sat there and waited for the war to end. It probably—certainly—would have saved a lot of lives. But General Hays had his orders. What if the negotiated peace fell apart? What if Hitler, instead of putting a bullet through his brain or whatever he did, had moved to his fortress in Bavaria and defended Germany from there? We couldn't take the risk. General Hays's orders were to deny the southern border to Fortress Europe. We had to press the attack.

Without the benefit of hindsight—with no perspective at all save that from their warm, spring foxholes—the men of the 10th waited amid the rumors and the blooming of cherry trees and the steady build-up of materiel. Great stockpiles of shells, small-arms ammunition, K rations, and supplies of all kinds grew by the roadsides. Both sides continued to drop propaganda leaflets from overhead. David Brower remembered:

> They delivered the papers in some sort of propaganda rocket that moaned over and popped. Their stuff arrived a little tattered, but no less amusing. One of their cleverest bits of copy was a bunch of instructions for fooling the medics and simulating various ailments that would enable a man to sit out the war in a hospital. . . .
>
> In one issue of the *Low Down* [the name of the monthly propaganda sheet] they insisted, on page 1, that they were going to keep on fighting and fighting, while on page 2 they argued that we should take no unnecessary risks in the European war, which had already reached "five minutes to twelve."

Bud Winter, who had returned to his outfit, wounds healed, in late March, noted in a letter to his mother that at least some of the enemy doggerel was appreciated. "The Jerries shell us with leaflets with a picture of a beautiful girl on one side and a skull and cross bones on the other. One side says Life and the other Death. . . . Well, anyway, it seems to raise the morale of most of the fellows because they hang the side with the beautiful girl up for a pinup and say to hell with the other side."

The Allies shot their propaganda sheet, *Frontpost*, overhead in 105-mm shells timed to burst high in the air over German lines. Included were "PW passports," which promised in several languages (the depleted German ranks included many east European and Russian "recruits") to give safe conduct to the deserting bearer on his way through Allied lines. "More than one prisoner had his safe-conduct pass neatly tucked away in his billfold," Brower recalled, "and produced it with a sheepish smile when he reached the interrogation point." Ever the editor, Brower couldn't resist adding, impishly, "Reaction to the *Frontpost* seemed very favorable;

the PWs' most frequent complaint was that the paper hadn't been delivered regularly enough."

Reading time would end abruptly for the men of the 10th with the commencement of the long-awaited Spring Push, code-named Operation Craftsman. This would be the last offensive, it was hoped, into the Po Valley and beyond. No one knew the final objective, other than the unconditional surrender of the German army in Italy. And to that end, the offensive would involve nearly every Allied unit in northern Italy, all tactical aircraft, and some fifty thousand Italian partisans who were being counted on to wage guerrilla warfare behind enemy lines.

Craftsman had three components. The first was a diversionary attack on the far left flank of the U.S. Fifth Army front near the Ligurian Sea. The 92d Division jumped off on April 5, augmented by the Japanese American 442d Regimental Combat Team. These soldiers effectively tied up some of von Vietinghoff's reserves around the town of Massa, preventing them from moving east to defend the Fifth Army's main point of attack.

On the east end of the front, the British Eighth Army, including divisions from New Zealand, India, and Poland, charged off on April 9 through the rugged Argenta Gap. The Brits would hug the Adriatic coast, destination Venice and ultimately Trieste—to get there before the Communists. In the middle of the front, Clark's Fifth Army was scheduled to jump off April 12 against the last stoutly defended hills, destination Bologna, and the 10th Mountain Division would spearhead the attack.

Once again 10th soldiers filled their ammo belts, checked their rifles, and steadied their minds for what the combat veterans knew would be a murderous opening day. But then came an unexpected reprieve: Fog over the airfields the morning of the 12th prevented the Air Corps from flying its dive-bombing missions. The attack was postponed a day. Then on the morning of the 13th, the troops learned of President Roosevelt's death the day before, at age sixty-three, of a cerebral hemorrhage, at his Little White House in Warm Springs, Georgia. As Bob Woody noted, "An era had ended. We had been first graders when FDR was first elected." The news and the fog and the fact that it was Friday the 13th added another twenty-four-hour postponement. John Jennings wrote in his diary:

> Each stay of 24 hours bringing great relief and jubilance . . . like a prisoner receiving a brief stay of execution. . . .
>
> It was in those hours that one really noticed the beauty of the world around him. It was spring. The drabness was gone. The grass was a delicate light green. Some of the trees were in bloom. Nameless birds twittered. The sun shone warm and restful from a clear blue sky. Yes, you could see now that Italy was beautiful.

And then the zero hour approached yet again and Jennings's thoughts turned darker:

> The brass hats way back there in Corps or Army headquarters, the rear echelon men, and the people at home welcome a big offensive, for it brings the end of the war that much closer. However, infantry soldiers don't see it that way; they are the ones that will have to do the killing and the dying, and nearly every one would be just as happy if it didn't come about, if it could be won on some other front. Nevertheless, when the final order comes, the infantryman loads his rifle, grits his teeth and sets off into Hell. That's how wars are won, I guess.

The emotional seesaw finally ended with a clear dawn on April 14. The Brazilian Expeditionary Force took up the left flank with the 10th Mountain Division next to them. To the 10th's right, the 1st Armored Division straddled Highway 64. The 6th South

African Armoured Division was next to them, and then the U.S. 88th, 91st, and 34th Infantry Divisions still further right. The 85th Division stayed in reserve. Allied artillery began firing about 4:00 A.M., and Harry Poschman remembered thinking, "Nothing could live in that wall of lead and steel we threw across the valley to the north. Next came the planes. Their combined efforts churned the ground and clouded the sky. The Germans were not firing back at us. I thought for sure they must all be dead."

At 9:45 A.M.—on what would be the bloodiest single day of the war for the mountain division—the 10th pushed off down the forward slopes of Monte della Spe, all three infantry regiments in a line abreast.

CHAPTER 12:

Race to the Alps

The Germans had had a month to prepare for an Allied push they knew would be coming. And they knew that this was probably their last real stand, their last line of defense against an Allied breakthrough. Lose this one and that was likely to mean the end to their long, fighting retreat up the spine of Italy. Hills always confer an advantage to defenders, but once in the big valley to the north, superior Allied numbers—mechanized units, tanks, and aircraft—would certainly tip the scales.

In anticipation of the push, General von Senger's 90th and 94th Panzer Divisions, along with elements of the 334th and 267th Divisions, fortified every defensible position across the complex, rolling, sometimes steep terrain north of Monte della Spe and west of the town of Vergato—a region of scattered farms and woods not unlike New York's Catskills or Vermont's Green Mountains. They buried countless thousands of mines. Some were glass-topped *Topf* (pot) mines, almost impossible for the American engineers and their magnetic mine detectors to find. They camouflaged hundreds of machine-gun nests in hedgerows and calibrated artillery in advance to blast the ridges and gullies the Americans would need to traverse. They made a fort of every stone barn and farmhouse still standing. They even rigged bins of chestnuts with wires and high explosives to booby-trap heedless GIs. Most importantly, they dug elaborate underground bunkers in which to wait out the inevitable Allied bombings.

The shelling began in the early morning of the 14th. First came the waves of heavy carpet bombers, followed by more waves of P-47 dive-bombers, followed by the pounding of thousands of rounds of artillery shells. With the Luftwaffe effectively eliminated from Italy, there was no German air defense, nothing for the German infantry to do but sit and take the beating. The shelling was designed to demoralize as well as bury as many of the defenders as possible. But despite the sound and fury, despite the impression Harry Poschman and many others had that nothing could have survived such an onslaught, when the big guns stopped firing, the Germans dug themselves out of their shelters ready to rain fire down on the advancing Americans. In the first hours, especially, they had plenty of targets to shoot at. North of della Spe's concealing knob, the landscape opened into a complex of small intersecting valleys, cut by country roads and nearly devoid of trees. The riflemen tried to run across, but with almost no natural cover they fell by the score before they even had a chance to climb the next set of hills.

Just after the jump-off, Capt. David Brower mused on the heavy responsibility an officer bears in the planning of such an attack. He recorded his thoughts in *Remount Blue*. "There is no security against the gnawing feeling of responsibility you have for the men out there whose safety—what there is of it—depends too much on luck and very much on the proper support the battalion must give and coordinate. So you just get gnawed at until there are mostly calluses left. You can step out [in Brower's case step out of the battalion command-post dugout on Monte della Spe], view the human devastation, and marvel only that there hasn't been more."

The hills the 10th attacked this time were less grand than those they'd left behind. Most didn't have names on the map; instead they were known by their elevations in meters above sea level. On the left, the 85th Regiment started up Hill 913, Hill 909, and Hill 915. The 87th Regiment, in the middle, tackled Hills 903 and 890 and the town of Torre Iussi at their foot. On the right flank, the 86th Regiment had as its objectives Hills 889 and 815, plus the very rocky and steep (and aptly named) Rocca (Fortress) Roffeno.

These hills would be the last that hundreds of men from the 10th Mountain Division would ever climb. Five hundred fifty-three mountaineers were killed or wounded that day. (By contrast, the Riva Ridge operation counted "only" 68 casualties over seven days' fighting. Nine hundred fourteen were lost over the twelve days it took to win and hold Monte Belvedere and della Torraccia.) The numbered hills were also witness to moments of great bravery amid the carnage. Hill 909 was where Pfc. John Magrath, a fresh-faced nineteen-year-old in G Company, 85th Regiment, earned the division's only Medal of Honor. Soon after crossing the line of departure, Magrath's company came under intense fire. His commander fallen and dead, radioman Magrath volunteered to accompany a small reconnaissance party forward, where he performed a series of astonishing solo feats, possessed, apparently, by the kind of inexplicable energy that had inhabited Hugh Evans on Gorgolesco. Running ahead of the group, with only his semiautomatic M-1 rifle, Magrath rounded the corner of a farmhouse and came face to face with a German machine-gun crew. He shot one man dead and forced the other to surrender. When five more enemy then sprung from their foxholes and began shooting at him, Magrath turned the German machine gun around and mowed down the lot, killing one and wounding the other four. Abandoning his M-1 in favor of the deadlier MG-34, he carried it across an exposed field, exchanging fire with yet another machine-gun position in the trees, killing two more and capturing that weapon as well. The rest of the company followed in amazement. Magrath's heroics and luck ran out later in the day, however, when he volunteered to dash through heavy shelling to gather a casualty report. In the middle of an open field, sprinting hard, he was killed instantly by mortar shells that exploded practically at his feet.

Sgt. Friedl Pfeifer, the Austrian skimeister with dreams of transforming Aspen from a backwoods ghost town into a thriving ski destination, led his squad onto Hill 903, where shrapnel from mortar or artillery fire tore through his back and pierced a lung. Pfeifer survived but spent the rest of the war in the hospital.

Perhaps the best-known victim on Hill 913 (at least in later decades), was a replacement soldier from Kansas named Robert J. Dole. Second lieutenant Dole, with I Company of the 85th, had never skied and had not been with the 10th at Camp Hale or in Texas. He was one of thousands of American Army replacements who were assigned to new companies to help bring them back up to strength after substantial losses in battle. (By the time the war ended, the 10th would include on its roster nearly seven thousand replacements in addition to the fourteen thousand men originally in the division.) That first night on Hill 913, Dole was leading a patrol when machine-gun fire killed two scouts and ripped into Dole's neck and arm. He spent the next forty months in army hospitals.

It was also on Hill 913, on the first night of the Spring Push, that soldiers of the 85th Regiment, 3d Battalion, dug in on their side of the hill and in a quiet respite began singing. When they sang "Lili

Marlene," German soldiers on the other side of the hill joined in. Then the Germans started a new song, and the Americans did their best to sing along. In the morning, both sides got up and resumed killing each other.

The 10th did not demonize its enemy across the line. Rather, 10th men recognized a certain shared heritage with these men, and common passions. "We had a grudging respect for the German mountain troops," recalls Bob Parker. "We knew they weren't Nazis, by and large, and at home were mountain guides, ski instructors. We knew that had they been home, Friedl Pfeifer and Sigi Engl would have been drafted into their mountain troops and might have faced us across the line. The fact of war convinces one that the sooner it is over, the better, for everyone."

Sadly, April 14 brought the end of the war for Bud Winter, one of the most beloved of the original Mountain Training Group. Winter was with M Company, 85th Regiment, on bloody Hill 913 that day. A forward mortar observer for a heavy weapons company, he was killed when a German mortar barrage fell in on top of him. Bud's last letter home was dated April 12: "Dear Mother, I went to a memorial service for the Belvedere dead. I was glad to be there as I knew many of the boys. Some were quite close friends, but I guess that comes with war." Not even the recent death of friends or the uncertain prospects ahead had dimmed Bud's love of fly-fishing, however. He ended the letter, "Please send the fishing tackle if you get a chance. Love to all, Bud."

By April 16, the hills were littered with bodies, machinery, and the bloated carcasses of little Italian mules both sides had used to carry supplies on the one-lane tracks that passed, in the convoluted terrain, for roads. The 10th had suffered mightily, but the German divisions facing them had been practically destroyed. The attack had severed the connection between the German 41st Mountain Division and General von Senger's 14th Panzer Division. The 90th and 94th Panzer Divisions had been routed; their foot soldiers surrendered by the hundreds or else fled in disarray. The speed of the 10th's advance had caught many a German unit off-guard. On the morning of the 16th, when the 87th Regiment arrived in the town of Tole—six miles north of della Spe and one of the last strategic road junctions leading to the open country of the Po Valley—they found that the commanding general of the 90th Panzers had abandoned his headquarters in such haste he'd left on the table a fresh piece of bread and jam, with one bite missing.

The 10th left the hills behind on April 20 and poured out onto the long downslope to the Po. In seven days of relentless forward movement, the division had lost 1,800 men—370 of them killed in action, the others wounded. But now that they had breached the German defenses, there was little resistance as they raced north miles ahead of the rest of the U.S. Fifth Army. Commanding Gen. Mark Clark sent a message forward to General Hays commending his "rapid progress and brilliant execution." Clark also said that he wanted Hays to stop there, at the edge of the valley, to let the 85th and 88th Divisions catch up and move through. The 10th had done its job, he said; now flatland infantry would continue the attack. Hays was livid. Bob Parker recounts Hays turning to his chief of staff with Clark's message in hand. "'Did you see this message?' [Silence.] Then he asked the radio operator, 'Sergeant, did you see this message?' [Silence.] And he took the paper and crumpled it up and threw it in the trash bin." The 10th had spearheaded the push, survived all the numbered hills and all the ones with names, and broken the back of the German defense, and now Mark Clark wanted him to stop.

Hays had been the one to see, before General Clark had, the wisdom in taking Riva Ridge prior to an attack on Monte Belvedere. Now that same instinct told Hays that this was not the time to stop and reorganize. Hays sensed the importance of pressing forward with all possible speed, sensed the chaos among the retreating Germans. To hell with reorganizing. To hell with Bologna; the big city on the 10th's right would soon be in the hands of other Allied divisions. Hays wanted to get to the Po River, another seventy miles to the north, before retreating Germans had a chance to blow the bridges across the water. General Clark may have wanted the 10th to slow up, regroup, consolidate, but Hays refused, shrugging, "They'll have to catch us first."

With the roads through the Apennines now in Allied hands, the 10th had at last become a mechanized division. The men rode on anything that promised to get them off their feet. They piled on jeeps and tanks, hitched rides with self-propelled artillery and six-by-six trucks. They drove captured German officers' cars, rode ambulances and horses and bicycles. And when they couldn't ride, they walked in long, dusty lines, finally free of the hills, down the gently sloping plain. Into the valley David Brower later said reminded him of home—his native California Central Valley. Two-thirds of Italy's farmland lay in the Po's 250-mile-long alluvial bowl. The land was a great patchwork of cultivated fields and orchards—wheat, corn, sugar beets, vegetables, peaches, plums, pears, apples, grapes, nut trees—every square separated from its neighbors by a canal, a well-worn path, or a line of poplars. Nearly every river in northern Italy, from the south side of the Alps to the north side of the Apennines, flowed into the Po, which meandered east to the Adriatic Sea south of Venice. In addition to farming, the Po also supported Italy's industry, with its most prosperous, modern cities: Milan, Turin, Bologna. The Germans had been right to throw everything they had into defending this river and its valley. But now they were running for their lives.

For two days the 10th streaked north toward San Benedetto Po, covering thirty-five miles a day, battalions leapfrogging, stopping only rarely to deal with streams of prisoners, or to catch a fleeting rest. Men slept wherever they plopped down: They slept in ditches, they slept in jeeps, they slept on the backs of clanking tanks. They even, as David Brower had predicted back at Camp Swift, slept while they walked. Bill Mauldin understood the phenomenon. In one cartoon, his Willie and Joe march along in a dogged, disheveled column, and Willie says, "Maybe Joe needs a rest. He's talking in his sleep."

The nonstop 10th outran its artillery support, outran its supply vehicles. The men ran right off the maps they carried with them. Occasionally they had to fight through pockets of German resistance. Often, these were units who were unaware that the American advance had actually passed by them. The Germans were shocked to find they were behind enemy lines.

Through their exhaustion, the men of the 10th felt something they hadn't felt before, a sense of exhilaration, a hint that the fighting might soon be finished. It was as if they were sliding downhill again—not on skis now, but as though riding something inevitable, like gravity. They'd been through their baptism of fire, gone from innocence and optimism and a false sense of invincibility, through the nighttime terror of the Belvedere climb; through the grinding, waiting, random death on della Spe and all the subsequent hills; through the unseen mines and the implacable, spitting machine guns; through all the running, the digging in, the struggling up to run again. They'd long since been robbed of any illusion about war's nobility or their own special place in it. But now, despite the familiar, interminable weariness and aching feet, there was the hint of something different, some kind of momentum (partly of their own making) heading irresistibly toward conclusion.

In many villages that the 10th passed through, women and old men appeared along the roadside with wine or eggs or bread. Seeing the Americans coming, they would run to the garden to dig up bottles of wine they'd hidden from the Germans. Little girls put flowers in GI's helmets. People cheered: "Bravo! Viva! Libaratore!" Without breaking stride, a trooper would take a glass of wine, down it, then hand the glass to the nearest child running alongside, who returned it for a refill, and the cycle began again. Bob Parker received a handful of eggs. Thinking fast, he stopped and built a quick fire under his helmet, added water, and hard-boiled the fragile gifts. Now he could carry them safely in a jacket pocket.

There actually was enough wine to cause a problem for some of the soldiers, but even if there had been none, the events around them would probably still have seemed hallucinatory. John Jennings recalled an encounter when they were speeding through the Po's villages: "A German tank roared out of a side road, fell in with one of our mechanized columns, finally recognized that we weren't retreating German forces, fired off a couple of rounds, and sped off."

Bob Parker ran head on into the chaos as he passed through another village. He was riding in a jeep, absent-mindedly manning the machine gun mounted on the back. "People came running out wanting to give us something. One woman threw a crusty, hard bread loaf at us as we went by, and I wasn't paying enough attention because it hit me right on the forehead." A minute later Parker's column stumbled into a firefight with some stubbornly resistant Germans; the bread was instantly forgotten.

That night at chow a medic sits down next to me and says, "Let me fix up that wound, soldier." I said, "What wound?" I had blood all over my face from a cut on my forehead. He bandaged me up and then handed me the form you filled out to receive a Purple Heart. I said, "No, I got hit by a flying loaf of bread." He said, "Go ahead, fill it out. Wounded in the line of duty." But I couldn't do it, not for failing to catch a loaf of bread.

So many Germans were surrendering, the 10th had a hard time dealing with them all. Hays didn't want to give up any of his men to escort prisoners to the rear, so scores of POWs were searched, tagged, and simply told to walk south on their own. In their mad dash north, Dave Brower's platoon spun some of those southbound prisoners around and had them carry packs for the tired Americans. At times, it was not easy to tell the captors from the captives. Some ski troopers wore souvenir German mountain caps or German sweaters. Others sported feathered Alpini hats. Everyone wore the same thick coat of road dust. Through confusion and irony, the motley parade surged northward.

Two days after General Hays's refusal to stop, the 87th Regiment reached the sandy dikes of the Po River, near the town of San Benedetto Po. Word of the 10th's approach had preceeded them, and as Hays had feared, the bridge lay in twisted wreckage sagging into the flow. The 10th would have to find another way to cross. The scuttled bridge would slow the mountain troops' advance, but it had other, unintended consequences as well: German troops fleeing north were also caught on the south bank. The men of the 87th watched from a distance as hundreds of Germans, including a general and his staff, swam the muddy current. More than a few drowned trying to reach the safety of the far shore.

The river here was about two hundred yards wide, not yet in full spring flood, moving languidly but powerfully, at about six miles an hour. Hays had no equipment for laying down a pontoon bridge; that had been assigned to II Corps, miles away to the east. Nor did he have assault boats; they were on their way to the 85th Division, also miles downriver, to the units Mark Clark had intended and expected to lead the crossing. Not only did Hays have no way to cross, he didn't know what lay on the other side. He didn't know if the enemy had reinforcements prepared to resist an American crossing. He didn't know if he'd have the support of Allied air power (still moving up from their Tuscan airfields) or artillery. Communication among American units was scanty, and new maps were still in the process of being prepared. What Hays did know was that he was the first to reach the river and should get across as quickly as possible, to establish a beachhead in case there was a fight. So, while the 87th settled in for the night on the south shore and the other two regiments moved up in the darkness to join them, the general called his engineers and told them, in no uncertain terms, to find him some boats.

The 126th Engineers were the resourceful bunch who had built the aerial tram up Riva Ridge. A couple of engineers—one of them Lt. Fritz Benedict, an architect who had worked with Frank Lloyd Wright before the war—and a supply warrant officer took off in a jeep. Somehow in the night they ran into a convoy of five flatbed trucks, each one loaded with ten plywood assault boats, bound for the 85th Division. Perhaps it was the patch the warrant officer wore—signifying 85th *Regiment*, not 85th Division—or perhaps the 10th men were just that convincing. At any rate, they persuaded the convoy commander to follow them; they'd lead him right where he wanted to go, they said. Instead of his scheduled destination, though, they took him to the 10th Mountain position at San Benedetto. They arrived at the river about midnight, hastily unloaded the boats, and sent the convoy on its way, none the wiser.

By noon the next day, April 23, companies of the 87th Regiment—in an unlikely reprisal of their landing on Kiska—made the first Allied amphibious crossing of the Po River. The boats came equipped with paddles—no motors. So the engineers paddled the ungainly craft, each one loaded to the gunwales with ten to twelve infantrymen. The first wave of boats triggered considerable artillery and mortar fire from beyond the far bank, and high-trajectory, antiaircraft flak burst in black rosettes above the water, but the fire seemed undirected, and the boats moved across with relatively few casualties en route. The first man ashore was Tech. Sgt. George Hurt of A Company. Hurt had been one of the members of the original 87th glee club back at Paradise in the earliest days of the ski troops.

Once on the far bank, the men splashed out and threw themselves against the sand dike expecting a shower of lead. But they encountered negligible resistance. They hopped over the top and discovered dozens of enemy dugouts but very few Germans manning them. Fritz Benedict was one of the first engineers across to the north side. He and a buddy captured a German inside one of the dugouts and took shelter there for a while against the sporadic shelling. The man talked to them in animated, insistent tones. Fritz spoke a little German and asked him to slow down. Finally, he understood. The prisoner was predicting the future. He was saying, "I don't know why you aren't fighting with us against the Russians. The Russians will be your enemies very soon."

Back and forth the engineers paddled. Once the 87th was safely across, they began ferrying the 86th and the 85th. Eventually, amphibious trucks called DUKWs (pronounced "ducks") arrived to take on some of the burden. The next day bridging equipment from II Corps arrived as well, and other engineers quickly spanned the flow with a floating pontoon bridge. Now the six-by-six trucks and tanks and artillery could move across and continue the drive north. At long last, General Clark caught up to the 10th. Once again he congratulated General Hays—the insubordinate cavalry charge out of the hills apparently forgiven. Clark pumped Hays's hand and, grinning, called him "the conqueror of the Po."

But General Clark's message was not all adulatory; he had a new assignment for the mountain division. While the speed of the Fifth Army advance had left von Vietinghoff's forces in a shambles, many thousands of them still had their heavy weapons and remained capable of a fighting retreat into the Alps, into Hitler's Final

Redoubt. Of course, there was skepticism about the existence of such a Götterdämmerung plan, but Clark and the Allied commanders couldn't afford to take the chance that it didn't exist. Clark's solution was to send the 10th to cut them off at the pass. Literally. If the 10th, with its speed and stamina, could beat the Germans to the Brenner Pass, on the Austrian border, and cut off this primary escape route, then surely the fighting on the southern front would be over.

And so the 10th took off again, as soon as its armor—jeeps and tanks and artillery—got across the Po. The troops skirted around Mantua and drove up Highway 62 toward Verona, stopping only briefly to wolf down K rations and maybe catch a few minutes of sleep. From Verona, they would begin climbing into the Alps, up along the Adige River into the Sud Tyrol, following the ancient route to Brenner Pass.

Slogging toward Verona with his D Company, 85th Regiment, Harry Poschman could at last see the snow-topped Alps, the inspiration for the ski troops in the first place. Harry felt his spirits lift. The resistance north of the Po had so far been light; soon, maybe, this would be over. He smiled to himself. "I will ski soon."

CHAPTER 13:

Tunnel of the Dead

As the 10th sprinted for the Alps, the American public focused on events in Germany and Okinawa. By April of 1945, doubts about Hitler's sanity were aired frequently, if not openly, within the highest levels of Nazi command. Hitler had proclaimed on the eve of the American armies' crossing the Rhine that "the [final] battle should be conducted without consideration for our own population." He ordered the destruction of Germany's critical infrastructure: the electrical plants, the waterworks, gas works . . . "all food and clothing stores" in order to create "a desert" in the Allies' path. He told his minister of war production, Albert Speer: "If the war is lost, the German nation will also perish. So there is no need to consider what the people require for continued existence." Even Speer, who had run Germany's slave-labor industry, was appalled at this callousness, and went behind the Führer's back to convince regional authorities to ignore the order.

By April 11, U.S. and British forces had reached the Elbe River, sixty miles west of Berlin, and stopped there, in fulfillment of the agreement between Eisenhower and Stalin. Two weeks later, Soviet divisions completely surrounded Berlin and linked up with the Americans on the Elbe. Also mid-month, U.S. and British forces liberated the concentration camps at Bergen-Belsen and Buchenwald, revealing for the first time the full horror of Hitler's plan for the extermination of Europe's Jews, his "Final Solution."

In the Pacific, Gen. Douglas MacArthur was making good his promise to return to the Philippines, rooting out the last Japanese resistance on the big island of Luzon. The British also made good progress southward through Burma toward Rangoon, while one of the major battles of the war raged on the island of Okinawa, south of the Japanese main islands. The drama on Okinawa, and on the surrounding waters of the East China Sea, riveted the nation from April 1—when U.S. Marines first landed. There was the failed suicide mission of the *Yamoto*, the greatest battleship in the world, sent south to Okinawa with only enough fuel for a one-way trip, in a desperate attempt to finish off the U.S. Fleet. And there was the horrific struggle for Okinawa itself, which resulted in forty-eight thousand American dead and wounded and in excess of one hundred thousand Japanese killed. The main islands of Japan were now within striking distance, but the willingness of Japanese soldiers to fight to the last man, and the intransigence of the Japanese leadership, complicated any hopes for imminent victory.

In northern Italy, with the end of the war in sight, danger and risk took on new meaning. There was the story, for instance, of what happened to John Jennings's company commander just north of the Po River. Jennings's F Company, 87th Regiment, had crossed the river without casualties and then moved inland to occupy a small town on the left bank. All seemed peaceful in the hamlet, and the men settled into defensive positions while the pontoon bridge was being built, waiting for the armor to cross. It was the first real rest any of them had had since the jump-off April 14. Capt. James Kennett found an abandoned bicycle and, entranced perhaps by the sweet spring air and the near-certainty that his war would soon be over, rode up and down the streets of the village. A lone sniper, left behind in a second-story window, fired once. The bike clattered to the cobblestones along with the mortally wounded captain. Jennings was nonplussed. "All through the fighting, as a radioman, I was up with the captain in the front of the company. . . . He came through the worst of it right out in front—unscathed—only to be killed when things were beginning to look easier."

Then there was the incident at Villafranca. Forty miles north of the Po and ten miles short of Verona, the 85th Regiment pulled into Villafranca di Verona after an all-night march with orders to secure the town and its airport. Shortly after their arrival, a German fighter pilot landed his plane and walked, astonished, into captivity.

At dawn D Company's four machine guns were set up to guard the north and south approaches to the town, while Harry Poschman befriended a local family and began frying up hotcakes, from a stash of Aunt Jemima ready-mix that had been sent from home. The fire was roaring and the girls of the family were fascinated by these *torte da farina* when all hell broke loose down the road. Harry had long since become accustomed to the noise of explosions in the distance as retreating Germans blew up their fuel dumps and ammo supplies. But this sound was different. These were his own gunners at the south entrance to town firing their water-cooled .30-caliber machine guns with a definite urgency. By the time Harry got there, it was all over but for the rounding up of prisoners—the ones who weren't burnt to a crisp—and Harry had to piece the story together.

Once again, the speed of the 10th's advance had resulted in deadly confusion. Bob Woody, who was there in Villafranca too, with C Company, remembered:

> [Two trucks were] hurtling up the road toward us. They were filled with Germans. . . . A German in the lead truck was spraying the road ahead with a machine gun on the cab roof. We were stunned. We had not expected any Germans from that direction. They were obviously stunned too, having come from the south into the rear of our column. They hadn't been able to stop in time or turn around. They were making a desperate dash.

And they almost made it through, but for the D Company gunners whose tracers ignited fuel drums in the second truck. (Ahead, the first truck turned over, spilling its passengers into the road.) Harry Poschman continues, "The driver was cremated in his truck. The man on top was blown up on the roof of a house very near. He still had some fight left and pointed his gun at someone in the street. One of our guys shot that man with one round from his carbine without taking his arm from around a cute little girl he was cuddling. The diehard Nazi fell dead from the roof, just like in the movies."

Woody ran forward, through the flames and charred bodies, to help with the prisoners. Most were just boys, with newspapers stuffed in their holsters where pistols should have been. No Americans died in the kamikaze rush, although one man was shot in the shoulder. Woody shook his head: "Caprice as much as courage determines who lives and who dies."

Later that same day, as if to prove that things could get even weirder, Harry and some mates discovered two large chests in the airport office at Villafranca—a German army payroll. The loot totaled ten million Italian lire, a hundred thousand dollars at the official exchange rate; it would double the pay (roughly $100 per month) of every man in the battalion. U.S. servicemen were not allowed to send cash home from Italy. But they could spend it in the country, and beneficiaries of Harry's find bought everything from jewelry to paintings—the trophies of which General Hays had spoken—and shipped them later to the States.

That night the order came down for the 86th Regiment to move through the 85th and take Verona, while the 87th, with the 85th at the rear, would shove off directly for Lake Garda. "Damn," Harry thought, "they're going to get all that wine and maybe Juliet, too . . . oh, well. The 1st Battalion of the 85th Regiment moved out of Villafranca with the coin of the realm bulging from every pocket."

The seesaw of emotion continued in the walled, pink-brick city of Verona. As the 86th entered the historic home of Shakespeare's Montagues and Capulets, they were shelled from south of the city. Worse, it soon became clear that the shells were not coming from German artillery but mistakenly from the U.S. 88th Division. One of the regular, flatland divisions on the 10th's right, the Blue Devil Division was not at fault. There had been a mix-up in the hastily prepared map overlays; Verona was on its liberation list too.

From far back as Roman times, Verona has marked a key crossroads. The road north leads up the Adige River to Austria and the rest of Europe. To the west is Milan and to the east Venice. It is also home to Bardolina, Valpolicella, and Soave, three of Italy's classic wines. David Brower and his 3d Battalion were looking forward to sampling the fruits of the city.

> Italians, in the streets and squares by the thousands, welcomed us with almost embarrassing enthusiasm. At each momentary stop vehicles would be covered with civilians, laughing, crying, and singing. Flowers covered the streets and colorful flags hung from the buildings. Balconies almost sagged with people. Signs were

scrawled on the sides of buildings, "Liberate," and "Vive Americani." Everywhere, damage from the explosions could be seen. Windows were broken, and buildings along the river had collapsed from the blasts.

The high point of the day came when the mayor of Verona stepped out on the city hall balcony to proclaim the war was over. This was it, we thought. Everyone went mad, soldiers included. Weapons were fired and people danced in the streets, drinking wine or whatever was available.

The celebrating among the GIs soon ended, however, when they were told that the mayor was referring only to Verona's war. The 10th's work still was not done.

The snafu with the 88th Division ended poorly for the 86th Regiment. Not only had the 88th shot at them, now they were usurping their accommodations to boot. Apparently, higher powers than David Brower had ruled in favor of the 88th. That night of April 26, as the Blue Devils moved in, the men of the mountain division had to move out. They gave up their pleasant beds in the homes of local families, shouldered their packs, and motored several miles out of the city to a bivouac area in a field. It was raining.

Worse yet, Brower remembered, "Along with the billets—and the spoils, we can assume, of war—they [the 88th] took credit for the liberation of the city."

Plans continued to change with the extremely fluid situation on the ground. Overnight, the 10th's assignment shifted from the Adige road and Brenner Pass to the shores of Lake Garda a few miles farther west. Garda afforded another escape route into the Alps, and concentrations of German artillery and tanks had been spotted moving up the lake's eastern and western shores.

Rain squalls frothed the surface of Lake Garda over the next two days as 10th battalions chased enemy units up the eastern shoreline.

They moved through the resort towns of Lazise and Bardolino, Garda and Malcesine, while German artillery batteries on the west shore fired across sporadically. Even in the drizzle, these were towns of sublime beauty, for centuries host to Europe's elite. Grand villas, including Mussolini's at Gargnano, dotted the shoreline. Shelley wrote "Ode to the West Wind" and "Adonais" there in the early nineteenth century. The great German writer and philosopher Goethe lived and worked at Malcesine, on the east shore, between 1786 and 1788. Surrounded by olive groves and citrus and palm trees, each town crowded down to a small boat harbor on the water, and each was crowned by a stone turret or other remnant of a medieval fort on the hill.

Even in the rain, the men could see that this was the true beginning of the mighty Alps. Lake Garda, Italy's largest lake, is shaped like a Chianti bottle with the south end spreading into the foothills at the edge of the Po Valley. Thirty-four miles north, the bottle's neck is pinched by tremendous walls of snow-capped gray granite, "like a glacier-carved fjord," to the eyes of Bob Parker. Escarpments on both sides rise as high as 7,000 feet above lake level and plunge so precipitously that the highway requires a score of tunnels to circumnavigate the northern shore. These tunnels, and countless galleries carved into the rock above them, were the scenes of bloody battles in World War I, when the northern half of the lake was still part of the Austro-Hungarian Empire. The Treaty of Saint-Germain in 1919 gave this end of the lake and the adjacent high mountains, the Sud Tyrol, to Italy.

On the morning of April 28, as the 2d Battalion of the 86th Regiment approached the first tunnel, German sappers set off charges that blew the entrance and covered the road in automobile-sized boulders. Over on the west shore, two miles across the water, German 88-mm cannon on railroad cars rolled out of tunnels, blasted the cliffs above the Americans, and rolled back inside. The 88s were the most feared artillery piece in World War II, with a range of up to twelve miles and better accuracy than any comparable Allied weapon. With each incoming shell, shrapnel and more rocks rained down on the ski troopers. There was no place to dig in, no place to hide, with water below and vertical rock cliff above.

The battalion moved back around a corner to relative safety and considered its options. There appeared to be three. They could wait for the 126th Engineer bulldozers to clear the tunnel and proceed up the lake road. But what would prevent the enemy from blowing other tunnels? And what about the 88s dialed in on the road? A second option involved climbing overland across the high spine of Monte Baldo ridge, which separated Lake Garda from the valley of the Adige. There was a trail from Malcesine to the summit of the escarpment and then from there north, up and down along the ridge, to a point above the town of Torbole, the regiment's objective, at the head of the lake. Third, they could try an amphibious skirting of the blown tunnel. Twenty-five-man DUKWs from the Po crossing were hot on the heels of the 10th's advance and could conceivably be used to get around the tunnel.

Capt. David Brower argued initially for the overland climb. "Wasn't this situation just what we were asking for? Hadn't we, as mountain troops, been trained for just such terrain? Shouldn't we be able to effect complete surprise by attacking along a route that the enemy—especially a disorganized enemy, few in number—would have to assume could defend it?" But one by one, Brower answered his own questions in the negative. From *Remount Blue*:

> Here we were, mountain troops, fighting in the Alps. But where was our mountain equipment? Presumably, it was back in Naples. The equipment and clothing with us was no different from the ordinary flatland GI's, right down to the last shred of

underwear—except that even most of the flatland apparel had been left behind when we jumped off [almost two weeks before], and we hadn't had so much as a change of underwear since then. Ropes, mountain boots, sleeping bags? Why ask about those? We hadn't yet captured enough German blankets to give more than one man in ten a blanket to his name.

Brower concluded that the 10th at that moment was less equipped for mountains and snow than the flatland soldiers had been prepared for Attu in 1943, when they had suffered so many needless casualties.

And what about the time factor? General Hays was in a race to cut off access to the high passes. Brower estimated, based on his own mountain experience, that "in good weather, with no snow on the trail, one man who knew a little about mountains and was properly dressed for them but otherwise climbing free of load, could have covered the high route to Torbole in about 17 hours. How would a battalion fare?" Brower also worried about the experience level of the force.

We may have had many men who knew a little about mountains when we hit Italy, but the division's 4,000 casualties had included too many of the original mountain men. We utterly lacked proper clothing and equipment. A battalion column would be four miles long, and flank protection would be all but forbidden by the steep slopes on either side of the trail. Without mules, we could hardly hope to secure such close artillery support as might be necessary. And finally, far from being free of loads, the men would have to carry weapons and ammunition. That would be bad enough for riflemen. Heavy weapons men would have tougher sledding still.

So, the road and the right flank were both out. That left the left flank, a risky boat ride in full view of enemy gunners, through storm-chopped waters around the blown tunnel. Here were the mountain troops, trained to ski and climb, about to rely, again, on a maritime maneuver. The 2d Battalion backtracked to Malcesine and boarded the DUKWs. The German 88s across the lake opened up on the string of ducklings hugging the shore. Timed fire burst in angry black puffs of flak over the soldiers' heads, and point-detonation shells sent geysers of foam fifty feet into the air. Shells blasted the cliffs above the fleet and sent rocks crashing into the water as well. The DUKWs moved further off-shore, but the shelling only intensified.

Watching from the lakefront at Malcesine, Brower and his 3d Battalion, who were next in line, assumed the little fleet would be annihilated. But then the surprising word came back that they'd made it, without casualties even. They had landed in a small cove between Tunnels 2 and 3, and had moved into the shelter of Tunnel 3, which was free of demolitions. Later DUKW loads were not so lucky. When the barrages came close, the men dove as best they could to the floor of the ungainly craft, but timed fire claimed a number of 3d Battalion men.

By nightfall of the 28th, two battalions of the 86th had hunkered down just shy of Tunnel 4. There was a break in the cliff wall here— the angle of the rock backed off somewhat—and the decision was made to send I and K Companies up a steep traverse and overland to Torbole while the rest pressed ahead on the coast road. In continuing drizzle, everyone tried to sleep. They had not rested well since the Po. They had not eaten properly; the best food of late had been the sausages in captured German rucksacks. The men were wet and worn, physically and emotionally. They weren't sure how much more they could endure. That hint of victory they'd tasted in the Po River valley had been replaced once again by the dry, tight throat of uncertainty.

In fact, though the frazzled men of the 10th could not have known it, their war was tantalizingly near its end. On the morning of the 29th, hundreds of miles to the south in the comfortable splendor of the royal summer palace at Caserta, the highest echelons—including Field Marshal Sir Harold Alexander, who was Allied commander in chief for the Mediterranean theater, and German Commanding General von Vietinghoff and SS commander Gen. Karl Wolff—signed surrender documents for all German forces in Italy and southern Austria. The problem was, the negotiations had been conducted in secret, without Hitler's knowledge or consent; the surrendering generals could not guarantee the documents' recognition by Berlin. Meanwhile, the fates of thousands of men hung in the balance as the 10th, and all of the other Allied divisions on the northern Italian front, continued to attack.

On the other side of the Alps, the U.S. Seventh Army rushed to deny northern access to a Final Redoubt. Its tanks raced southward up into the Austrian Alps through Landsberg, Germany, in whose famous fortress/prison Hitler had written *Mein Kampf* (My Struggle), the Third Reich's doctrinal guidebook. Across northern Italy, following the crossing of the Po River, Allied divisions fanned out swiftly toward the eastern and western borders. Elements of the British Eighth Army reached Venice on the 30th and kept driving north and east toward Trieste, in a race for that port city with Marshal Tito's Yugoslav Communists. On the west, elements of the U.S. Fifth Army neared Milan; Turin would be next. In a moment as symbolic as it was grisly, Italian partisans on the 28th caught Benito Mussolini, his mistress Clara Petacci, and twelve cabinet ministers in a convoy attempting escape into Switzerland. Jailed by King Victor Emmanuel III in 1943, Mussolini had escaped (with the help of German commandos) and installed himself as puppet dictator of German-occupied northern Italy. Now, in a vengeful fury, partisans executed all fourteen fugitives outside a village near Lake Como. The next day, the bodies of Clara and Il Duce were brought to Milan and hung upside down from lampposts in the square where, a year before, fifteen anti-Fascist partisans had been executed. A crowd crazy with revenge spat upon the bodies and shot them full of holes.

As for the 10th Mountain Division, what happened next epitomized the needless waste of war. Brower's 3d Battalion entered Tunnel 4 on the morning of the 29th, but couldn't get out the other end. A German machine gun sprayed the exit from a World War I–era embrasure carved out of the granite beside Tunnel 5. M Company gunners brought forward one of their own .50-caliber machine guns to "seal off" the offending rock window with fire more deadly than the Germans could return. "Under this cover," Brower recalled, "riflemen spurted forward and tossed grenades through a doorway in the wall of the next tunnel. Two of the room's occupants staggered out into the tunnel to die; another six lay where they were. The tunnel was ours, and advance elements of L Company moved quickly through the black interior."

At the far end, they stumbled over a pile of debris that was at first inexplicable. This was the tunnel later known as the Tunnel of the Dead, and death was not finished with it. For the Americans, who had seen enough horror to numb them almost completely, here was a scene of special hideousness. Apparently, a rear-guard crew of about twenty Germans—it was impossible to discern exactly how many—had been hand-moving a 20-mm antiaircraft gun to a new defensive position to their rear, preparatory to blowing the tunnel up. "Somehow," Brower writes, "they ran afoul of their own demolitions. . . . Their war ended quickly, if not prettily.

The explosion set fire to their own ammunition and to them. Pieces of men were scattered as far as fifty feet out of the tunnel. Part of the massive rock roof of the tunnel collapsed and fell to the floor. But there was too little rock to complete the burial or to extinguish the smoldering."

The 3d Battalion men picked their way gingerly over the pile of rock and flesh and advanced another mile to the entrance of Tunnel 6, the last tunnel before Torbole. This tunnel curved in the middle, its far end lining up directly on the town of Torbole. Germans in the town had no intention of letting the Americans safely out of this tunnel either; they sprayed machine-gun and pom-pom (20-mm antiaircraft) fire into their end of it. Ricochets reached all the way to the south entrance, where L Company stopped short.

A meeting of 86th Regiment officers and noncoms gathered just outside the Tunnel of the Dead to plan what relief they could for L Company. Suddenly, a trio of 88-mm air bursts rent the air overhead and sent all of the men scrambling into the tunnel—back in among the German dead.

At this time David Brower's battalion command post was located quite comfortably behind Tunnel 4 at the only spot where he could maintain radio contact with both the overland traversing companies and with L Company ahead.

It was sunny, shrubs and annuals around us were showing their springtime greenery, and a few men went down to the lake to fill their canteens with mountain water. An ominous message came back from the Battalion Commander's radio operator: "Send up all the litter teams you can get!"

Soldiers don't pale easily. But Lt. Butterwick, who came running back to our CP about then, was pale. A piece of shell fragment an inch across had ripped into, but had not entered, the top of his steel helmet and was still imbedded there, although he didn't know it. "Major Drake's been hit," he said. "'They got a direct hit inside the tunnel."

A one-in-a-thousand shot from the town of Riva (not to be confused with Riva Ridge), two miles beyond Torbole, had burst fifty feet inside the tunnel entrance. Those who were not hit with shell fragments or rock splinters were torn apart by the tremendous concussion, artificially contained within the walls. The lucky ones stumbled away stunned and deafened. In agony, men screamed "Medic! Medic!"—words that were too often last words. The toll in the Tunnel of the Dead—the American toll, not counting the German bodies underneath them—was seven dead and forty-four wounded.

Other units of the 10th had a somewhat easier time of it on Lake Garda, although they suffered needless casualties as well. On April 30, Companies K and M of the 85th Regiment took off across the lake in twelve DUKWs. They came ashore in the town of Gargnano without significant opposition and took possession of Mussolini's thirty-seven-room villa there, in addition to capturing German tanks and artillery. On the way back, however, afternoon winds capsized one of the DUKWs, and all hands but one were lost.

The 1st Battalion of the 87th Regiment took off overland from Garda's east shore toward the town of Spiazzi, where the Germans were known to have a noncommissioned officers' school. The German NCO candidates and their instructors battled the 87th in furious house-to-house fighting. Some ski troopers took refuge in a school and others in a hospital, both of which the Germans then attacked with antitank rockets. After two days of fighting, seventy enemy were counted dead with forty wounded. When the shooting stopped, a booby-trapped building exploded, killing one 87th man and wounding nine.

"Those guys were fierce to the last," recalled Bob Parker. Parker's Headquarters Company also participated in what surely was one of the most unlikely scenarios of the war. While the tunnel road was blocked, neither British artillery nor American tanks could move north in support of the 86th, clawing its way toward Torbole. The solution was once again a maritime operation, but there was no way the two-and-a-half-ton DUKWs could carry either a five-inch canon or the heavy tanks. The answer required Parker and others, mostly from the engineer companies, to sail the armor up the lake on commandeered native wooden sailing barges. Under full sail, and riding the afternoon southerly winds, the ponderous barges approached Torbole's waterfront blasting away like brigantines.

With flanking help from the barges, the 3d Battalion took on the stubborn defenders of Torbole, who fought from building to building and with tanks of their own. The two overland companies from 1st Battalion came in from the rear, after descending a long switchback trail off the ridge. The climbers had suffered a tragedy of their own when, in the predawn darkness, a German bomber, probably just trying to jettison his weapons, dropped them on Company B. It may have been the only time a 10th unit was bombed by German aircraft. Harris Dusenbery came upon the scene in daylight. "Someone had made a partial attempt to clean up. Along the trail there was a gunny sack of arms and legs." Nine men were killed.

But Torbole was in American hands by noon on the 30th. The 2d Battalion of the 86th took the larger town of Riva at the lake's northwest corner by 2:00 P.M. Reeling remnants of the German Fourteenth Army withdrew deeper into the mountains toward Trento, Arco, and Bolzano up the river Sarca. No one knew it, but the last battle for Italy had ended.

There was still time, however, for one more tragic twist of fate.

Col. William O. Darby, who had led the task force successfully up the lake, was in Torbole meeting with assistant division commander Gen. David Ruffner and regimental staff about continuing the attack toward Trento. The officers had just finished lunch at a hotel in the rubble-strewn downtown when they heard a single 88-mm shell explode somewhere in the town. No one commented on it, and meeting adjourned, the group walked outside in the sunshine to Ruffner's jeep. Darby climbed into the backseat while the general discussed something with an aide. At that moment another 88 shell hit the building above them. A piece of shrapnel pierced Colonel Darby's chest, killing him instantly. A young sergeant major was hit in the head and also died.

Stunned by Darby's death and in desperate need of rest, the 10th took the next two days in and around Riva and Torbole to regroup. The men were issued new clothing for the first time since the jump-off and, David Brower noted, "sleeping bags!" "There were higher, colder mountains to the north"—very high, glacier-draped mountains that dwarfed anything the ski troops had seen in Colorado or Washington. The Germans' last-ditch Redoubt was very much on everyone's mind.

And then, at 6:30 P.M. on Wednesday, May 2, new word came by radio. The German army in Italy had surrendered unconditionally. The same broadcast noted the double suicide of Hitler and Eva Braun in his bunker in Berlin two days earlier, but that news caused scarcely a ripple at Lake Garda. Harris Dusenbery remembered the official announcement word-for-word in his *North Apennines and Beyond*: "Italian Theater armistice in progress. Commanding General 10th Mountain Division orders cease firing except in self-defense. All patrols are called off. There will be no firing of arms in celebration. More details to follow."

Harry Poschman got the news in a restaurant in Malcesine. Harry's weapons platoon had been camping out in an olive grove for the previous two nights. Each evening they went down to the harbor with orders to board the DUKWs and motor across to the west shore as part of an effort to encircle the retreating Germans. But each of the last two nights the operation had been postponed because of the bright moonlight. A good thing, too, Harry thought. "The Germans could have picked us off with their 88s just like shooting fish in a barrel." The word was, they were going the night of May 2, moon or no moon. So, Harry and his friend John Pierpont were enjoying a "last supper" of potato soup and Chianti ("the only things to be had") when the news came over the radio.

"We toasted with that Chianti. We toasted some more. The Italians went crazy. Their land was free at last. Now I *knew* I would ski. Shots rang out. The Italians, and Americans too, fired their guns out the windows. I grabbed my soup and wine and jumped into the fireplace, a readymade foxhole."

John Jennings was sitting in the little town of Torri di Benaco with his company, getting ready to push off again to the north, when he heard. "Most of us were too tired, too dazed to realize the full import of this news, so there was no gay celebrating. Here and there you might hear a murmured 'Thank God,' or a very tired 'Well, I made it.' The infantry had suffered too much, lost too many comrades to be jubilant."

Bob Parker's I&R platoon was out "chasing down this SS unit that had fired on us," when word came. "We chased them over a pass. We could hear them, see their nail-boot tracks in the mud. They got away."

Bob Woody heard the news in the form of a cacophony approaching on the road. "There was heavy rifle fire up the road, which was coming our way and increasing in volume. Soon a jeep came bouncing along with tin cans tied on the rear with a guy yelling 'The war is over.' Then my company took up the fire with delirious joy. Never have I heard such noise. Rifles, BARs, machine guns all burning up ammunition. Finally, officers had to order us to stop firing for fear someone would be hurt."

On May 3 David Brower's battalion struck off for Resia Pass near the point where Switzerland, Austria, and Italy come together. (The 88th Division had earlier been sent to occupy Brenner Pass to the east.) Past Bolzano and on into the night, Brower thought to himself, "Why not turn our lights on?" Throughout the war, tactical situations always required blackout driving. But now the war was over, why not see the road and speed up the column? Lt. Col. John Hay, at the head of the column, had no objection "so a lighted column eight miles long passed through Merano about midnight and continued up the Adige Valley toward Passo di Resia."

By dawn they were winding up the final grade below the pass at 4,947 feet of elevation. The air was cold, and new snow coated the meadows on either side of the road. The column stopped and sent a jeep forward to make contact with the German area commander. The jeep returned a short time later with, as Brower tells it, a disturbing story.

The surrender in Italy, the German commander had believed, did not apply to [his] outfit across the border, which was still resisting the advance of the American Seventh Army. When they heard that our task force was coming up the valley from Merano, they turned part of their artillery around and registered on the road to prevent our attacking their rear. They had their hands on the lanyards. When our column came into range with lights ablaze, the Germans assumed that something must have happened that they didn't know about, otherwise we would not have dared to use lights. They took their hands off the lanyards, we advanced to the border, and Jerries and Yanks peacefully patrolled the line—with Yanks in the better billets.

Best of all, many of those billets contained ski gear used by German border patrols. For the weary ski troopers it was the most fitting of rewards. "We took over not only the quarters," Brower recalled with relish, "but the skis as well, plus the patrol route that included part of the Swiss border and some fine open slopes above timberline for recreational skiing." The 10th Mountain Division had come home.

CHAPTER 14:

Mountain Idylls

D ave Brower's group were not the only ones making pleasant discoveries. Soon after the surrender announcement, K Company of the 87th Regiment entered a series of caves near the Swiss border and found them stacked to the ceilings with cases of French champagne and cognac. It was good-quality stuff, too—Mumm, Reims, Ponsardin—all of it stamped RESERVED FOR THE WEHRMACHT. General Hays ordered the loot trucked to the 10th's division supply depot. It took fifty-five truckloads to bring it all down. Every man in the division was issued two bottles of champagne and one of cognac. For a time, champagne was free while beer still cost ten cents. The men joked that only the rich drank beer.

Jacques Parker, the illustrator whose sketches of the Riva Ridge climb made page 1 of the *Blizzard*, took his ration of bubbly to the

Lake Garda shore, where he contemplated the miracle of his having survived the war. "This is fascinating," he thought, through his alcohol haze. "This is where Shelley lived and wrote his poems. So, I lay down on the edge of the lake and looked up at the clouds. It was so quiet and peaceful—the war was at last over. I fell asleep then and woke up at dawn the next morning, hearing these little noises. It was the lake, lapping at my head."

In the sudden hush of peacetime, division commander Gen. George Hays praised the 86th Regiment assembled in Torbole, near the square where Colonel Darby had been killed. Dave Brower was there and recalled Hays's words in *Remount Blue*: "The entire 10th Mountain Division crossed the Po Valley with enemy to the front, unprotected flanks to the right and to the left, and no protection to the rear. . . . Never in its days of combat did it fail to take an objective, or lose an objective once it was taken. Never was so much as a single platoon surrounded and lost."

Had the 10th's mountain training contributed to these successes, of which the general was so proud? Clearly, mountaineering skills, especially with ropes and pitons, had made the surprise attack on Riva Ridge possible. The troopers were able to scramble up an escarpment that German defenders had considered "unclimbable"— at least for a battalion-sized force. But what about after Riva, when the division functioned as a standard infantry division, albeit in rugged terrain? Had climbing and skiing somehow better prepared 10th soldiers for what John Keegan calls "the strain [of war] thrown on the human participants"?

In *The Face of Battle*, Keegan says, "Mountains, like battlefields, are places inherently dangerous for the individual to inhabit; . . . the risk of death always stalks the climber." Soldiers and mountaineers face "objective dangers." In peacetime, mountain risks may include collapsing cornices, snow avalanches, falling rock, or the risk of slipping and tumbling. But soldiers must also face the weapons of war: rifles and machine guns, buried mines, artillery, and aerial bombardment. And something the mountaineer doesn't have to deal with—a clever, conscious enemy. Both groups are subject to "exposure" in "the killing zone." Climbers are said to be exposed when a fall from the rock would mean certain death. Skiers are exposed when crossing an avalanche path. In war, as with a siege on a mountain, the most exposure falls to the men on the leading edge, the lead climber or skier, the division spearheading an attack. The 10th had been the point on the Fifth Army spear in breaking through the Winter Line.

The relieved and inebriated survivors at Lake Garda credited luck more than anything for their having made it through. John Jennings wrote in his pocket diary: "Slowly, it was beginning to sink in just what it all meant. I realized how lucky I had been to have gone through it safe and somewhat sound. Shrapnel had once grazed a scratch on my thumb and had torn a hole in my shirt, but that's all except for some near misses. Damn lucky, when you consider that our total regimental casualties were about 1,400. That is 50 percent, even including those headquarters men in the rear."

Bob Parker also praised luck over any other factor. On the day his unit drove down into the Po Valley, Parker's jeep came under artillery fire. The driver ditched the vehicle off the roadside, and Parker dove for the cut bank. Lying there as flat and small as he could make himself, Parker heard a terrific whoosh and felt a pounding of dirt and rock across his body. When he could at last look up, he saw the 88-mm shell imbedded in the embankment fourteen inches from his face. Had it exploded, he knew, his corpse would not have been recognizable. But it didn't explode; it was a dud. Later, when Parker learned about them, he said a silent prayer to the OSS saboteurs, brave conscripts and foreign workers forced to toil in German munitions plants, who risked their lives to jinx the fuses of every third or fourth shell that passed through their hands.

There had been myriad close shaves, lucky moments. Everyone had them. And everyone had seen the shattered bodies of men who, in the purposefully casual argot of the living, "got it." Got it through no fault of their own, no lack of bravery or skill. "Such fantastic luck," Parker said more than once, shaking his head.

The German army may, in the end, have given the 10th more credit than the exhausted infantrymen gave themselves. Despite early propaganda that belittled the ski troops as "sports personalities and young men from wealthy or politically significant families," the Germans who fought across the line from the 10th were impressed, and they said so. Gen. Fridolin Rudolph Theodor von Senger und Etterlin, known more simply as von Senger, wrote in his "War Diaries": "The 10th Mountain Division [was] my most dangerous opponent." His forces had been sent reeling as the 10th, by itself, routed five German divisions, including at least one mountain division, and helped cause "the complete disintegration of the [German] 14th Army."

When von Senger was presented surrender documents, he asked as a point of honor to be allowed to surrender to Gen. George Hays and the 10th Mountain Division. Appropriately, the surrender documents were delivered to von Senger's Bolzano headquarters by the young New Hampshire ski racer, Steve Knowlton. As part of the 86th Intelligence and Reconnaissance Platoon, a nervous Knowlton drove north from Lake Garda in a four-jeep convoy.

> Over this ridge was about a jillion Germans, still armed. We didn't know if they knew the war was over. . . . We came to a little castle and went in. It was just like a movie. There was a guard there, and he gave the Nazi salute and I saluted back and went up to the second floor. The door was open and there, sitting at a desk, was this German officer with a white turtleneck and a blond crew cut. I went over and saluted and handed him the envelope.

Von Senger spoke perfect English. He had studied at St. Johns College, Oxford, before World War I. He was a professional soldier, not a doctrinal Nazi. In this war, he had fought on three fronts, including the Russian, and participated in the brutal, five-month siege of Cassino. He knew about bravery and toughness, and he praised the 10th on both counts. He said later that when his mountain troops were facing the Americans in the Apennine hills, and when he saw the men of the 10th running up the mountainside with fixed bayonets at their positions, he "never in the world [would have] believed that there were American troops with that kind of spirit and that kind of physical condition."

It was true, Bob Parker remembered: "Our spirit and our mountain conditioning is what got us through the hardest times." And General Hays put an exclamation point on that in his speech beneath a ruined church tower in Torbole. Standing, hands on hips before a sea of 10th Mountain helmets, he said, "When you soldiers go home, no one will believe you when you start telling them of the spectacular things you have done. There have been more heroic deeds and experiences crammed into these days than I have heard of."

All in 114 days. The 10th was the last U.S. division to enter the war in Europe, but it had been given one of the most daunting assignments in Italy and consequently suffered the highest casualty rate, per combat day, of any division in the southern theater. Nine hundred seventy-five 10th Division men were killed in four months; 3,849 were wounded. Ten other U.S. infantry divisions fought in Italy. Of these the 34th suffered the highest total casualties—16,401 over twenty months, for a casualty rate of 820 a month. The 88th Division incurred 13,111 casualties over fourteen months—937 a month. The 10th's casualty rate figured out to 1,209 per month. General Hays's high praise had come at a high cost.

The thrill of victory in Italy lasted only a few days. VE Day (May 8) came and went "with little excitement," according to Harris Dusenbery in *The North Apennines*, in part perhaps because the Army had just released photographs of the atrocities in the concentration camps: Bergen-Belsen, Dachau, Auschwitz. Reality set back in. The United States was still at war in the Pacific. Even though Japan faced a hopeless situation, similar to Germany's in the last weeks, official Japanese propaganda promised that her people would fight to the death. Experience on Okinawa proved this. What would it be like for American servicemen charged with invading the Japanese homeland? Tenth men didn't want to think about it, but rumor swirled, as always: The invasion was planned for the rocky coast north of Tokyo, where mountain troops would be called on to scale the sheer sea cliffs, no doubt defended by desperate fanatics . . . and so on. The dogfaces wouldn't hear about it, but on May 25 General MacArthur was ordered to plan Operation Olympic, the invasion of the southern island of Kyushu, to commence November 1. The War Department estimated hundreds of thousands of U.S. casualties and as many as two million Japanese dead. And the 10th was slated to lead the attack.

Two weeks after von Senger's surrender, the 10th's disparate units, spread around the high country north of Lake Garda, were ordered back down into the Po Valley. This was a blow to the mountain men, most of whom were savoring their first taste of the Alps. These summits were no higher, most of them, than the peaks around Camp Hale, but the valleys cut much, much deeper. Average elevations for the glacier-carved valley floors were between 1,000 and 3,000 feet above sea level, versus 7,000 to 9,000 feet in Colorado. Peak-to-valley elevations might span 10,000 vertical feet, double the relief of most climbs in North America outside Alaska. Multiplying the feeling of immensity, timberline in the Alps is much lower—a good 5,000 feet lower—than it is in Colorado. So, the vast majority of this high country qualifies as alpine: naked rock, tundra, snow, and ice. This unobstructed distance, and the huge vertical relief, are what led Shelley to write: "I never knew what mountains were until I saw the Alps." Many in the 10th had the same epiphany. They were transported by the beauty, and not at all eager to leave.

Having to come down was particularly hard on John Jennings, whose unit had settled into the idyllic little town of Folgaria, in the Dolomite Range. With time on their hands, they had set up an impromptu rock-climbing school; they relaxed with the local people and climbed frequently on days off.

> I arrived on a peak from which I had one of the most breathtaking views I ever hope to behold. I could see for miles and miles in all directions across the Alps. I'm pretty sure that was Switzerland in the hazy distance. . . . There were numerous old emplacements, caved-in dugouts, trenches and caves on the peak I climbed and on some of the surrounding promontories and ridges. These were used in the last war, which was rather intense in this area. The Austrians and the Italians battled back and forth for some time through this unbelievable country.

(Mountaineers who did any rambling at all saw the old fortifications, defensive bulwarks that gave David Brower a subjunctive chill: "Had we not beaten the retreating Germans to them . . .")

For Jennings, the hardest part of leaving was saying goodbye to the Rizzardi family, "consisting namely of the signorinas Sandra, Maria, and Piera, whose mountainside home we visited quite frequently. My particular favorite was Maria, a girl of about my own age. Here there was a little social life for a change, and even a couple of dances."

That all ended with relocation to the dusty, flat Po, now overlain with the heat of early summer. Bob Woody groused, only half facetiously: "Shaves, close-order drills, and all the chicken shit was to be re-imposed. Incredible. We had just won a war! We were heroes."

Some of the heroes had enough points to go home. You accumulated points for months of duty and months in combat. You got five points for each battle star—Northern Apennines, Po Valley, etc.—and five for any medals you earned: Purple Heart, Bronze Star, Silver Star, and so on. (Woody's nascent writing career got a boost when certain noncoms, who "knew of my way with words," asked him to help with their commendations for a Bronze Star. "Sure, I said, creating in my mind or embellishing events in the officialese of the citations: 'In spite of wounds to an embarrassing part of his anatomy, Sgt. So and So refused evacuation and stayed with his squad. . . .'") Anyone with enough points could, at any time, leave for home. A few in the 10th did just that.

The rest were saved from the heat and boredom of duty in the valley—guarding prisoners, cleaning weapons, and the incessant marching—by another potential conflict, a phantom conflict happily, on Italy's border with Yugoslavia. On May 20, the division was ordered to Udine. Tensions between Tito's ragtag Yugoslav forces, Italian partisans, and Italian Communists ran hot for a time. The U.S. Fifth and British Eighth Armies were to quell the isolated skirmishes and secure the border. The great benefit for the 10th was that they were in the mountains again, and relatively free to pursue their passions.

On June 3, a collection of former MTG men reunited on Mount Mangart, in the Carnic Alps, for a long-imagined ski race. Using gear appropriated from Axis warehouses, they climbed Mangart's 8,927-foot height and set a course in the vestigial spring snow. At last, Harry Poschman could lean into his elegant Arlberg turns. Everyone admitted that the skiing muscles had suffered from long neglect, and there were some humorous "rubber-leg" scenes at the finish line, but the day was a grand one. They all agreed it was only right that the fastest skier of the day should be Sgt. Walter Prager, the former Dartmouth coach and 87th Regiment instructor on Mount Rainier.

With time and a jeep at their disposal, Bob Parker and Sigi Engl took off across Austria—to Innsbruck and Kitzbühel—to see if they could find Sigi's uncle. John Jennings made the short hop over the border into the Austrian state of Carinthia for some sailing on the Wörther See. David Brower and a number of his Sierra Club mates took advantage of the fine summer weather to climb some of the classic routes in the Alps.

Raffi Bedayan attempted the Matterhorn (Monte Cervino) from the Italian side but was chased down by bad weather. He did succeed in climbing Austria's highest summit, the 12,470-foot Grossglockner, as well as the massive snow dome of Mont Blanc, the tallest mountain in central Europe at 15,771 feet. Astride the border of France and Italy, rising nearly 13,000 feet above Chamonix on one side and 12,000 feet above Courmayeur on the other, Mont Blanc resonated with a special significance. It is the literal birthplace of mountaineering (beginning with its first ascent in 1786) and a physical and spiritual mecca for climbers ever since.

The writer and climber James Ramsey Ullman stated the fact in no uncertain terms in his classic, *High Conquest: The Story of Mountaineering*: "The Alps were the first place where it ever occurred to men to climb mountains—where not merely a sport was born, but an idea." David Brower, very much an idea man as well as climber, found himself in a kind of heaven for the two months the 10th occupied northern Italy. Here was the myth and lore of climbing, the stuff he'd read about since his youth. Brower helped to establish division climbing and ski schools at Trafoi in the Dolomites, at Passo del Predil in the eastern Julian Alps, and on the tremendous glaciers of the Grossglockner. With fellow 86th trooper Leo Healy, he got to within 800 feet of the Matterhorn's summit of 14,691 feet, where Healy was stricken suddenly with headache and nausea—acute mountain sickness. They were forced to retreat, but Brower remained thrilled with the attempt. "It is a big mountain. You climb for hours, and it still rises more hours above you. The exposure—the thousands of feet of precipice plunging to the glaciers below—is, and I can think of no better word, classical."

Most of Brower's time was spent in the Dolomites, the Italian range that is home to a particular gray-and-pink limestone rock, and bolts vertically out of lush, green pasture. It was here that some of the highest-standard rock climbing was practiced. After working their way through barbed wire left over from a World War I machine-gun position, Brower and his 3d Battalion buddies climbed Piccola Cima, one of the three famous spires in the Tre Cime di Lavaredo. Then it was off to France for a successful two-day ascent of the Grepon, one of the famous Chamonix rock needles.

The Grossglockner eventually became the site of several regimental "refresher" schools, where former MTG instructors led classes for both neophyte and experienced mountaineers. *Grossglockner* means "big bell" in German, and the massive, bell-shaped mountain, draped on all sides with glaciers, offered plenty of summer ice and snow routes. The 86th set up its school in the Glocknerhaus, an inn owned by the Austrian Mountain Club. The 85th took over the Pasterzenhaus nearby. Equipment had to be scrounged from all over northern Italy and southern Austria. "Our American equipment would have suited us better," wrote David Brower, "but it was still in Naples and no transportation was available to get it to Austria." Soon, however, "ropes, pitons, axes, crampons, carabiners, boots, parkas, skis, pants, rucksacks, and various minor items of mountaineering equipment were pouring in."

Harry Poschman remembers:

[I] couldn't take my eyes off the huge mountain, the constant rumbling slides and big snow fields. The ice field at the head of the Pasterzen glacier loomed big and bright even at night, and several of us decided we would go up there at the first opportunity. It was early July. I didn't care if I never went home, what with skiing, the great Austrian beer, climbing, beer, pleasant people, free food, and let's not forget beer at $1.50 a barrel.

Fifty school graduates made the difficult ascent to the peak itself, up the glacier, across great crevasses and through a jumbled mass of ice seracs, overnight at the Oberwalderhütte and on to the summit. There were more ski races on the lower slopes. Harry and his crew eventually made the long hike to the Oberwalderhütte "in anticipation of a beautiful run down the next morning." The hut was filled with pleasant people and conversation. Germans and Austrians, former enemies, reflected on the war with their American counterparts. The morning dawned clear and cold; the skiers would wait until the sun warmed the snow to perfect corn [the skiers' term for "melting crust"] before skiing down.

We watched the sun gradually creep across that vast expanse of snow till it lit up a tiny figure far away. The figure was approaching. Byron Johnson arrived long before the snowfield was soft enough for our descent. He was a messenger. The message was "Go." Immediately—not when the snow was soft enough to enjoy the run, but right now. (The run down was terrible—more like ice skating.) The 10th had left the mountains and gone back to Florence. We would get the bad news on our arrival there.

Bob Woody was in the Franz Joseph Hut on another shoulder of the Grossglockner when a different messenger brought the exact same message. "We were being summoned to Florence. The whole division was to be shipped to the United States for amphibious training and the assault on Japan."

That assessment seemed confirmed when the 10th was replaced in Udine by the 34th Infantry Division, the division with the

223

longest service in the European theater of operations; they'd been overseas since November 1942. It wouldn't have been right to send those long-suffering dogfaces to Japan. Let them stay in peaceful Italy and send instead the division with the fewest days in combat. It made sense, but it didn't make the mountaineers happy. In Florence, the orders became more specific: Once home, the 10th was to reassemble after a thirty-day leave for a planned November 2 attack on Kyushu.

In late July, in balmy weather, the 10th's three regiments boarded three different ships and steamed for home. Despite smooth seas, tension lurked just below the surface. Woody thought, "What would the Japanese soldier be like? We had survived one war. Not likely the next one. I had once considered myself immortal. No longer. I was *certain* I would get it in Japan."

Then on August 6, word came that would change everything. A new kind of bomb had been dropped on Hiroshima. "We had no idea what an atomic device was," Woody recalled in his memoir:

> Hiroshima in my mind was some Japanese military camp on a palm-lined island in the South Pacific. All humans had simply vanished in atomic disintegration leaving barracks and palms intact. Geelan [Pfc. Thomas] talked about atomic theory. He was always a bit more erudite than the rest of us.
>
> And then [on August 11] we were passing the Statue of Liberty as a flotilla of tugboats and fireboats steamed toward us and presented us with a victory fountain from their hoses. There were pretty girls on those fireboats, too. We crowded en masse to the side. The *Marine Fox* began to list dangerously under our collective weight. The ship's loudspeaker warned us to move back from the railing.

Japan surrendered four days later.

CHAPTER 15:

"We Could Do
Almost Anything"

S gt. Friedl Pfeifer would make good on his promise to return to Aspen after all. Landing back in the States, Pfeifer was sent to Camp Carson, in Colorado Springs, to recover from the grizzly wounds he'd suffered at Torre Iussi. By mid-September, missing half a lung but well enough to drive, he made his first trip up to the old silver town and immediately felt "the same incredible sense of coming home that had hit me two years before when I'd marched into Aspen with Company A, 87th Regiment."

Discharged from the Army on October 16, he moved straightaway into a little frame house on Third Street, just a few blocks from where the formal Victorian grid met the north face of the mountain. Pfeifer's vision of an Aspen to rival his hometown of St.

Anton was no small feat of imagination, for Aspen in 1945 still languished in its silver-bust doldrums of nearly fifty years. Most of the buildings had either burned or fallen down, or were boarded up against the town's roving bands of semi-wild dogs. Most of the population of six hundred souls—down from a turn-of-the-century high of twelve thousand—either believed against all logic in the return of silver or else had become resigned to a life of inexorable, if not altogether unpleasant, decline. This was Aspen in what the locals called "the quiet years." And but for a handful of risk takers like Laurence Elisha and the lumber merchant Tom Sardy, Friedl might not have got his dream off the ground.

Pfeifer's furrowed-brow intensity rubbed off on Elisha, proprietor of the only hotel and president of the fledgling Aspen Ski Club. Together, they tackled Pfeifer's to-do list, which included widening the only ski trail on the mountain, the serpentine Roch Run, and cutting a new trail off the summit into Spar Gulch, one that would be less intimidating to intermediate skiers. Pfeifer also wanted to renovate the infamous Boat Tow toboggans, and build a rope tow for beginners' lessons. These he accomplished with astonishing speed, utilizing crews of ski club volunteers who cut timber some nights long after dark by the lights of their miner's helmets. Sardy extended a generous line of credit.

A ski area needs a ski school, and Friedl staffed his with two friends who had worked with him at Sun Valley before the war, John Litchfield and Percy Rideout. Both also were 10th veterans and Dartmouth alumni. Litchfield had been with division headquarters, and Rideout (F Company, 86th Regiment), a former ski team captain, had been on the Riva climb.

Army doctors had told Pfeifer that he probably would never ski again. But every day throughout the fall, Friedl hiked the mountain, learning its every curve and gaining back his strength. When the first real snow arrived in early November, he skinned to the summit and skied back to town, tears of joy streaming down his cheeks. With the arrival of the second big storm just before Thanksgiving, the ski school and the lifts were ready for their first customers. Tickets were to be sold out of Mike Magnifico's shoe-repair shop downtown. Pfeifer, Litchfield, and Rideout stood by the ski school sign and waited. Nobody came.

Then, at last a Mrs. Nichol appeared. Pfeifer wrote in *Nice Goin': My Life on Skis*, "She was a 70-year-old lady who had skied in Europe a little bit and was staying with friends in town. She was out there every morning for at least an hour or so, usually getting half way up the [rope tow] before her hands lost their grip. Percy, Litch and I tossed a coin every day for the privilege of teaching Mrs. Nichol and getting paid."

Pfeifer knew that a handful of skiers, a ski school, and a simple lift do not a world-class ski resort make. He had much bigger plans—for more trails and more and better lodgings in town, for a restaurant on the mountaintop, and, most important, for chairlifts to the summit, like the ones that had vaulted Sun Valley to instant acclaim in the late 1930s. Friedl figured, no doubt accurately, that "few people would be willing to drive 250 miles [then about eight hours] from Denver to ski a hill with a small lift."

But all of this development would cost money, a lot of money. Pfeifer estimated he'd need $250,000 to pay for it all, a sum that "might as well have been $10 million" for the impoverished, idealistic skiers involved. The answer came in the unlikely form of Chicago industrialist Walter Paepcke. Unlikely, because Paepcke was not a physically adventurous person himself, not a skier. But his wife was, and Elizabeth Paepcke finally convinced her husband to visit moribund Aspen in the summer of 1945, a few months before Friedl Pfeifer's return. Paepcke's Container Corporation of America, which produced innovative cardboard packaging, had made him a rich man, and that allowed him to indulge his passions for philosophy, modern art, and a nearly evangelical zeal to reform American intellectual life. Paepcke believed in the Greek ideal of a healthy mind in a healthy body. He thought that mid-century industrial America was lacking on both counts and that a conscious recombining of art and work, of humanistic study and physical activity, could right the cultural ship. He had long imagined creating a "summer university" for corporate executives in a pristine setting far from urban distractions. In Aspen, he believed, he'd found that place, and he proceeded to buy up whole blocks downtown, along with several of the best-preserved Victorian houses. He took out leases on the Jerome Hotel and the shuttered Wheeler Opera House and commenced plans for their renovation. "Here," a friend wrote, "was to be another Renaissance, with Paepcke as Medici in chief."

Teaming up with Friedl Pfeifer and his ski-area dreams seemed as natural as the snow. Paepcke needed the physical component to his Greek ideal, and Friedl needed the kind of people Walter Paepcke could bring into the ski business. In early 1946, Paepcke, Pfeifer, Johnny Litchfield, Percy Rideout, and a number of other investors, including Minnie Dole, formed the Aspen Skiing Corporation. Secretary of the Navy Paul Nitze, an ardent skier and Elizabeth Paepcke's brother, was the single biggest shareholder, contributing $75,000.

That summer Paepcke's money and Pfeifer's expertise built the world's longest chairlift on Aspen Mountain. Actually, it was two chairlifts, one after the other, from the edge of town to the top of Roch Run. The chairs traveled nearly three miles and gained over 3,000 feet of elevation. They were single chairs, like Sun Valley's, with footrests and blankets attached for the long ride—forty-five minutes bottom to top. Lift tickets cost $3.75 a day; a season pass sold for $140. When the snow came, skiers queued up for the chance to ride so high to such great terrain. Lift lines became an instant fact of life. Friedl also got his restaurant that summer, the mountaintop Sundeck, co-designed by Fritz Benedict, the architect, who also had come back to Aspen. On January 11, 1947, the official party began. A special train arrived bearing the governor of Colorado, assorted senators and congressmen, and a huge media contingent. There were skiing and jumping exhibitions, ice skating, fireworks, parades, and a black-tie dinner hosted by the Paepckes at the newly resplendent Jerome. A little more than a year after Friedl Pfeifer's return, not even a year and a half since the end of the war, Aspen was being hailed by *The New York Times* as "the winter sports center of America."

The same story, with somewhat less fanfare, unfolded at hundreds of American ski centers. Tenth veterans across the country, thrilled to be alive and reconnected to the sport they loved, jump-started a boom that was unprecedented in the history of outdoor recreation. Where before the war, a few hundred rope tows dotted the northern landscape, by 1970 there were over seven hundred full-fledged ski areas in the United States, most with chairlifts and base lodges and trail-grooming machines descendant from the 10th's snow-going Weasels. A few hundred thousand skiers ballooned into something on the order of 13 million.

Vail founder Pete Seibert told *The Denver Post* in 1985 that "the ski industry would have developed without us, but probably ten years later." In retrospect, that statement seems too modest. The energy that 10th vets brought to the ski business—as coaches, racers, ski instructors and patrollers, ski school directors, filmmakers, shop owners, publishers, writers, and equipment manufacturers and importers, as well as ski-area developers—would have been difficult to replicate. Surviving the war had given many 10th men a new sense of purpose. And, as Bob Parker says, "Our mountain training gave us two things. One, an unusual work ethic. And two, we knew we could do almost anything we asked our bodies to do in terms of physical effort and mental effort." The ski troops naturally fell back in with each other, drawing on the camaraderie of battle, yes, but even more from their days together at Camp Hale and Mount Rainier. "The men of the 10th formed a small but determined self-elected elite," writes historian Morten Lund in *Ski Heritage*, "that constituted a brotherhood in the sport."

That brotherhood created outright a score of new ski areas, including Arapahoe Basin, Aspen, and Vail in Colorado; Snow Valley in California; Mount Bachelor in Oregon; Mission Ridge and Crystal Mountain in Washington state; Lutsen Mountain in Minnesota; Sugarbush and Pico Peak in Vermont; New York's Burby Hollow; Sandia Peak and Santa Fe Ski Basin in New Mexico; Iron Mountain and Pine Mountain, Michigan; Seven Springs, Pennsylvania; and Otis Ridge, Massachusetts. Sixty-two ski areas were either managed by or had ski schools directed by 10th alumni, and an estimated two thousand ski troopers became ski instructors. Vets played key roles in forming the National Ski Areas Association, the Professional Ski Instructors of America, the trade group Ski Industries America, and various regional umbrella groups such as Colorado Ski Country USA, Ski Utah, and Ski New England.

Camp Hale had already been substantially demolished by the time the ski troops returned, but Colorado, with its history and its reliable, high-elevation snow, remained a magnet. At Aspen, Friedl Pfeifer ran the ski school until 1964. He recognized the need for a true beginners' mountain (Aspen Mountain was and is unrelentingly steep) and so developed Buttermilk Mountain just outside of town in 1958. He created the world's first professional racing circuit in the 1960s. Hollywood discovered Aspen, as it had Sun Valley a decade earlier, and Friedl squired the likes of Gary Cooper and Lana Turner around the mountain, his impeccable hair and aviator glasses as stylish as his low, swooping turns.

Steve Knowlton (Headquarters/86th Regiment) became the

town's first ski bum. He swept out Mike Magnifico's shop and repaired skis at night, so that he could ski and train all day. He trained well enough to compete in the 1948 Winter Olympics in St. Moritz on a team with fellow troopers Gordy Wren (E/87), Dev Jennings (I/85), Wendell Broomhall (A/87), and Joe Perrault (126th Engineers). Sgt. Walter Prager, back coaching at Dartmouth, also coached that Olympic team.

Pete Seibert (F/86) recovered from wounds suffered on della Spe (shrapnel to the face and knee) and joined the vets in Aspen. Despite one leg noticeably shorter than the other, he became a legendarily beautiful powder skier while nursing dreams of starting his own ski area. With 10th men Ben Duke (L/86), Bill "Sarge" Brown (L/86), and Jack Tweedy (E/86), Seibert built his dream from scratch out of a Colorado sheep meadow near Vail Pass, terrain that is an hour's ski tour north of the Resolution Creek–Ptarmigan Pass area of D-Series fame.

Vail opened in 1962 with Colorado's first gondola, a pedestrian village patterned after the little Alpine towns Seibert had seen during the war, and a young marketing director named Bob Parker. Parker's path since the war had been a serpentine but not altogether atypical one. He went back to school, not to St. Lawrence but to the University of Washington to study English. Parker knew, as a nineteen-year-old, the first time he set eyes on Mount Rainier that "this was god's country" and that assuming he survived the war, he would spend the rest of his life out west. With his degree in hand, he returned to Europe as an education advisor to the Army. In Germany, he skied in the Army championships, spent time with Sarge Brown, who ran the Mountain Training Center in Bavaria, and worked as a stringer, or "European correspondent," for Bil Dunaway (10th Recon/MTG) who had succeeded Dick Wilson (M/85) as editor of *Skiing* magazine, which was started in 1946 by Merrill Hastings (A/86). The brotherhood was already well established.

Parker, the man who went through Italy wearing a "liberated" pair of German mountain boots, tells this story about a visit he paid to the famous ski-boot maker Hans Rogg in 1951:

> When we reached the Po River, our squad took jeeps along the river to look for the big guns that were shooting at us. Lying on the levee bank, we heard small-arms fire, and saw Germans swimming for the other side, pursued by bullets hitting the water. Our sergeant told the GIs who were firing to quit shooting at helpless Germans, which they did. Meanwhile, we watched this little guy with long black hair tiring, and beginning to sink. A big blond German grabbed him with a perfect lifeguard's carry, swam him to the north bank, dragged him out, and they disappeared over the north levee.
>
> In 1951, I was in Hans Rogg's little shop in the basement of a bombed-out building in Munich to be fitted for a pair of his superb ski boots. We got to chatting about the war—both of us were in the mountain troops opposite each other. Turned out he was the little guy with the long hair. His life-saving buddy was a German Olympic swimming champion.

At Vail, Parker admits, "None of us knew much about marketing." But along with Seibert and Brown, they had an eye for ski terrain and a nose for what the skiing public wanted. By the time Parker retired in 1997, Vail had become the biggest, most successful ski resort in North America—biggest single-mountain acreage (five thousand acres and counting) and over a million skier visits per season.

The boom was fueled early on by the sudden availability of inexpensive war-surplus gear. Hundreds of thousands of civilians got their start skiing on white-painted Army skis and white bamboo poles with baskets as big as dinner plates. And it wasn't just the leftovers from Camp Hale; the War Department had ordered tens of thousands of skis that were never used. New skis could be had for $5 a pair. A complete outfit, including skis, boots, poles, parka with fur-trimmed hood, wool pants and gaiters, long underwear, and mittens, would set you back in the neighborhood of $75. And it wasn't just ski gear flooding the market. Thousands of olive-drab nylon climbing ropes were for sale too, ropes that were far better— stronger and suppler—than anything the mountaineering commu- nity had seen prior to the war. Climbers and hikers snapped up the 10th's fine multipurpose mountain boots with the revolutionary Vibram soles and luxuriated in the first down sleeping bags to be widely available. Thanks to the Mountain and Winter Warfare Board, much of this surplus gear was superior to anything produced commercially. For many years into the peace, 10th Mountain Divi- sion equipment went along on first ascents (and first ski descents) across America and indeed all over the world.

Tenth men dove with gusto into the business of manufacturing and distributing ski equipment. John Woodward (HQ/87), one of the original patrol leaders and MTG officers, managed a ski shop in Seattle and later became a partner in the Anderson & Thompson Ski Company, an early distributor of cable bindings, steel ski poles, and ski racks for automobiles. In the 1960s Anderson & Thompson introduced the fabulously successful, American-made K2 skis. Hans Hagemeister (10th Recon) imported skis and skiwear from Europe. Sun Valley ski instructor Don Goodman (E/87) designed and manufactured the Goodman Release Binding, one of the first safety release bindings.

Several 10th men got involved in the ski-lift business, which took off in symbiosis with the ski areas. After graduating from Dartmouth in 1948 (and winning that year's coveted four-event title for skiing in downhill, slalom, cross-country, and jumping), John Jennings went to work for the Heron Company in Denver.

This was the same Bob Heron who had engineered the tram used for evacuation and resupply on Riva Ridge. The same Bob Heron who cobbled together old mine cable and equipment purchased by Friedl Pfeifer and fashioned Aspen's historic Lift 2. The same Bob Heron who built the world's first double chairlift at Berthoud Pass west of Denver, and the first-ever triple and quad chairs at Boyne Mountain, Michigan. Over the years Heron-Poma (the Denver company was eventually swallowed up by the French giant Pomagalski S.A.) designed and installed over 120 chairlifts and several aerial tramways, including the ones at Squaw Valley, California, and Cannon Mountain in New Hampshire.

Harry Poschman didn't want to build ski lifts; he just wanted to ski the mountains they opened up. That first December home, December 1945, Harry found that he couldn't return to his beloved Sun Valley; the lodge was still being used as a Navy hospital. So, he took off for the mountains of Utah, where Alta, which had stayed open throughout the war, was just about the only place with lifts running. Harry got a job the day he arrived. "I swore I'd never pick up another shovel after the service. But my first job in Alta was shoveling snow!" For four years, through Alta's typically prodigious storms, Harry worked as a lift operator by day and a bartender by night. In 1949 he moved briefly back to southern California and the mountains of his youth to help John Elvrum (HQ/86)) put up the first chairlift at Snow Valley, near Lake Arrowhead. Then it was off to Aspen, where Friedl Pfeifer proffered a job with the ski school. That was it, heaven-on-earth for the Arlberg style-master. Harry bought a house with six bedrooms, turned it into the Edelweiss Inn, a chalet-style bed and breakfast, and settled in with his wife and two children. And he never missed a powder day for the next twenty-five years.

Bob Woody, one of the youngest recruits when he joined the 10th in 1944, was still only twenty years old when the Army let him go.

Did the war make me a man? No. I still got sweaty palms when asking a girl on a date, and one time when I went in to buy a suit after the war, the salesman said, "Hey, sonny boy, what do you want?" I came home with fantasies of the good life. College. Coeds. A career as a foreign correspondent in trenchcoat and eye patch and dangerous liaisons with beautiful blond spies. Then the perfect pipe-smoking tweedy job in some ivy-covered academia.

Instead he went to Dartmouth (no coeds until 1972) along with his best war buddy Newc Eldredge. After school, international ambitions notwithstanding, the romance of skiing worked its magic. Pulled west—first to rural Colorado, then to Idaho, and finally to Salt Lake City—he traded on his facility with words at various small newspapers. Then one day at Alta, in two feet of fresh powder on Sunspot—the moment still sparkles in his mind—"I realized, this is it; I'm staying." He had his skiing; by then he had a growing family; and he had his words. The trenchcoat didn't seem so important. He remained business editor of the Salt Lake Tribune for more than thirty years. And to this day, he teaches skiing every week of the winter for a University of Utah program on the nearby slopes at Alta.

CHAPTER 16:

A New World Outside

On a blustery day in May 1995, eight 10th Mountain Division veterans sat in the park in Telluride, Colorado, and talked about their war and the world they came home to. (All eight were featured in the film *Fire on the Mountain*, a documentary look at the mountain division, which premiered that weekend at Telluride's annual Mountainfilm Festival.) Some of the former ski troopers wore their white canvas anoraks, and they all sported the 10th's versatile mountain cap with visor and earflaps. They had brought along examples of their rucksacks, box-toed mountain boots, trigger-finger mittens, and other pieces of gear. White-haired David Brower (HQ/86) of Berkeley sat on the left with even whiter-haired Paul Petzoldt (MED/85) of Jackson Hole, next to him. Then came Bob Parker (HQ/87) from Santa Fe, sporting an elfin gray goatee, and Phil Lunday (126th Engineers), also of Santa

Fe. Bob Woody's friend, Newc Eldredge (L/85), of Newport, New Hampshire, was there with his trademark handlebar mustache. Boulder's Hugh Evans (M/85) stood next to Ben Duke (L/86) from Littleton, Colorado, and Dick Wilson (M/85) of Grantham, New Hampshire. A bottle of Jack Daniels whiskey sat on the table in front of them. It was cold enough for a nip—isolated snowflakes swirled through intermittent sunbeams—but none of the men needed help in loosening up.

Bob Parker began by telling the audience—clad in the latest Gore-Tex and pile, "You're looking at a bunch of old ski bums from World War II."

Which was true, but only a very small part of their story. These men not only revolutionized ski sport in America after the war; they represented a revolution in the way Americans today think about the outdoors, how they spend their money and their leisure time, and how they view the planet as a whole.

In the prosperity of the postwar years, recreation changed. And the most dramatic shift occurred away from the lined court and the measured field, and out into the natural world. The new sports were self-propelled, individual pursuits, with no winners and losers and no scorekeeping. Hiking, camping, backpacking, trail running, fly-fishing, mountain biking, trekking, adventure racing. The gravity sports: skiing and climbing, whitewater kayaking, surfing, hang gliding, BASE (building-antenna-span-earth) jumping. Sports that required knowledge of, indeed intimacy with, natural forces and environments—weather, altitude, wind, water, snow, and rock.

The returning mountain soldiers didn't by themselves create all of this, but they did a lot to drive it, by example and with their business endeavors, and in the process they passed along their passion for the outdoors to future generations. They were an exceptionally influential bunch. (Harry Poschman complains, half-seriously, that "the legend of the 10th Mountain" spread wider after the war than it ever had during training or combat in Italy.) Far from simply inspiring a few ski bums, as Bob Parker wryly put it, the 10th's elemental love helped create a new awareness in America of wild landscapes and of how an active generation might claim a place in it. Inevitably, in the process, Americans discovered how fragile the environments are that support this new recreation, how finite wilderness is, and how important its preservation.

Some 10th veterans actively fostered these notions, made this their life's work—people like David Brower, who became the first executive director of the Sierra Club, and Paul Petzoldt, who founded the National Outdoor Leadership School. But it wasn't just the outspoken teachers who made a difference. Hugh Evans became a mining engineer; Bob Parker, after his time at Vail, studied to become an archeologist (and fifty years after the fact, was finally able to write about some of his war experiences, including Punchboard Hill); Jacques Parker worked as an illustrator. They either moved to the mountains or skied every day they could, and they passed the tradition on to their children.

Did the 10th Mountain Division create exceptional men, or was it the other way around? Certainly, exceptional people were drawn to the mountain troops in the first place. And Minnie Dole's insistence on a selective process (at least in the beginning) guaranteed that the 10th would not be like other Army divisions. Friedl Pfeifer and Paul Petzoldt, for example, were consummate mountain men before the Army and no doubt would have continued their careers after the war, whether or not they'd joined the mountain troops. Others, perhaps, were more directly shaped by their mountain training—the thousands of nonskiers, for example, who learned from the experts and came to love the snow and cold, and the feel of warm rock under their hands. An extraordinary number of them came out of the service, despite the horrors they'd seen, with a preternatural optimism. However difficult the task, they seemed to have the attitude, "This can't be so hard; we can get this done."

Many of these men seem now to have been endowed with the best qualities in the American character: individualism and cooperation, independence and entrepreneurship, inventiveness and a need for freedom—in this case the freedom of the hills. The "romance" of war did not infect them. Very few stayed in the military after the war. Their loyalties were to the mountains, to their comrades, and to what Fritz Benedict described as "the life you were going to lead, that was the important thing."

Participation in World War II did not, by and large, pose a moral dilemma for most of these men. Not the way that war today inspires ambivalence. The stakes were clear: Either the democracies rallied to defeat fascism, or they faced the possibility of a world in which moral choices were not allowed a man of conscience. After helping to ensure the outcome in Italy, David Brower was free to follow his sense of duty in the aid of a ravaged natural world. While still overseas, he wrote what he called a "lament" and sent it to the *Sierra Club Bulletin* in Berkeley. It began:

> Death isn't a pleasant thing to see, but you can get used to it. You may get so that you can just count the bodies; or you may study them academically, to see just how death occurred. The waste of human future is too appalling to ponder upon. Besides, you know that the death of a man is irrevocable. However tragic it may be that he was young and died unnecessarily on a battlefield, you can, because of that irrevocability, learn to accept it.

The death Brower refers to was meant to be both literal and metaphorical. He goes on:

> This is not the only death I have seen. In such parts of the mountains of Italy, Austria, Switzerland and Yugoslavia as I have been

able to observe are the shattered remains of what must have been beautiful wildernesses. These wild places had their one-time inaccessibility to defend them—their precipices, mountain torrents, their glaciers and forests. But they lost their immunity; they felt the ravages of a conqueror. And now they're dead. Their death isn't irrevocable, as is that of [a] man; but still, in time, you become callused to it and merely wonder, academically, what caused the demise.

The *Bulletin* published Brower's essay under the title "How to Kill a Wilderness." David Brower's fifty-five-year run as point man and conscience of the conservation movement had begun.

Brower had witnessed first-hand the scars of two world wars on the once-pristine Alps. But even more devastating to true wilderness, he concluded, were the degradations inflicted by the well-intentioned but heedless "improving" of God's handiwork: the ubiquitous trails and roads; the dams and flumes and penstocks leading to powerhouses and power lines webbing the landscape; the houses and huts and even hotels built right up on the highest ridgelines; the mining excavation and debris; and the myriad fortifications of war.

As a young man, Brower had spent five whole summers, and parts of many others, in the Sierra high country. He led his blind mother on long walks through tall-grass meadows, describing everything he saw. He made seventy first ascents on Sierra rock. He and his friends could walk for days, living on beans and onions, without seeing another soul. He knew the "Range of Light" as John Muir, the Sierra Club's first president (1892–1914), knew it. Dave Brower believed in the club's motto: "To explore, enjoy, and render accessible the Sierra Nevada and other scenic resources of the United States."

Compared with the Alps, the Sierra remained relatively

unspoiled. But even then, Brower worried about "the apparently democratic notion that you must produce the greatest good for the greatest number." Where wildness was concerned, greater numbers—of trails, roads, vehicles, people—inevitably meant greater damage, and the shrinking of a finite resource. "Render accessible" therefore became problematic, and Brower, a board member since 1941, successfully lobbied to change the wording to "enjoy and preserve."

After the war, in the midst of the unprecedented explosion in outdoor recreation, Brower helped refocus the club's mission to one of preservation—of air, water, soil, and particularly, of wilderness. Once opened up (to logging, mining, and commercial skiing, for example), he realized, wilderness was effectively gone—dead. In the decades to come he would transform his beloved Sierra Club from a regional hiking club with two thousand members to the world's most powerful environmental organization with a roster today of over seven hundred thousand members. He led the fight to create the Wilderness Act, which passed Congress in 1964 and has to date set aside over one hundred million acres of wild land in Alaska and the Lower 48. He succeeded in stopping the building of dams in Dinosaur National Monument and in the Grand Canyon. (Although in saving the Grand, to his eternal regret, he believed he had bargained away the equally spectacular Glen Canyon of the Colorado.) He steered the club into publishing politically powerful books of photographs by Ansel Adams, Eliot Porter, and others, books that spotlighted the beauties of the American continent and the dangers facing them. He traveled and spoke ceaselessly, right up until his death in 2000 at the age of eighty-eight. The postwar life and work would not make you think right away of the soldier. He spoke softly, ironically, often with a self-deprecating humor. But he was a soldier, a warrior for a few years in the service of democracy, and then for the rest of his life, a warrior for wilderness.

One of the first projects Brower tackled on coming home from Italy was the designation of Southern California's highest mountain, the 11,502-foot San Gorgonio Mountain, as off-limits to development. Conservationists hailed the 1947 decision to protect the big peak northwest of Palm Springs. Others, including Harry Poschman, hated it. Harry had spent countless hours as a young man skiing and winter camping on Gorgonio's bald dome. He'd always hoped that some day ski lifts would make his ascents easier.

Controversy found the outspoken Brower ever after. In 1952, he was named the Sierra Club's first executive director by then-president Dick Leonard, the same Dick Leonard who contributed so much to the 10th's development and testing of the nylon climbing rope. But by 1969, in a battle over a nuclear power plant on California's central coast, Leonard refused to support his old climbing partner, and the board voted to fire Brower. Undaunted, Brower started Friends of the Earth and the Earth Island Institute, which together help foster environmental activism in other countries and broaden the perspective of Americans on how their actions affect the world ecosystem. Dave Brower was too modest to admit it, but he became his heroes, became the John Muir, the Henry David Thoreau of the second half of the twentieth century. He was nominated three times for the Nobel Peace Prize. He didn't win it, but he succeeded, perhaps as much as the first photographs of Earth from space had, in changing the way earthlings see their world.

Brower found himself on the opposite side of the fence from some of the 10th alumni who were carving new ski areas out of the forest lands. But he kept skiing himself, the way he always had, in the backcountry with skins and a rucksack and an explorer's eye. Similarly, he witnessed an invasion of sport climbers—brought on in part by the nylon rope—to the crags, and most particularly to his sacred Yosemite Valley. There was nothing he could do to stop them. Nor would he have wanted to, so long as these new converts to the mountains tread lightly and left no scars. He believed in "a new renaissance": "The old one found a way to exploit. The new one has discovered the earth's limits. Knowing them, we may learn anew what compassion and beauty are, and pause to listen to the earth's music."

In 1994, Paul Petzoldt set out with friends on what he hoped would be a seventieth anniversary climb of his beloved Grand Teton, a 13,770-foot-high shark's fin soaring above Jackson Hole. The sixtieth anniversary ascent ten years earlier had gone swimmingly: up to the glacier the first afternoon, then on summit day, roped together and working deliberately up the knife-edge Petzoldt Ridge to the top, and down again on the route he had pioneered in 1924. This time around, things did not go as well. Petzoldt's glaucoma had progressed so that his climbing, even with the help of friends, slowed to a snail's pace. The group had to turn back at 11,000 feet. The decision was Paul's. He took the setback with typical grace, commenting, "There are old climbers, and there are bold climbers. But there are no old, bold climbers."

It was a smart, safe decision, the kind of judgment call that, along with boldness and great strength, characterized Petzoldt's career as a guide and teacher. After the war Paul returned to his guiding business in Wyoming. People from around the world wanted to climb the sharp spires in the Tetons group, and Petzoldt made a decent living guiding them. He further enhanced his reputation for innovative rescue work (a reputation burnished in the 10th) on a couple of high-profile rescues in the 1950s. One involved a risky winter climb deep inside Grand Teton National Park to the spot where a DC-3 passenger plane had crashed on the snowy flank of Mount Moran. The rescuers found no one left alive. The other one, on Devils Tower in northeastern Wyoming, dragged on for days and was attended by television cameras, search lights, and a national media horde. A stunt artist had parachuted onto the summit of the sheer-sided Tower but didn't know how to get down from there. Navy guns were brought in to shoot ropes up 1,000 vertical feet to the man, but when that didn't work, Petzoldt and a hotshot rescue crew had to climb up to get him. By this time, the media frenzy was in full swing. Searchlights blinded the climbers and their hapless charge on the painstaking rappel down. Petzoldt remembers thinking he wanted to roll rocks down on the insensitive cameramen. "We got a lot of loot out of that one, though," Petzoldt said, with a twinkle, of the food and whiskey and Chesterfield cigarettes that had been dropped by local pilots to sustain the man during his ordeal.

Even more than guiding, Petzoldt believed in teaching. In the early 1960s, he helped bring the Outward Bound School from its birthplace in England to the United States. His was the perfect personality—magnetic, forceful, and extremely able—to implement the school's twenty-six-day wilderness courses, and in 1962 the Colorado Outward Bound School was born. For chief instructor, Petzoldt hired Tap Tapley, the Sun Valley ski patroller and fellow 10th vet famous for his survival skills (and for a few legends, including the shooting down of low-flying aircraft with bow and arrow). Together they designed the school's recipe for life-affirming adventure. The courses thrust people together in physically demanding settings, winter or summer. Climbing, skiing, and extended backpacking trips led—now and then through a personal heart of darkness—to new awareness of one's capabilities and new appreciation for the natural world. The results were not entirely dissimilar to the way recruits bonded at Camp Hale. They even had a motto—"No whining"—that could have come from the 10th's rigorous time at Hale. Coincidentally, the Outward Bound School's main Colorado base camp was for years located in Leadville, just south of Tennessee Pass and the 10th's abandoned camp.

With the passage of the Wilderness Act, Petzoldt felt an additional responsibility to teach a backcountry ethic that would later be called "leave no trace." His inspiration came from the wording of the act itself, where wilderness is defined as a place "where the earth and its community of life are untrammeled by man, where man himself is a visitor who does not remain." This meant, according to Petzoldt, that "the time-honored practices of legendary outdoorsmen and mountain guides [and, one might add, World War II mountain soldiers] were no longer acceptable: no longer break off pine boughs for beds, dig trenches around tents, build bonfires in a circle of rocks, pollute streams and lakes with cooking grease and soap or litter campsites with glass, tin and foil."

There was no bible for such a code, so Petzoldt wrote *The Wilderness Handbook*. And in 1965 he broke away from Outward Bound and formed his own school, the National Outdoor Leadership School, or NOLS, to train new generations of guides and teachers. Typically generous, Petzoldt turned almost no one away, instead scribbling "pay back when able" scholarships for students with no money. Petzoldt based NOLS in Lander, Wyoming, hard by the east escarpment of the Wind River Range, a fiercely wild and largely uninhabited mountain range protected by three Wilderness Areas. NOLS graduates went forth to man the proliferation of postwar institutions devoted to outdoor education, experiential education, adventure travel, and ecotourism. With Tapley's help, NOLS developed programs in Alaska and the Yukon, in Mexico, Patagonia, India, Africa, and Australia.

In 1977, as David Brower had been from the Sierra Club, Paul Petzoldt was ousted from NOLS by his very own board of directors. Nevermind. Petzoldt, like Brower, simply started anew, creating the Wilderness Education Association, which provides courses through colleges and universities for future outdoor professionals in the fields of recreation, forestry, and conservation.

*　　*　　*

Like a lot of climbers, Paul Petzoldt had a mind for organization. The activist David Brower dreamed of a society that knew the value of its wild heart. Petzoldt organized an army to live Brower's dream. Bill Bowerman (G/86) had a genius for innovation. After the war, he returned to his alma mater, the University of Oregon, to coach the track and field team there, winning NCAA championships in 1962, 1964, 1965, and 1970. He trained thirty-three Olympians and sixty-eight all-Americans, and coached the 1972 U.S. Olympic track team.

The fiery Bowerman was not just a great coach who attracted great athletes to his program; he was a crusader for physical fitness, a value that was cemented by the 10th's training and its impact in Italy. In the 1960s he started jogging and racing programs throughout Oregon that bloomed into a national running craze, a movement that led directly to the boom in marathoning, to triathlons, and to ultramarathons nonstop across whole mountain ranges. Bowerman became a kind of pied piper of the running movement, having an impact parallel to that of James Fixx and his seminal 1977 bestseller, *The Complete Book of Running*.

But even that influence, huge as it was, pales compared with the revolution Bowerman sparked in the design and marketing of athletic shoes, indeed in the shaping of contemporary consumer culture. The story is legend now, apparently true, and is told in reverential tones in boardrooms and on basketball courts and track infields around the world. It happened in 1972. Bowerman and a former athlete of his named Phil Knight had set up a small business importing running shoes from the Japanese company Onitsuki Tiger. Bowerman's athletes liked the shoes, but everyone agreed there were no models anywhere that gave good traction on Eugene's famously muddy running trails. Knight and Bowerman settled into the latter's kitchen one morning with a batch of latex rubber, a bit of leather, some glue, and Bill's wife's waffle iron. The waffle iron was not fit thereafter for cooking breakfast, but the result of their tinkering was the world's first molded waffle outsole. Bowerman and Knight each chipped in $500 and built three hundred pairs of running shoes in Bowerman's garage. Four of the top seven finishers in the 1972 Olympic marathon wore those shoes, which by then were selling under the name Nike.

Nike, which Bowerman co-founded, took the manufacture of athletic shoes to unheard-of places in terms of performance science; they invented the wedge heel and the cushioned insole, among other innovations. They built shoes for every conceivable specialty, including climbing, hiking, bicycling, kayaking, trail running, beachcombing, and river rafting—all of the new outdoor passions except skiing, it seemed—on top of the traditional court sports. Even more telling culturally, Bowerman and Knight moved athletic shoes into the realm of fashion. The Nike swoosh, a near-universal symbol of cool, became a paradigm of the new global economy. Bill Bowerman died a wealthy man in 1999 at the age of eighty-eight, having given the world (according to Damian Cave writing for Salon.com) "a new way of looking at feet, a reason to exercise, and a new form of cultural expression."

Meanwhile, in Aspen, there were some who felt the roaring success of the postwar ski industry had gone too far. By the 1970s, real estate had replaced ski lessons and lift tickets as the engine driving ski-town economies. The ski culture was evolving away from the adventure and athleticism of the early 10th Mountain cadres and toward a safe and predictable, amusement-park experience, one among many recreation options in a resort setting. Many of the pioneers, including Pete Seibert and Friedl Pfeifer, had long since been eased out of management in favor of corporate, bottom-line types. Skiing was becoming less a way of life than a business, an amenity.

Fritz Benedict, of the 126th Engineers and Aspen, had contributed as much as any man to the rapid development of Colorado skiing, but he, too, came eventually to decry the crowds and the cars, the industrialization of the sport he loved. He'd "discovered" Aspen before the war, before Pfeifer and Knowlton, when he hitchhiked up from Arizona, with his backpack and his skis, for the 1941 National Championships on Roch Run. At the time, Fritz was a student at Frank Lloyd Wright's Taliesin West, in Scottsdale, Arizona. When he moved permanently to Aspen in September 1945, he was the town's only architect.

Benedict's organic, Wrightian stamp can be found on scores of buildings in Aspen, from the Sundeck restaurant atop the ski mountain to the Prairie-style Pitkin County library to the first passive solar house (1946) built in the valley. From the beginning he was asked to contribute to base villages at many of Colorado's flagship resorts: Vail in 1962, Snowmass in 1967, Breckenridge in 1971, Winter Park, and Steamboat. At Snowmass, Fritz envisioned a car-free village, like the ones at Zermatt and Saas Fe in Switzerland, with lodging right on the slopes so that "kids can ski home without ever crossing a road." The slopeside lodging was indeed built and became a model for future designers. But other parts of the plan were too far ahead of their time; he had underestimated the power of the automobile in shaping American design. The pedestrian village was scrapped, and in its place a hideous heated roadway, called Snowmelt Road, was constructed to get the cars up to Fritz's lodges.

As time went by, Benedict's enthusiasms evolved away from town and toward the backcountry trails, where he had always felt at home. He thought about building a trail system linking Aspen and Vail to the north, across some of the terrain the 10th had explored from Camp Hale. How about a trail sprinkled with rustic huts, each one a day's ski from the next, like the Appalachian Mountain Club huts in New Hampshire or the alpine huts linking Zermatt and Chamonix along the classic, six-day Haute Route? Such a trail might, Fritz hoped, "help preserve a kind of simple enjoyment of the mountains."

Other skiers around the country were forsaking the lifts and the manicured trails for the backcountry, becoming reacquainted with free-heel bindings and climbing skins. Enthusiasms were coming full circle, and in 1980 Fritz's idea tapped into a groundswell of interest in skiing's self-propelled, wild-snow roots. The new traditionalists could have been quoting from David Brower's introduction to the 1942 edition of *The Manual of Ski Mountaineering*: "We have nothing against the practice slopes and the standard runs; but if that's all you know, you have missed something special, something lost behind the ranges, a sparkling new white world with its hard edges covered over for the winter, and you its discoverer."

Fritz also wanted to honor the ski troops, and so his idea became the 10th Mountain Division Trail and Hut System. The U.S. Forest Service gave its blessing. Tenth veterans, including Bob Parker and Bill Bowerman, got involved. Fritz donated an office, designed the first two huts, and enlisted a small army of trail cutters, cabin builders, fund-raisers, and reservations takers. The huts had wood stoves for cooking and heating, solar-powered lights, and bunks for up to twenty people. Skiers would carry their own bedding, food, and wine; drinking and washing water would come from melting snow in big pots on the stove. All the rest was there, everything grand about the 10th's winter forays onto the peaks—the camaraderie, the spectacular vistas, the sharp air and powder snow—without the misery of C rations and snow caves.

The first two huts opened for the winter of 1981–82. Twenty more have been added since, completing a jagged, three-hundred-mile circle around the Holy Cross Wilderness: from Aspen north and east to Vail, then south across Tennessee Pass to Leadville, and west again to Aspen. Twenty thousand skiers glide through the system in a typical season. Most ski in for a night or two. A few, with strong lungs and a long holiday, make the complete circumnavigation. Hut 8, the 10th Mountain Division Hut, was funded entirely by 10th veterans, Bill Bowerman in particular. It sits at 11,370 feet overlooking Slide Lake and Homestake Peak, site of the early regimental training "disaster." The ninth hut, Uncle Bud's Hut, was built from stone on the site and named in honor of Bud Winter, the eager MTG stalwart and prolific letter writer. It is perched high on the side of Galena Mountain just off the route Winter and the others took on their famous "trooper traverse" from Leadville to Aspen in February 1944. The hut's log contains a poem by Bud's father, Fred, written soon after the family learned of Bud's death. It reads, in part: "Sleep peacefully my buddy boy, beneath Italian skies / . . . And may God give you silver skiis, to ski celestial hills, / And fishing rods and lines and reels, to fish those streams and rills."

Despite two heart surgeries in his seventies, Fritz insisted on skiing at least twice a week on the cross-country trails around Aspen and, on occasion, up to the huts, where he loved to drink bourbon and count stars with his skiing buddies. He died in 1995 at age eighty-one. In 1997, two small huts at 10,900 feet up Hunter Creek east of Aspen were added to the system in honor of Fritz and his wife, Fabi. Fritz's wish for "an American Haute Route" to honor the nation's first and only Army mountain division had become reality.

There were hundreds more who affected the world outdoors. Some we know about; many we don't. John Jay finished up his war editing publications for the Air Force in the Philippines and occupied Japan. Then when he came home, he went right back to what he loved most: shooting, editing, scoring, and narrating ski movies.

For the next twenty-five years he traveled the world's great ranges, skiing and filming, and set the standard by which all subsequent ski films and travelogues were judged.

Monty Atwater, a Harvard grad who wrote juvenile fiction as a first career, took his Camp Hale experience with Rocky Mountain snow and turned it into a career as America's preeminent avalanche-control expert. Atwater hired on at Alta soon after the war and began immediately to experiment with explosive control of dangerous slide paths. Drawing on Colonel Ruffner's artillery exercise at Homestake Peak in 1943, Monty became the world's first practitioner to regularly shoot down slides with military weaponry, including the 10th's artillery piece, the 75-mm pack howitzer. Monty proved the then-radical notion that avalanches can be controlled. Atwater demonstrated how, rather than simply issuing warnings, as they had done in the past, in vulnerable areas, like ski resorts and slide-prone highways, snow rangers can trigger avalanches artificially and bring them down before they become monsters.

Another 10th man, Morley Nelson, moved to Idaho after the war, worked for the Soil Conservation Service, and became one of the nation's foremost experts on raptors. Known as the "Birdman of Boise," Nelson not only raised and rehabilitated dozens of birds, he campaigned tirelessly against the rampant shooting of birds of prey, designed safer power lines to protect birds from electrocution, wrote and lectured and lobbied for the establishment of the Snake River Birds of Prey Natural Area and the Peregrine Fund's World Center for Birds of Prey. He also brought raptors into millions of living rooms and theaters by contributing to thirty films about birds of prey, including Disney's *The Eagle and the Hawk*.

So many of these men lived, and continue to live, long and energetic lives. Their nonprofit 10th Mountain Division Association is one of the most active veterans organizations to emerge from

World War II. Seventy-eight hundred 10th alumni were members at its peak. It still listed twenty-seven hundred members in 2003, though the roster—sadly, inevitably—shrinks almost daily. The related 10th Mountain Division Foundation raises money for college scholarships, for handicapped skiing, and for various memorials, including the 10th Mountain Division Trail and Hut System.

Minnie Dole gave the opening speech at the very first 10th reunion in 1946. He called his talk "Birth Pains of the 10th Mountain Division," and in it he referred with parental affection to "our division." He admitted that "my life was wrapped up in the division for the past five years, and your departure left a tough void to fill." Following the war Minnie went back to the insurance business, but he never stopped pressing the Army to make ski training an integral part of military service. And he stayed close to many ski troopers, including General Hays, through the association. Minnie Dole died in 1976 at the age of seventy-six.

In 1980, together with mountain soldiers from eight other nations—Austria, France, Germany, Italy, Poland, Slovenia, Spain, and Switzerland—10th vets organized the International Federation of Mountain Soldiers. Former allies and adversaries now get together regularly to remember the dead, no matter their nationality, and to strengthen their common bonds. To that end, the IFMS organized a reenactment of the 10th's Riva Ridge climb fifty years to the day after the historic event. On February 18, 1995, a score of still-fit 10th troopers, including seven who had actually fought on Riva, made the climb up C Company's route to Monte Serrasiccia. Now well into their seventies, they climbed it in daylight, and they had help from comrades in the Italian Alpini and from a handful of young men with the reactivated 10th Mountain Division (Light Infantry). At the summit they were met by family and friends, and by German and Austrian soldiers, at least one of whom had been taken prisoner by the Americans that day fifty years before. Under flags of many countries, and some former enemies, the assembly dedicated a new twelve-mile long Peace Trail, the first of many planned for the Northern Apennines and the Alps.

The new 10th Mountain Division (Light Infantry) was activated in 1984 at Fort Drum in upstate New York. Forty-nine years after the original 10th was disbanded, the Army reassigned the name to a division trained for combat in "any terrain or climate." Not a ski troop per se, it is a "rapid-deployment force" designed primarily for security and peacekeeping duties. Since 1992, the new 10th Mountain has been the most-deployed division in the Army, serving in southern Florida following Hurricane Andrew, in Somalia, Haiti, Bosnia, Kosovo, Uzbekistan, Afghanistan, Cuba, Kuwait, and Qatar. Johnny Litchfield (HQ/DIV), one of the original ski instructors with Friedl Pfeifer in Aspen, says of the new 10th, "We have a heritage, and they are carrying it on. The mission has changed . . . but the [Mountain Division] patch remains the same."

Every year, the men who still ski—and there are a lot of them—congregate at a ski area out west for a reunion. It's not just an annual meeting of the association but a real reunion with plenty of time for sliding on the mountain and drinking and singing the old songs together. Talk only rarely veers back to Camp Hale or Italy. Mostly, they talk about new skis and dear friends, and how John Woodward, in his nineties, still beats everybody to the bottom of the hill. (As former *Skiing* magazine and *Aspen Times* publisher Bil Dunaway said at a recent gathering, "Once you're addicted to the outdoors, it's pretty hard to stop.")

Early on, the reunions were held at Vail, on Pete Seibert and Bob Parker's mountain. In recent years, they've been hosted by Keystone Resort, also in Colorado. The men usually pick a day and drive over to Cooper Hill on Tennessee Pass for some skiing on the old Camp Hale trails. The T-bar has been replaced with a chairlift, and the area is now run by the community—not the Army—but the high, thin air and dry snow on the Continental Divide remain essentially unchanged.

After skiing, the troopers gather at the pass before an immense slab of polished Italian granite on which are inscribed the names of the 997 mountaineers lost in battle. Someone speaks a brief prayer. Someone else, usually Hugh Evans or Earl Clark, then leads the gathering in song. The voices are mostly still strong; a couple of brave tenors mix in harmony with many others deep and cracked with age. Finally, someone else reads a poem by Sgt. Ed Currie (G/85).

> now who will sing
> the April song?
> the fluting voice
> the silvered spear
> lie crumpled on the ground,
> and all we know of youth
> and friendship
> rattles in the gourd
> we carry in our hearts . . .
> Italia's slopes are green
> birds nest in leafless trees
> the fluting voice,
> the silvered spear . . .
> lie crumpled on the ground.

There is no attempt either to cover up the horrors of the war or to glorify their part in it. As Art Delany (L/87) of Denver said, "It was a big war. Dead bodies are scattered all over the world. We did our share, and we did it well. That's about as much congratulation as a person should take for the effort, I think."

Instead of credit, the remaining men of the 10th Mountain

Division want most to hold on to the feeling they all had at one time or another in the mountains. Ralph Lafferty (HQ/86) said it best in the film *Fire on the Mountain*: "You get to the top of a mountain, and you feel happy about the whole thing. You start to sing. That's the spirit we had in the 10th."

ACKNOWLEDGMENTS

Every summer, 10th Mountain Division veterans living in New England gather to climb New Hampshire's Mount Washington, the highest peak in the Northeast. In August of 2001, I invited myself along and was graciously welcomed by the group, which included John Imbrie, Newc Eldredge, Bob Traynor, and Carlton Miller. We climbed the Boott Spur Trail, nearly ten miles and 4,000 vertical feet up to the Lakes of the Clouds Hut, where we spent the night before hiking on to the summit the next morning. It was slow going. These men are in their seventies and eighties now, and the trail winds through steep boulder fields much of the way. They never lost their good humor, though. At one point late in the day, I heard a clarion downeast accent: "We're not to the top yet. But you could *roll* to it from here."

They could have driven to the top, as indeed many more of their mountain division comrades did the next day for the annual memorial service. But those who can still make the climb prefer to hoof it. It's in their blood.

Each of us carried a bottle of red wine in our packs. (Newc made sure to spread the weight around.) And at dinner that night in the hut, the men toasted the mountain and all the mountains they have known. They celebrated their own great good fortune and remembered those who had gone before them.

A book like this one would not be possible without the help and encouragement of surviving 10th Mountain Division veterans, a generous, inclusive bunch. In particular, I am indebted to Bob Parker, John Jennings, Robert Woody, and Harry Poschman, who loaned me their journals and other writings, shared their stories and memorabilia, and invited me into their lives.

At the same time, no book on the 10th would ever come together

257

ACKNOWLEDGMENTS

without the encyclopedic guidance of Debbie Gemar and Barbara Walton at the 10th Mountain Division Resource Center in the Western History/Genealogy Department of the Denver Public Library.

Many thanks to filmmakers Beth and George Gage, who generously shared 10th contacts; to John Imbrie, tireless 10th historian, for lightning responses to questions on anything and everything; to Newc Eldredge, 10th film librarian; Jacques Parker, unofficial division illustrator; Phil Lunday, database and map man extraordinaire; Onno Wieringa for the wonderful things he saved; Mike Meyers and Georgianna Contiguglia for information on the 10th's equipment and clothing; and to Dean Rolley, for sharing video of the veterans' seminar in Telluride.

Special thanks to Ed Pitoniak, Gibbs Smith, Greg Poschman, Morten Lund, Heritage Aspen, The Colorado Ski Museum, and the 10th Mountain Division Hut and Trail Association.

Countless details came from countless hours of conversation with charitable 10th men Thomas Brooks, Bill "Sarge" Brown, Earl Clark, Hugh Evans, Bob Frausen, Leon Goodman, Nick Hock, Howard Koch, Ralph Lafferty, Bud Lovett, Jacques Parker, Crosby Perry-Smith, John Pierpont, Pete Seibert, Ernest "Tap" Tapley, Duke Watson, Onno Wieringa, Dick Wilson, John Woodward, and Herbert Wright.

And finally, thanks to Sarah McGrath and Erin Curler at Scribner, to alert copyeditor Linda Stern, and Elizabeth Kaplan of the Elizabeth Kaplan Literary Agency.

SELECTED BIBLIOGRAPHY

Atwater, Montgomery M. *The Avalanche Hunters*. Philadelphia: Macrae Smith Company, 1968.

Black, Andy, and Chuck Hampton. *The 10th Recon/MTG*. Privately printed, 1996.

Bradley, Charles C. *Aleutian Echoes*. Fairbanks: University of Alaska Press, 1994.

Brower, David, ed. *The Manual of Ski Mountaineering*. Berkeley: University of California Press, 1942.

———. *For Earth's Sake: The Life and Times of David Brower*. Salt Lake City: Gibbs Smith Publisher, 1990.

———. *Remount Blue: The Combat Story of the 3d Battalion, 86th Mountain Infantry*. Privately printed, 1948.

Burton, Hal. *The Ski Troops*. New York: Simon and Schuster, 1971.

Cohen, Stan. *A Pictorial History of Downhill Skiing*. Missoula, Mont.: Pictorial Histories Publishing Company, 1985.

Dole, Charles Minot. "Birth Pains of the 10th Mountain Division." Unpublished speech, 1946. 10th Mountain Division Collection, Denver Public Library.

Dulles, Allen. *The Secret Surrender*. New York: Harper and Rowe, 1966.

Dusenbery, Harris. *The Northern Apennines and Beyond with the 10th Mountain Division*. Portland, Ore.: Binford and Mort Publishing, 1978.

———. *Ski The High Trail, World War II Ski Troops in the High Colorado Rockies*. Portland, Ore.: Binford and Mort Publishing, 1991.

Fire on the Mountain. Directed and produced by Beth and George Gage, First Run Features Home Video, 1995.

Harrer, Heinrich. *The White Spider*. London: Harper Collins, 1958.

Imbrie, John, and Hugh Evans. *Good Times and Bad Times, A History of C Company 85th Mountain Infantry Regiment 10th Mountain Division*. Quechee, Vt.: Vermont Heritage Press, 1995.

SELECTED BIBLIOGRAPHY

Jay, Lt. John C. *History of the Mountain Training Center.* Army Ground Forces Study No. 24, 1944. 10th Mountain Division Collection, Denver Public Library.

Keegan, John. *The Face of Battle.* New York: Viking Press, 1995.

Lund, Morten. "The 10th Mountain Miracle." Skiing Heritage: The Journal of the International Skiing History Association, Vol. 7, No. 2 (fall 1995).

Lunday, Philip, and Charles Hampton. *The Tramway Builders, A Brief History of Company D, 126th Engineer Mountain Battalion.* Printed privately, 1994.

Mauldin, Bill. *This Damn Tree Leaks.* Reprinted from *Stars and Stripes,* 1945.

Pfeifer, Friedl, with Morten Lund. *Nice Goin': My Life on Skis.* Missoula, Mont.: Pictorial Histories Publishing Company, 1993.

Poschman, Harry. *The Birth and Death of the 10th Mountain.* Unpublished memoir, 1983.

Putnam, William L.. *Green Cognac: The Education of a Mountain Fighter.* New York: American Alpine Club, 1991.

Ringholz, Raye. *On Belay! The Life of Legendary Mountaineer Paul Petzoldt.* Seattle: Mountaineers Books, 1998.

Ski Patrol. Directed and produced by John Jay, John Jay Films, 1943. Denver Public Library, 10th Mountain Division Collection.

The Sun Valley Skiers. Directed and produced by David Butterfield, Centennial Entertainment, Ketchum, ID, 2000.

Ullman, James Ramsey. *High Conquest: The Story of Mountaineering.* New York: J. B. Lippincott, 1941.

Von Senger und Etterlin, Generalleutnant Fridolin. "War Diaries." Unpublished, 1945. Denver Public Library, 10th Mountain Division Collection.

Whitlock, Flint, and Bob Bishop. *Soldiers on Skis: A Pictorial Memoir of the 10th Mountain Division.* Boulder, Colo.: Paladin Press, 1992.

Winter Warriors. Written and produced by Martin Gillan, A&E Television Networks, 2001.

Woody, Robert. *Charlie Red One, Over and Out.* Privately Printed, 1995. Denver Public Library, 10th Mountain Division Collection.

INDEX

INDEX

atomic bomb, 224
Attu:
  battle for recapture of, 56, 69–70, 71
  Japanese garrisoned on, 56, 57, 58, 69–79
Atwater, Monty, 252
Auschwitz concentration camp, 218
Austin, Tex., 111, 113
Austria:
  Nazi takeover of, 12, 33
  surrender of German troops in, 203
  10th Mountain in, 221, 222–23
avalanches:
  control of, 252
  as military weapon, 62–63, 252
  and MTG's Aspen hike, 98–99
  10th Mountain's training and climbing sessions and, 100–101
Axis Sally, 171

Badoglio, Pietro, 80, 92
Bagni di Lucca, 4, 123
Bankart, Debbie, 51, 52, 53–54, 157–58
Basic Principles of Skiing, The, 49–50
Bastrop, Tex., 106, 110
battle shock, 162, 165
Bedayan, Raffi, 221
Belgium, Nazi occupation of, 18
Benedict, Fabi, 250
Benedict, Fritz, 189, 190, 229, 240
  postwar career of, 229, 249–51
Bennett, Nelson, 31
Bergen-Belsen concentration camp, 194, 218
Berlin, Soviet troops on outskirts of, 173, 194
Bingham, Roy, 155
Birth and Death of the 10th Mountain, The (Poschman), 62
"Birth Pains of the 10th Mountain Division" (Dole), 11, 253

Black, Andy, 85
Blaise, William, 155
Blanc, Mont, 221
Blizzard, The, 100–101, 114, 168–69, 213
Bologna, Italy, 120, 121, 158, 176, 185
Bowerman, Bill, postwar career of, 247–48, 250
Bradley, Charles, 30, 34–35, 38, 39, 42
Braun, Eva, 208
Brazilian Expeditionary Force (BEF), 121, 177
Brelsford, Corporal, 62
Brenner Pass, 191, 198, 210
Bright, Alex, 8, 30
Britain, Battle of, 27–28
Bromaghin, Ralph, 36
Brower, David, 19, 24, 84–85, 86, 87, 88, 95, 99, 113, 122, 123, 128, 136, 143–44, 166, 175–76, 180–81, 185, 186, 197–98, 200–202, 204–6, 208, 210–11, 214, 219, 221–22
  environmental concerns and projects of, 240–44, 250
  Sierra Club and, 23, 84, 239, 242, 243, 246, 250
Brown, Bill "Sarge," 231, 232
Browning Automatic Rifle (BAR), 3, 4, 5, 6
Brown Palace Hotel (Denver), 102
Buchenwald concentration camp, 194
Burkett, Douglas, 22
Burma, in World War II, 106, 114, 138, 194
Buttermilk Mountain (Colo.), 230
Butterwick, Lt., 205–6

Camp Hale, 4, 38, 45–46, 66–67, 245, 254
  drawbacks of, 54–55
  in movies, 50, 53

262

INDEX

INDEX

Made in the USA
San Bernardino, CA
03 November 2019